T0305092

The Labour Market Triangle

GLOBALIZATION AND WELFARE

Series Editors: Jane Lewis, *London School of Economics, UK,* Denis Bouget, *MSH Ange Guépin, France,* Giuliano Bonoli, *Swiss Graduate School of Public Administration (IDHEAP), Switzerland and* Jochen Clasen, *University of Edinburgh, UK*

This important series is designed to make a significant contribution to the principles and practice of comparative social policy. It includes both theoretical and empirical work. International in scope, it addresses issues of current and future concern in both East and West, and in developed and developing countries.

The main purpose of this series is to create a forum for the publication of high quality work to help understand the impact of globalization on the provision of social welfare. It offers state-of-the-art thinking and research on important areas such as privatization, employment, work, finance, gender and poverty. It includes some of the best theoretical and empirical work from both well established researchers and the new generation of scholars.

Titles in the series include:

The Labour Market Triangle

Employment Protection, Unemployment
Compensation and Activation in Europe

Edited by

Paul de Beer

*Henri Polak Professor of Industrial Relations, University of
Amsterdam, the Netherlands*

Trudie Schils

*Assistant Professor of Economics, Maastricht University,
the Netherlands*

GLOBALIZATION AND WELFARE

Edward Elgar
Cheltenham, UK • Northampton, MA, USA

© Paul de Beer and Trudie Schils 2009

All rights reserved. No part of this publication may be reproduced, stored
in a retrieval system or transmitted in any form or by any means, electronic,
mechanical or photocopying, recording, or otherwise without the prior
permission of the publisher.

Published by
Edward Elgar Publishing Limited
The Lypiatts
15 Lansdown Road
Cheltenham
Glos GL50 2JA
UK

Edward Elgar Publishing, Inc.
William Pratt House
9 Dewey Court
Northampton
Massachusetts 01060
USA

A catalogue record for this book
is available from the British Library

Library of Congress Control Number: 2009936765

Mixed Sources
Product group from well-managed
forests and other controlled sources
www.fsc.org Cert no. SA-COC-1565
© 1996 Forest Stewardship Council
FSC

ISBN 978 1 84844 478 2

Printed and bound by MPG Books Group, UK

Contents

Figures

Tables

Contributors

Jean-Claude Barbier, Director of Research at the Centre National de la Recherche Scientifique (CNRS), and Senior Researcher at the University Paris 1, Panthéon Sorbonne, Centre d'Economie de la Sorbonne.

Paul de Beer, Henri Polak Professor of Industrial Relations, Amsterdam Institute for Advanced Labour Studies, University of Amsterdam and the Centre for Industrial Relations (de Burcht), Amsterdam.

Jochen Clasen, Professor of Social Policy, School of Social and Political Studies, University of Edinburgh.

Johan De Deken, Assistant Professor of Sociology, Department of Sociology, Faculty of Social and Behavioural Sciences, University of Amsterdam, and Research Fellow of the Amsterdam Institute for Advanced Labour Studies, University of Amsterdam.

Bernhard Ebbinghaus, Professor of Sociology, University of Mannheim, Director of Mannheimer Zentrum für Europäischen Sozialforschung (MZES), and Academic Director of the Centre for Doctoral Studies in Social and Behavioural Sciences.

Werner Eichhorst, Deputy Director of Labour Policy at the Institute for the Study of Labour (IZA).

Per Kongshøj Madsen, Professor of Economics, Department of Economics, Politics and Public Administration, Aalborg University, Research Affiliate at the Centre of Labour Market Research, Aalborg University, and Research Fellow of the Institute for the Study of Labour (IZA).

Trudie Schils, Assistant Professor of Economics, Department of Economics, Faculty of Economics and Business Administration, University of Maastricht, and Research Fellow Amsterdam Institute for Advanced Labour Studies, University of Amsterdam.

Eskil Wadensjö, Professor of Labour Economics, Swedish Faculty of Social Sciences, Stockholm University, and Research Fellow of the Institute for the Study of Labour (IZA).

Abbreviations

AAH	Allocation d'Adulte Handicapé (disability allowance, France)
ABVV	Socialist Trade Union (Belgium)
ACAS	Advisory, Conciliation and Arbitration Service (UK)
ADG	Arbeitsamt der Deutschsprachigen Gemeinschaft (Employment Office for the German Community, Belgium)
AFR	Allocation Formation Reclassement (retraining allowance scheme, France)
AGB	severance pay insurance for blue-collar workers (Sweden)
AGE	severance pay insurance for white-collar workers in the private sector (Sweden)
ALG I	Arbeitslosengeld I (contributory, earnings-related unemployment insurance, Germany)
ALG II	Arbeitslosengeld II (means-tested unemployment assistance, Germany)
ALMP	Active Labour Market Policy
AMS	National Labour Market Board (Sweden)
APW	average production wage
ArGe	Arbeitsgemeinschaft (joint agency of BA and municipalities, Germany)
API	Allocation de Parent Isolé (lone parents' allowance, France)
ASS	Allocation de Solidarité Spécifique (minimum income benefit, France)
ASSEDIC	Assocation de l'Emploi dans l'Industrie et Commerce (regional agencies for employment in industry and commerce, France)
ATP	Arbejdmarkedets Tillaegs Pension (labour market supplementary pension scheme)
AUD	Allocation Unique Dégressive (standard social security benefit, France)
BA	Bundesagentur für Arbeit (Federal Employment Agency (formerly Office), Germany)

BERR	Department for Business, Enterprise and Regulatory Reform (UK)
BGDA-ORBEM	Brusselse Gewestelijke Dienst voor Arbeidsbemiddeling – Office Régional Bruxellois de l'Emploi (Brussels Employment Office, Belgium)
CAF	Caisses d'Allocations Familiales (family funds, France)
CB JSA	Contribution-Based Job Seekers Allowance (UK)
CBI	Confederation of British Industry
CDD	Contrat à Durée Déterminée (fixed-term contract, France)
CES	Contrat Emploi Solidarité (subsidized contract, France)
CDI	Contrat à Durée Indéterminée (open-ended contract, France)
CGT	Confédération Générale du Travail (General Labour Confederation, France)
CNE	Contrat Nouvelle Embauche (new recruitment contract, France)
CPAG	Child Poverty Action Group (UK)
CPE	Contrat Première Embauche (New recruitment contract for the young, France)
Ctsv	College van toezicht sociale verzekeringen (Monitoring Board for Social Insurance, Netherlands)
CWI	Centrum voor Werk en Inkomen (Centre for Work and Income, Netherlands)
DTI	Department of Trade and Industry (UK)
DWP	Department for Work and Pensions (UK)
EEA	European Economic Area
EES	European Employment Strategy
EMU	European Monetary Union
EPL	employment protection legislation
ERM	Exchange Rate Mechanism
ET	Employment Tribunal (UK)
EU	European Union
FFESZ	Fund for Financial Balance in Social Security (Belgium)
FOREM	Office Communautaire et Régional de la Formation et de l'Emploi (Walloon Vocational Training and Employment Office, Belgium)
FSO	Fonds Sluiting Ondernemingen (Redundancy Payments Fund, Belgium)
GDP	gross domestic product
HRW	Hoge Raad voor de Werkgelegenheid (High Council for Employment, Belgium)

HVW	public unemployment benefits payment body (Belgium)
IAF	Unemployment Insurance Board (Sweden)
IAP	intensive action period (UK)
IB JSA	Income-Based Job Seekers Allowance (UK)
ILO	International Labour Organization
IRO	Individuele Re-integratie Overeenkomst (Individual Reintegration Contract, Netherlands)
ITB	Industrial Training Board (UK)
IWI	Inspectie Werk en Inkomen (Inspection for Work and Income, Netherlands)
JSA	Jobseeker's Allowance (UK)
KSZ	Kruispuntbank van de Sociale Zekerheid (Social Security Bank, Belgium)
LAS	Job Security Law (Sweden)
LEC	Local Enterprise Council (UK)
Lisv	Landelijk Instituut Sociale Verzekeringen (National Institute for Social Insurance, Netherlands)
LO	confederation of blue-collar unions (Sweden)
MEDEF	Mouvement des Entrepreneurs Français (main employers' organization, France)
MSC	Manpower Services Commission (UK)
MIB	minimum income benefit
ND25+	New Deal for people aged 25-plus (UK)
ND50+	New Deal for people aged 50-plus (UK)
NDDP	New Deal for Disabled People (UK)
NDED	New Deal Evaluation Database (UK)
NDLP	New Deal for Lone Parents (UK)
NDYP	New Deal for Young People (UK)
NI	National Insurance (UK)
NIF	National Insurance Fund (UK)
OECD	Organisation for Economic Co-operation and Development
OMC	open method of coordination
OSA	sheltered work in the public sector (Sweden)
PAP	Plan d'Action Personnalisé (personalized action plan, France)
PARE	Plan d'Aide au Retour à l'Emploi (back-to-work support plan, France)
PES	Public Employment Service
PPAE	Plan Personnalisé d'Accès à l'Emploi (Individual reintegration agreement, France)

PPE	Prime pour l'emploi (tax credit, France)
PTK	association of the major trade unions for white-collar workers in the private sector (Sweden)
PSL	private sector led partnerships (UK)
PWA	Local Employment Agency (Belgium)
RDBB	Regionale Dienst Beroepsopleiding Brussel (Regional Vocational Training Agency, Belgium)
RMA	Revenu minimum d'activité (mininum income benefit, France)
RMI	Revenu minimum d'insertion (minimum income benefit, France)
RSA	Revenu de Solidarité Active (earned income supplement, France)
RSZ	Rijksdienst voor Sociale Zekerheid (National Office for Social Security, Belgium)
RVA	National Employment Office (Belgium)
RWB	District Unemployment Office (Belgium)
RWT	reduction of working time (France)
RWI	Raad voor Werk en Inkomen (Council for Work and Income, Netherlands)
SER	Social and Economic Council (Netherlands)
SER	regional parity-based advisory council (Belgium)
SUWI	Act on organizational change in social insurance (Netherlands)
SVr	Sociale Verzekeringsraad (Social Insurance Council, Netherlands)
TEC	Training and Enterprise Council (UK)
TUC	Trades Union Congress
UB	unemployment benefit
UI	unemployment insurance
UNEDIC	Union Nationale pour l'Employ dans l'Industrie et le Commerce (National Union for Employment in Industry and Commerce, France)
Uvi	Uitvoeringsinstelling (administration office, Netherlands)
UWV	Uitvoeringsinstituut Werknemersverzekeringen (Social Security Agency, Netherlands)
VAT	value added tax
VDAB	Vlaamse Dienst voor Arbeidsbemiddeling (Flemish Employment Service and Vocational Training Agency, Belgium)
VERP	Voluntary Early Retirement Pensions (Denmark)

Preface

The future of the welfare state is inextricably bound up with its capacity to foster a well-functioning labour market while maintaining its traditional task of providing protection against the vagaries of a modern market economy. Experience has shown that there are no simple ways to realize this twin goal. All countries that were heralded as a paragon of an optimal policy mix at one point in time, such as Sweden, Japan, the Netherlands, New Zealand and Finland, were confronted with serious problems later on and had to give up their model status. Nevertheless there is increasing understanding that countries should learn from each other's experiences. Although it is an illusion to think that one could copy the formula for success from one country to another, learning from other countries' experiences is indispensable in order to design a well-considered policy mix. This is now a central element of the so-called open method of coordination (OMC) of the European Union (EU), which has been employed in the areas of employment policies, social inclusion, pensions and health care.

However, one of the problems for policy learning in the EU is that it is often quite hard to establish which policies are successful and which are not. We are convinced that, in order to gain real insight into the effectiveness of social policy, we have to go beyond simple statistical indicators for policy measures and perform an in-depth study that covers the formal laws and regulations as well as the practice of administration and implementation of social policy. This is the main purpose of the seven chapters in this volume that discuss the social policy in a number of European countries. Experts from Belgium, Denmark, France, Germany, the Netherlands, Sweden and the United Kingdom analyse the policies with respect to unemployment insurance, employment protection and active labour market programmes and assess the strengths and weaknesses of the policy mix in their country. In the introductory and the concluding chapter we bring together the results from these overviews and draw some general conclusions with respect to the effectiveness of social policy.

We believe that the European social model is worthy of being cherished and protected against the assaults of the prophets of a liberal free-market economy. With this book we hope to add to the understanding of the strengths and weaknesses of European social policy. Thus, it might contribute to strengthening the European social model and making it ready for the challenges that lie ahead.

Paul de Beer and Trudie Schils, February 2009

Acknowledgements

The study on which this book is based was financially supported by Stichting Instituut Gak, a Dutch foundation that emanated from the largest social insurance fund in the Netherlands. Today, this foundation is one of the main sponsors of social policy research in the Netherlands.

This book would not have been possible without the contribution of a number of experts from various European countries, who wrote the country chapters in this book. We would like to thank Jean-Claude Barbier, Jochen Clasen, Johan De Deken, Bernhard Ebbinghaus, Werner Eichhorst, Per Kongshøj Madsen and Eskil Wadensjö very much for their contributions. They were all almost immediately prepared to write a chapter for this book when we asked them and were willing to comply with our demands with respect to the topic, the structure, the size and the deadline of their chapter. Thanks to their very cooperative attitude, this is probably one of the few edited books of which the manuscript was finished in time!

1. Introduction: achieving an optimal social policy mix

Paul de Beer and Trudie Schils

A PARADIGM SHIFT IN SOCIAL POLICY: FROM PASSIVE TO ACTIVE MEASURES

Since the 1990s it has become more or less conventional wisdom in most European countries that the predominant passive character of social policy should be replaced by more active measures. The welfare state that was built up in the post-Second World War period in Western Europe might have been quite successful in reducing poverty and providing income protection, but it proved unable to cope with the sharp rise of unemployment and the rapidly increasing numbers of benefit claimants after the oil shocks of the 1970s. Moreover, in the 1990s it became widely accepted that the rising number of beneficiaries was at least partly caused – or aggravated – by the passive character of the welfare state. From a failing solution to the problem of a malfunctioning economy, the welfare state became the problem itself.

During the 1990s, two main approaches were advocated to tackle the problems of the welfare state. The first was the (neo)liberal approach of welfare state retrenchment. To put it bluntly, this approach tries to remedy the flaws of the welfare state by reducing it and creating more room for the market and the private provision of income insurance. The main weakness of this approach is, of course, that it neglects the reasons why the welfare state was introduced in the first place, that is, to compensate for market failures. Shifting the responsibility for social protection from the state back to the market can give rise again to the unfavourable social consequences of market failures, such as high poverty levels, large income disparities and social exclusion of weaker groups. The second approach boils down to activating the welfare state. This approach was inspired by the alleged success of the Nordic welfare states, which for a long time were able to combine a high standard of social protection, low unemployment rates and high labour participation rates. The success of these welfare states is often attributed to their active labour market policies, which stimulate and support the unemployed to get back to work and facilitate the integration of all citizens in the labour market. During the 1990s, however, Sweden, the Scandinavian welfare state par excellence, experienced a deep economic crisis and record levels of unemployment, which forced the Swedish government to reform its welfare state, cut back expenses and reduce the generosity of social benefits. Although the Swedish economy has recovered, it is still questioned whether its welfare state will be sustainable in the end (Lindbeck 1997).

If the liberal approach guarantees the economic sustainability of the welfare state at the risk of increasing poverty and income insecurity, and the Nordic approach safeguards social protection without being sustainable in the long run, the obvious way out seems to combine the two approaches. This could be achieved by creating more room for a well-functioning self-regulating labour market on the one hand, while maintaining social protection and introducing activation measures on the other. Recently, a labour market policy concept has been developed that intends to achieve this. This so-called flexicurity approach is now an official goal of the European Union (EU), calling on the member states to 'promote flexibility combined with employment security' (EC 2005, p. 5) and 'convergence of views on the balance between flexibility and employment security, or flexicurity' (EC 2006, pp. 75–6). In 2007, the European Commission proposed a set of 'common principles of flexicurity' (EC 2007).

The flexicurity concept is not fully developed yet, nor is there a universally accepted definition. An important characteristic of the concept is that it refers to particular goals, namely flexibility and security, and not to particular instruments or measures. This probably explains its present popularity, since it fits nicely with the strategy of the open method of coordination (OMC), currently the common method for social policy in the EU. The OMC is tantamount to stating goals only, by means of so-called guidelines, and leaving it up to the EU member states to devise the measures to implement these goals. This allows each member state to choose the policy mix that fits its specific problems and circumstances best.

As pointed out by Wilthagen et al. (2003) the terms 'flexibility' and 'security' have various meanings. They distinguish four elements of flexibility and four kinds of security, and theoretically there can be 16 different combinations of flexibility and security. This makes the concept very broad and not very manageable for practical purposes. From the perspective of the welfare state debate, however, the most important elements of security seem to be income and employment security,[1] and the most important element of flexibility the movement of individuals between jobs and between employment and non-employment (including unemployment and positions outside the labour market).[2] This is also the position taken by the European Commission, which states: 'Flexicurity can be defined, more precisely, as a policy strategy to enhance, at the same time and in a deliberate way, the flexibility of labour markets, work organizations and labour relations on the one hand, and security – employment security and income security – on the other' (EC 2007).

Still, numerous policies affect these two kinds of security and this particular kind of flexibility. The literature, however, focuses on three categories of policies which specifically aim at a particular element of flexicurity. First of all, social security, and in particular unemployment benefits, is an important means for safeguarding income security by providing a social benefit to those who lose their job and/or are involuntarily out of work. Second, active labour market policies aim at promoting employment security, by enhancing the chances of finding a (new) job for those who lose their job or who enter the labour market. Third, labour market regulation generally reduces the flexibility of the labour market by restricting the unfettered working of the market. Deregulation, such as relaxing employment protection legislation, might be a means to enhance labour market flexibility and increase the flows between employment and non-employment.

In the next three sections, we successively discuss these three policy instruments to enhance flexicurity, and show that none of these on its own is sufficient to realize the intended combination of flexibility and security. Consequently, we discuss whether a combination of these measures yields better results and whether this might be called a 'golden triangle' of social policy.

THE CORE OF SOCIAL PROTECTION: UNEMPLOYMENT BENEFITS

At the core of each welfare state is a system of social security that provides income replacement for those who are involuntarily out of work and cannot, or are not required to, fall back on another source of income (such as capital income or income support from family members). All welfare states include a system of unemployment insurance, which provides either an earnings-related or a flat-rate cash benefit to employees who are (involuntarily) dismissed. There is a massive literature on the impact of these unemployment benefits on both income security and labour market flexibility. The general conclusion is that unemployment benefits enhance income security at the cost of reducing the outflow from unemployment to employment.

To be more precise, there is ample empirical evidence that unemployment benefits reduce income disparities by transferring income from employed to unemployed workers (see Korpi and Palme 1998). It should be noted, however, that most empirical studies look at the direct impact of social benefits on income disparities by comparing the inequality of pre-tax and pre-transfer market incomes with the inequality of post-tax and post-transfer incomes. In other words, they compare the existing income disparities with the counterfactual in which there would be no social benefits, but everything else would be the same. This assumption is, of course, highly implausible, since most people would change their behaviour if they were no longer protected against the income loss caused by unemployment. One way to analyse these behavioural responses is by building a complex micro-econometric model, which includes individual choices between work and leisure time and the budget restriction that individuals face, due to the social security and tax system. However, these models are very sensible to the underlying assumptions and the estimated labour supply elasticities, which casts substantial doubt on the reliability of the outcomes of such models. An alternative method to study behavioural responses to variations in the social security system is by comparing different countries. Such cross-country comparisons are, however, hampered by the fact that countries differ in many respects, which makes it difficult to attribute income disparities to one particular element. Nevertheless, there is convincing empirical evidence that a more generous social security system reduces income inequality, even if one takes the behavioural responses of the population into account (Moller et al. 2003).

There are also numerous studies on the impact of unemployment benefits on the flexibility of the labour market, in particular the outflow from unemployment to work (some recent studies are Røed and Zhang 2003; Jenkins and García-Serrano 2004; Lalive and Zweimüller 2004; Pollmann-Schult and Büchel 2005). In a neoclassical economic framework it is self-evident that unemployment benefits cause a rise of the unemployment level, since the benefit itself reduces the costs of unemployment for the individual. Benefit recipients will search less intensively or raise their reservation wage (the lowest wage at which they are prepared to accept a job), which will prolong their unemployment duration, elevating the unemployment level. However, this simple economic model may not be very relevant in practice, since in the real world eligibility to unemployment benefits is subject to specific qualifying conditions, including the obligation to apply for jobs and to accept a job offer (Atkinson and Micklewright 1991).

Most of the empirical studies use micro-level data to analyse the impact of unemployment benefits on the behaviour of individual unemployed persons. These studies usually find relatively small and sometimes negligible effects of the benefit level on unemployment duration or the outflow to work. However, they often find much larger effects of a change of the benefit level, for example due to expiration of entitlements (for an overview, see Holmlund 1998). Moreover, sanctions (such as benefit reductions when not searching intensively enough) reduce the duration of unemployment and increasing the monitoring intensity even increases the exit probability of the non-sanctioned unemployed (Lalive et al. 2005).

Macro-studies usually take the form of cross-country comparisons of unemployment rates whereby the level of unemployment, among other factors, is related to the social security system. This is mostly accomplished by taking the so-called replacement rate (the benefit level as a percentage of the average wage) and/or the maximum benefit duration as a measure of the generosity of unemployment benefits. These cross-country studies are subject to the same criticism as studies that attempt to estimate the impact on income inequality, since it is very difficult to disentangle the effect of unemployment benefits from other factors. Nevertheless, there is some evidence of a positive relationship between the benefit generosity and the unemployment rate and the share of long-term unemployed in particular (Layard et al. 1991; Nickell et al. 2005).

In sum, there is broad agreement that a system of unemployment benefits reduces income inequality by narrowing the income gap between the employed and the unemployed population. There is less convincing evidence that unemployment benefits enhance unemployment by prolonging unemployment duration and reducing the outflow from unemployment to work.

THE NEW ELEMENT: ACTIVE LABOUR MARKET POLICIES

One reason why international comparisons do not show a strong relationship between unemployment insurance generosity and unemployment rates is that, for a long time, the Scandinavian countries succeeded in combining a generous social security system with low unemployment levels and small numbers of long-term unemployed. This success is often attributed to the active labour market policies that are carried out in these countries in addition to the social security system (sometimes called passive labour market policies) (Calmfors et al. 2002). Various measures to help the unemployed back to work are assumed to mitigate or even fully offset the unfavourable effects of generous benefits on unemployment.

These measures include job brokerage, counselling, training, job sharing, direct job creation and specific measures for youth or for the disabled. If participation in these programmes is a precondition for receiving a benefit, these measures might also compensate for the disincentives caused by generous unemployment benefits (Madsen 2006 calls this the motivation effect of active labour market policy).

Although it seems obvious that active labour market policies promote the reintegration of the unemployed in the workforce, the majority of evaluation studies of specific programmes show only weak and often negligible effects. Some programmes are even found to be counter-productive, due to a locking-in effect, which tends to prolong unemployment spells merely because the unemployed individual cannot search for work while participating in an intensive training programme. In their survey of evaluation studies Martin and Grubb (2001) show that only some measures for some particular groups are effective, especially for women re-entering the labour market. Kluve (2006) gives an overview of 95 micro-evaluation studies and concludes that 'services and sanctions' (including job search assistance, vocational guidance and counselling) and 'private sector incentive schemes' (such as wage subsidies) are the most effective activation programmes (although he does not estimate their average effectiveness).

As with unemployment benefits, one can also explore the macro-impact of active labour market policies by comparing countries that differ in their efforts with respect to their activation policies or by studying changes in such policies in one particular country over time. Once again, one needs to disentangle the effect of activation strategies from the effect of other factors. Moreover, expenditures on active labour market policies tend to change countercyclically, since spending usually increases as unemployment rises. There is thus a bi-causal relationship between spending on activation and unemployment, which makes it even harder to estimate the impact of active labour market policies on unemployment. The few estimates of the macro-impact of active labour market policies that are available suggest that they only have a small or even negligible impact on the unemployment rate, and an even smaller impact on the employment rate (for an overview, see Kluve 2005, pp. 181–4).

In sum, although there is broad agreement among policy makers and politicians these days on the desirability of shifting the balance of social expenditure from passive to active labour market policies, the available empirical evidence hardly suggests that this is a promising way to counteract the unintended negative consequences of a generous unemployment insurance system.

THE MISSING LINK: EMPLOYMENT PROTECTION LEGISLATION

Both unemployment benefits and active labour market policies aim at softening the unfavourable consequences of unemployment, either by providing income maintenance or by shortening unemployment spells. However, neither kind of policies directly affects the functioning of the labour market by reducing the risk of dismissal or increasing the number of people that are hired. This might be one explanation for the small effects of active labour market policy found in empirical research. Even if activation policies increase the probability of unemployed individuals getting back to work, it does not affect the total number of job hires, and thus might have only a small impact on the aggregate unemployment rate (although there might be a positive indirect effect by shifting the unemployment–vacancies curve to the left).

The number of dismissals and job hires and, consequently, the flows between employment and non-employment are influenced by the regulation of the labour market. Various laws and regulations affect these flows, including working time regulations and statutory minimum wages, but arguably the most important is employment protection legislation. This legislation states the conditions under which an employer may dismiss an employee. In most countries, employment protection legislation distinguishes permanent or regular contracts from temporary or fixed-term contracts. Often, there are also different rules and procedures regarding individual dismissals and collective dismissals.

Economic theory predicts that employment protection for permanent contracts has two opposing effects. On the one hand, it raises the costs of firing an employee and increases job tenure, lowering the inflow into unemployment, especially during an economic downturn. On the other hand, employment protection makes it more costly to hire someone who one might have to dismiss in the future, and reduces the number of job hires. Consequently, the outflow out of unemployment decreases. Theoretically, it is unclear which effect is larger and, thus, whether employment protection increases or decreases the unemployment rate. Since employment protection legislation unambiguously reduces the flows between employment and unemployment in both directions, it results on average in longer job tenures and longer unemployment spells, hence raising the share of the long-term unemployed (Bentolila and Bertola 1990). If protection for permanent contracts is stricter than that for temporary contracts, as is usually the case, this is expected to raise the share of temporary employment in total employment.

These theoretical expectations of the impact of employment protection on (un)employment and (un)employment duration are largely confirmed by empirical studies (for an overview see the survey by Deelen et al. 2006). Unemployment protection legislation (EPL) does not significantly affect the aggregate employment rate and unemployment rate, but it does reduce the reallocation on the labour market and increases average job tenure and average unemployment duration. Consequently, relaxing employment protection legislation will not raise the employment rate or reduce the unemployment rate, but will only have an impact on the distribution of employment and unemployment over duration classes.

IS THERE AN OPTIMAL COMBINATION OF UNEMPLOYMENT BENEFITS, ACTIVATION POLICIES AND EMPLOYMENT PROTECTION?

Despite the broad consensus on the desirability of shifting the balance of social policies towards active measures, to date there is not much empirical evidence that supports the benefits of such a shift. On the one hand, a generous social security system and strict employment protection legislation do not seem to have a large impact on the overall employment or unemployment rate. On the other hand, both evaluation and macro-studies show only small or negligible positive effects of active labour market policies. One reason for these small estimated effects might be the existence of complementarities between the various measures. The impact of one instrument may very well depend on another instrument. While each policy separately might only have a negligible effect, a well-chosen combination of policies might be more effective than the sum of the separate policies. There can be various reasons for such complementarities (Blanchard and Tirole 2004; Eichhorst and Konle-Seidl 2005). If the unemployment benefit replacement rate is high and eligibility criteria are weak, the obligation to participate in an activation programme might compensate for the disincentives of the benefit, through the so-called motivation effect discussed before (Madsen 2006). If benefit levels are much lower and the incentives to leave unemployment much stronger, the motivation effect will not make much difference. Mandatory training programmes might thus be more effective, the higher the replacement rates are. A high replacement rate also makes it less costly for employers to dismiss workers, since employees will not resist dismissal fiercely if they only expect to suffer a small income loss. Hence, the employer can shift most of the (social) costs of unemployment on to society. This may result in excessive numbers of dismissals, which can be counterbalanced by strict employment regulation. If replacement rates are low, employment protection might lead to too few dismissals and thus hinder reallocation on the labour market. Furthermore, very strict employment protection might reduce the effectiveness of active labour market policies, since there are little job openings and even qualified job seekers might find it difficult to find a job.

If there are indeed complementarities between the various social policies, then there might be an optimal combination of unemployment insurance, active labour market policies and employment protection that renders the best results in terms of both flexibility and security. The European Commission states: 'A successful flexicurity strategy has to balance carefully the income insurance function of the unemployment benefit system with an appropriate activation strategy designed to facilitate transitions into employment and boost career development' (EC 2007, p. 7). Recently, it has been suggested that Denmark might be close to such an optimal combination of policies, for which reason some authors even refer to it as the 'golden triangle' (Bredgaard et al. 2005; EC 2007, p. 36). The three angles of the Danish policy triangle include generous unemployment benefits, high spending on active labour market policies and weak employment protection legislation. The first guarantees income maintenance in case of job loss, the second secures a quick return to the labour market for those who lose their job and the third stimulates a flexible labour market with large flows between employment and unemployment.

Although Denmark is one of the best-performing Organisation for Economic Co-operation and Development (OECD) countries with respect to the employment rate, the unemployment rate and the share of long-term unemployment, one can nevertheless question whether this good performance is really caused by this combination of policies. Does Danish social policy indeed constitute a golden triangle? To date, there are only a few studies that estimate the impact of the combination of various policies on labour market performance. Boone and van Ours (2004) analyse the joint impact of unemployment benefits and activation policies and conclude that the effect of training on the unemployment rate is larger the higher the replacement rate is. They do not find any complementarities between unemployment benefits and other elements of active labour market policies, such as, public employment services and subsidized jobs. However, they do not include employment protection legislation in their analysis. Belot and van Ours (2004) analyse the interaction effects of benefit generosity and tax rates, employment protection and centralization of bargaining, and union density and centralization of bargaining. They conclude that institutions matter and that they interact. The interaction between tax rates and benefit generosity, in particular, explains the reduction of unemployment rates in most European countries. However, they do not analyse the interaction effect of employment protection and unemployment benefits, and active labour market policy is left out of their study.

Kluve (2006) performs a meta-analysis of micro-evaluation studies of active labour market policies and finds that stricter employment protection reduces the likelihood that specific labour market programmes are effective, but he does not find a significant impact of unemployment benefit replacement rates. In a study of the OECD (2006) interactions are tested between benefit replacement rates and employment protection on the one hand and the overall institutional framework (measured by union density, collective bargaining coverage, the extent of corporatism and product market competition) on the other. The conclusion is that 'no firm conclusions can be drawn regarding the presence of specific interactions between the policies and institutions included in the baseline specification' (OECD 2006, p. 214). Moreover, it is stated that 'policy complementarities are estimated to amplify the unemployment effects of separate reforms by only 12 to 19 per cent' (OECD 2006, p. 216). However, of the three policy areas discussed above, this part of the analysis only includes unemployment benefits. In another analyses the OECD finds 'that the adverse impact of unemployment benefits is lower in countries that spend more on ALMPs' (OECD 2006, p. 217).

In conclusion, the empirical evidence for complementarities between various elements of social policy is limited and rather weak. The few available studies do not seem to warrant the existence of a golden triangle, which renders an optimal combination of flexibility and security. However, none of these studies analyses the possible complementarities between unemployment benefits (UBs), active labour market policies (ALMPs) and employment protection legislation simultaneously. Therefore, in the next section we present the results of an explorative empirical analysis that does take all three elements of social policy into account at the same time.

A STATISTICAL ANALYSIS OF THE JOINT IMPACT OF UB, ALMP AND EPL

For the analysis, we use data for 25 OECD countries covering the period 1985–2004. Data are retrieved from the OECD Labour Force Surveys, the OECD Social Expenditure Database and the CEP-OECD Institutions dataset (see Nickell 2006). Our analysis differs in a number of aspects from that in OECD (2006) and Bassanini and Duval (2006). We include the three components of the policy triangle and their interaction terms simultaneously. Our main interest is in the long-term impact of policy instruments on structural unemployment and trends in labour market flows. Therefore we base our analysis on five-year averages, leaving us with four time periods: 1985–9, 1990–4, 1995–9 and 2000–4. Consequently, we do not analyse the short-term impact of the various policies on the evolution of the unemployment rate over the business cycle, but the long-term impact on trends in average unemployment rates over consecutive business cycles. Although the use of period averages reduces the number of cases for our analysis, and thus makes it harder to find statistically significant effects, if we do find significant effects they are more likely to be robust. To faciliate interpretation of the estimated effects, we use deviations from the means in the relevant period. [3]

As dependent variables we include not only the overall unemployment and employment rates, but also the flows between employment and non-employment. After all, we are especially interested in a mix of policies that increases both security and flexibility. Labour market flexibility is better measured by labour market flows than by the stocks of employed and unemployed at a particular point in time. As a proxy for these labour market flows we take the share of long-term unemployment (unemployed longer than one year), the inflow into unemployment and the inflow into employment. The inflow into unemployment is calculated as the number of persons who are unemployed for less than one month, multiplied by 12, expressed as a percentage of the population aged between 15 and 64. This indicator measures the probability of becoming unemployed within a year for the average member of the working-age population. As a proxy for the inflow into employment we take the number of persons who are employed for less than one year as a percentage of total employment.

In addition, we construct a new indicator to measure income (in)security or the expected income loss due to unemployment, reflecting the difference in the expected income when unemployed and the average wage. It is calculated as the probability of being unemployed multiplied by the average replacement income during an unemployment spell (which is calculated as total expenditure on unemployment benefits divided by the number of unemployed) as a percentage of the average wage. This expected relative replacement income is subtracted from 100 to get the expected relative income loss due to unemployment (refer to the Appendix to this chapter for the technical details). This gives us a proxy for the 'security' part of flexicurity in each country.

The independent variables included in the models reflect the three policy instruments discussed above: that is, employment protection, unemployment insurance and active labour market policy. For employment protection legislation we take the OECD Employment Protection Legislation Index (OECD 2004). To reflect unemployment insurance we use the average OECD overall gross replacement rates for the first five years of unemployment, summarized over four different family types and three different income levels. Finally, as a proxy for active labour market policies we use the expenditures on active labour market policy expressed as a percentage of gross domestic product (GDP). This is the only cross-country measure available. However, we acknowledge the problems of bi-causality with active labour market policy and labour market outcomes such as the unemployment rate. In part we try to minimize this problem by using five-year averages. In addition, we try to correct more formally for this by using a two-step analysis (see the Appendix to this chapter for details on this method). In a first regression we estimated the relation between activation policies and GDP growth to find the cyclical part of expenditure on active labour market policy. From this regression we take the country fixed effects, that represent the policy part of the expenditure on active labour market policy, and include these in the analysis for the effect of the policy instruments on labour market outcomes. In doing so, we hope to reduce the problem of bi-causality to a minimum.

Apart from estimating the direct effects of the three policy variables on the labour market outcomes, we include the interactions between each pair of policy variables, as well as the interaction between the three policy variables. If a golden triangle really exists, we expect this last interaction term in particular to be significant, since that would imply that the full composition of the policy triangle matters. Detailed information on the analyses (such as the methods used, descriptive statistics of the included variables and the exact regression results) can be found in the Appendix to this chapter; Table 1.1 summarizes the estimation results.

The results of this explorative analysis are illustrative. Our analysis shows hardly any direct effects of the policy instruments, only expenditure on activation is positively related to the unemployment rate, the share of long-term unemployment and the expected income loss due to unemployment. The positive relation with the unemployment rate has been found before in the literature, when using this measure for active labour market policy and might still be caused by the bi-causal relation between the two variables (Calmfors et al. 2002). However, it might also be evidence of the earlier-mentioned locking-in effect of activation policies.

Although there are few direct effects, the results show a number of interesting bilateral interaction effects of the policy variables. First, the interaction between employment protection and unemployment benefits is significant in four models. When employment protection is stricter, more generous unemployment benefits result in a lower employment rate, a higher unemployment rate, a larger share of long-term unemployment and a larger expected income loss due to unemployment. This was expected from theory, since more strict employment protection reduces the number

Table 1.1   Summary of regression analysis of labour market policy on labour market outcomes

	Employment rate	Unemployment rate	Share of long-term unemployment
EPL	0	0	0
UB	0	0	0
ALMP	0	+	+
EPL*UB	−	+	+
EPL*ALMP	+	−	−
UB*ALMP	0	0	0
EPL*UB*ALMP	0	0	+

	Inflow into unemployment	Inflow into employment	Expected income loss due to unemployment
EPL	−	0	0
UB	0	0	0
ALMP	0	0	+
EPL*UB	0	0	+
EPL*ALMP	0	0	−
UB*ALMP	0	0	0
EPL*UB*ALMP	0	0	0

Note: For full regression results, see the Appendix of Chapter 1.

Source: Authors' own calculations.

of job hires and the mobility on the labour market, reducing the exit probability out of unemployment. This latter effect is aggravated by more generous unemployment benefits, that minimize the negative income effects of unemployment, raising the reservation wage. Apparently, the effect of the higher unemployment risk on the expected income loss is larger than the effect of a higher replacement rate.

Second, the interaction between employment protection and active labour market policy has a significant impact on four of the dependent variables, basically showing the reverse effects of the interaction between employment protection and unemployment benefits. As the employment protection becomes stricter, spending more on activation policies results in higher employment, lower unemployment, less long-term unemployment and a smaller expected income loss due to unemployment. It seems plausible that the higher activation expenditure offsets the unfavourable impact of strict employment protection (or the reduced flexibility of the labour market). The theoretical expectation of a diminished effectiveness of active labour market policies when employment protection is stricter is not supported by our analysis. Thus, it appears that large expenditure on active labour market policy has some unfavourable effects if employment protection is average, but has a positive impact if it is strict.

Third, there is no significant interaction effect of unemployment benefits and active labour market policy. This is somewhat surprising since it is generally believed that stronger activation policies can offset the negative effects of benefit generosity on unemployment duration. Finally, the estimation results show hardly any overall interaction effect between the three policy instruments, apart from a weakly significant effect on the share of long-term unemployment. More strict employment protection combined with higher unemployment benefit generosity and higher expenditure on active labour market policy is associated with a larger share of long-term unemployed. Interestingly, this occurs in addition to and in the opposite direction of the above-mentioned bilateral interaction between employment protection and expenditure on activation policies. This means that although spending more on activation is more effective if employment protection is stricter, this favourable effect is weaker the more generous unemployment benefits are.

In short, the estimation results show that only employment protection and active labour market policy have a direct effect on some of the labour market outcomes, both in an unfavourable direction. The observed bilateral interaction effects between the labour market institutions in our analysis on the labour market outcomes suggest that complementarities between the policy instruments exist and should be accounted for in labour market analyses. Moreover, our statistical search for the golden triangle seems to be bogged down. We found only minor interactions between all three angles of the policy triangle. This raises the question whether a golden triangle of social policy that renders an optimal combination of security (low unemployment rate and high income security) and flexibility (large flows between employment and unemployment) exists. However, this should not be interpreted to imply that the social policy mix is irrelevant, since the combination of measures explains roughly between one-third and half of the variance of the dependent variables in our regression analyses.

IMPLEMENTATION AND ADMINISTRATION

There might be various causes for the weak statistical evidence for consistent policy complementarities between the three policies. Before lapsing into the conclusion that the social policy mix has no role at all to play in improving labour market performance and income security, we prefer to examine another possible cause, which is that the indicators used in the statistical analysis are too general and too crude to serve as measures of the subtleties of social policy in practice. Measuring active labour market policy by aggregate public expenditure as a percentage of GDP simply misses the large variety in activation strategies in different countries. For example, spending 0.3 per cent of GDP on subsidized jobs may have a completely different effect than spending the same amount on job broker-age or training (Calmfors et al. 2002; Kluve 2006). Likewise, the OECD employment protection indicator summarizes a wide range of compo-nents of labour law into one figure. This has led to some criticism, mainly because of the rather crude and subjective coding frame (Bertola et al. 2000). In addition, the indicator only takes account of national legislation, while in some countries employment protection is further regulated in collective agreements (Schils, 2007). Two countries scoring equally on the OECD indicator may very well have strongly diverging systems of employ-ment protection. Finally, the overall OECD indicator for the replacement rate is a summary measure of the replacement rate in a number of different situations, but does not include entitlement conditions. Although it would be possible to disaggregate these general indicators into their constituent parts, the number of indicators that are available for a statistical analysis would soon exceed the number of observations, making a statistical analy-sis impossible.[4] To get a better insight into the impact of these specific elements of the policy triangle one has to resort to a qualitative, in-depth analysis of social policy in a number of countries.

A further reason why the indicators used may not be adequate for deter-mining the impact of social policy, is that they only measure the 'intensity' of social policy, in terms of income replacement (UB), spending (ALMP) and rights (EPL), but they do not take into account the way these policies are put into practice. The indicators give no information about the actors that are responsible for implementing and administering these policies.

Which actors are involved in social policy? Most studies and debates since the 1980s have focused on the roles of the state and the market, strongly suggesting that there is a dichotomy with respect to the distribu-tion of responsibility. However, as early as 1985, Streeck and Schmitter (1985) pointed out that there is a third kind of actor involved, namely intermediate organizations or associations, including trade unions and employers' associations.[5] In many countries these so-called social part-ners have played and still play an important role in social policy. In some countries they merely have an advisory role to the government on social policy, whereas in other countries the trade unions are involved in the actual administration of unemployment insurance (Belgium, Denmark, Sweden). The social partners may play a role in implementing active labour market policies as well, and collective agreements between trade unions and employers (or their associations) may include additional provisions with respect to unemployment benefits, employment protection and training measures. However, these extensions of the legal provisions are not included in the indicators used for our statistical analysis.

It is likely that the particular role of the various actors matters quite a lot for the effectiveness of social policy. For example, if the actor that pays out unemployment benefits is also responsible for implementing active labour market policy, it is more likely that these policies are coordinated and attuned than if different actors are responsible for them. After all, it is more profitable to increase the budget for active labour market policy if one can claw back part of the extra spending by reducing the number of persons who claim unemployment benefits. Likewise, if statutory unemployment benefits are paid out by a public body while a top-up is administered by the social partners, this might harm the coherence of unemployment insurance policy. Moreover, it is likely that a principal–agent problem arises when different actors are responsible for the legislation and the implementation of social policy, since the legislator (the government) and the administrator (an independent body) may not have the same objectives.

The importance of the role of the social partners with respect to policies to promote flexicurity is acknowledged by the European Commission, as it states: 'active involvement of social partners is key to ensure that flexicurity delivers benefits at all', and: 'Social partners are best placed to address the needs of employers and workers and detect synergies between them' (EC 2007, p. 8). This makes it essential to take account of the role of the social partners in assessing the impact of social policy. However, hardly any study in this field has paid explicit attention to their role. Therefore, this will be an important contribution of the in-depth country studies in this book.

FROM QUANTITATIVE TO QUALITATIVE ANALYSIS: THE PURPOSE OF THIS BOOK

For the reasons spelled out in the preceding section a purely quantitative, statistical analysis will not do in finding out the best combination of unemployment benefits, employment protection and active labour market policy to enhance flexicurity. We have to investigate the peculiarities and idiosyncrasies of social policy in separate countries to determine which characteristics are essential in explaining the successes and failures of these countries with respect to social protection and labour market performance. To accomplish this we have to perform a qualitative, in-depth study of the social policy triangle in each country separately. Therefore, the main part of this book consists of a number of case studies of social policies to tackle the unemployment risk in a selection of European countries. The selection of these countries is based on two principles. First, we include countries that are somewhat similar with respect to their socio-economic context, so that it is likely that differences between these countries regarding (income) security and labour market performance are for a considerable part due to differences in their social policy. Second, we need sufficient variation in the kind of social policies and the role of various actors (government, social partners, private companies) to be able to attribute differences in performance to these factors. These criteria resulted in the selection of Belgium, Denmark, France, Germany, the Netherlands, Sweden and the United Kingdom.

The next seven chapters give an extensive overview and discussion of the social policy triangle in these countries. Each chapter discusses the main changes in each of the three policy areas since the 1990s and then describes the main characteristics of the present policy, including the administration and the distribution of responsibility between the various actors involved. The last part of each chapter discusses the interaction between the three components of the social policy triangle and tries to assess its effectiveness with respect to flexicurity. In the final chapter we compare the design of social policy in the seven countries, establish the main differences and similarities and find out whether the social policy mix in the various countries is converging or diverging. Finally, we draw some conclusions from the lessons learned in the country chapters and try to answer the question whether there exists something like a 'golden triangle' after all.

NOTES

1. Wilthagen et al. (2003) distinguish employment security from job security, which refers to the security of keeping one's present job, but one could also consider job security to be a specific element of employment security. Their fourth element of security is combination security, which refers to the combination of paid work and other, unpaid activities, such as child care. This kind of security will not be discussed in this book.
2. This roughly coincides with what Wilthagen et al. (2003) call 'numerical-external flexibility'. However, this term seems to refer primarily to the need of flexibility of the employer and does not include the outflow out of unemployment or inactivity into work. The other elements that Wilthagen et al. distinguish are numerical-internal flexibility (such as overtime and part-time work), functional flexibility (such as multitasking, job rotation) and wage flexibility, which we will leave aside.

3. Details on the variables and methods used are presented in the Appendix to this chapter.
4. In some empirical studies (Nickell et al. 2005) more explanatory variables are included by using a pooled time-series cross-section analysis in which each year for each country is an observation, which increases the total number of observations strongly. However, such a regression analysis mainly explains the short-term cyclical variation in the dependent variable and does not give much insight into structural shifts in the long run.
5. Streeck and Schmitter (1985) include community as a fourth actor, but this actor will be left aside in our study.

REFERENCES

Atkinson, A.B. and J. Micklewright (1991), 'Unemployment compensation and labour market transitions: a critical review', *Journal of Economic Literature*, **29**(4): 1679–1727.

Bassanini, A. and R. Duval (2006), 'Employment patterns in OECD countries: reassessing the role of policies and institutions', OECD social, employment and migration working papers no. 35, Paris.

Belot, M. and J.C. van Ours (2004), 'Does the recent success of some OECD countries in lowering their unemployment rates lie in the clever design of their labour market reforms?' *Oxford Economic Papers*, **56**: 621–42.

Bentolila, S. and G. Bertola (1990), 'Firing costs and labour demand: how bad is Eurosclerosis?' *Review of Economic Studies*, **57**(3): 381–402.

Bertola, G., T. Boeri and S. Cazes (2000), 'Employment protection in industrialized countries: the case for new indicators', *International Labour Review*, **139**: 57–72.

Blanchard, O. and J. Tirole (2004), 'The optimal design of unemployment insurance and employment protection: a first pass', mimeo.

Boone, J. and J.C. van Ours (2004), 'Effective active labour market policies', IZA discussion paper no. 1335, Bonn.

Bredgaard, T., F. Larsen and P.K. Madsen (2005), 'The flexible Danish labour market: a review', Aalborg University/CARMA research paper 01:2005, Aalborg.

Calmfors, L., A. Forslund and M. Hemström (2002), 'Does active labour market policy work? Lessons from Swedish experiences', Institute for Labour Market Policy Evaluation working paper no. 2002-4, Uppsala.

Deelen, A., E. Jongen and S. Visser (2006), 'Employment protection legislation. Lessons from theoretical and empirical studies for the Dutch case', CPB Netherlands Bureau for Economic Policy Analysis document no. 135, The Hague.

EC (European Commission) (2005), *Integrated Guidelines for Growth and Jobs (2005–2008)*, communication to the Spring European Council, Brussels: EC.

EC (2006), *Employment in Europe 2006*, report of the Directorate-General for Employment, Social Affairs and Equal Opportunities, Brussels: EC.

EC (2007), *Towards Common Principles of Flexicurity: More and Better Jobs through Flexibility and Security*, report of the Directorate-General for Employment, Social Affairs and Equal Opportunities, Brussels: EC.

Eichhorst, W. and R. Konle-Seidl (2005), 'The interaction of labour market regulation and labour market policies in welfare state reform', Institute for Labour Studies (IZA) discussion paper no. 1718, Bonn.

Holmlund, B. (1998), 'Unemployment insurance in theory and practice', *Scandinavian Journal of Economics*, **100**: 113–41.

Jenkins, S.P. and C. García-Serrano (2004), 'The relationship between unemployment benefits and re-employment probabilities: evidence from Spain', *Oxford Bulletin of Economics And Statistics*, **66**(2): 239–60.

Kluve, J. (ed.) (2005), *Study on the Effectiveness of ALMPs*, report for the European Commission, Essen: Rheinsch-Westfaliches Institut für Wirtshafsfatschung (RWI).

Kluve, J. (2006), 'The effectiveness of European active labour market policy', Institute of Labour Studies (IZA) discussion paper no. 2018, Bonn: IZA.

Korpi, W. and J. Palme (1998), 'The paradox of redistribution and strategies of equality: welfare state institutions, inequality, and poverty in the Western countries', *American Sociological Review*, **63**(5): 661–87.

Lalive, R. and J. Zweimüller (2004), 'Benefit entitlement and unemployment duration: the role of policy endogeneity', *Journal of Public Economics*, **88**: 2587–616.

Lalive, R., J. Zweimüller and J.C. van Ours (2005), 'The effect of benefit sanctions on the duration of unemployment', *Journal of the European Economic Association*, **3**(6): 1386–417.

Layard, R., S. Nickell and R. Jackman (1991), *Unemployment: Macroeconomic Performance and the Labour Market*, Oxford: Oxford University Press.

Lindbeck, A. (1997), 'The Swedish experiment', *Journal of Economic Literature*, **35**: 1273–319.

Madsen, P.K. (2006), 'How can it possibly fly? The paradox of a dynamic labour market in a Scandinavian welfare state', in Johan A. Campbell, Johna A. Hall and Ove K. Pedersen (eds), *National Identity and the Varieties of Capitalism: The Danish Experiment*, Montreal: McGill Queen's University Press, pp. 321–55.

Martin, J.P. and D. Grubb (2001), 'What works and for whom: a review of OECD countries' experiences with active labour market policies', *Swedish Economic Policy Review*, **8**: 9–56.

Moller, S., E. Huber, J.D. Stephens, D. Bradley and F. Nielsen (2003), 'Determinants of relative poverty in advanced capitalist democracies', *American Sociological Review*, **68**(1):22–51.

Nickell, S. (2006), 'The CEP–OECD institutions data set 1960–2004', Centre for Economic Performance discussion paper no. 759, London.

Nickell, S., L. Nunziata and W. Ochel (2005), 'Unemployment in the OECD since the 1960s: what do we know?' *Economic Journal*, **115**: 1–27.

OECD (2004), 'Employment protection regulation and labour market performance', in *OECD Employment Outlook 2004*, Paris: OECD, pp. 61–125.

OECD (2006), 'Reassessing the role of policies and institutions for labour market performance: a quantitative analysis', in *OECD Employment Outlook 2006*, Paris: OECD, pp. 207–31.

Pollmann-Schult, M. and F. Büchel (2005), 'Unemployment benefits, unemployment duration and subsequent job quality: evidence from West Germany', *Acta Sociologica*, **48**(1): 21–39.

Røed, K. and T. Zhang (2003), 'Does unemployment compensation affect unemployment duration?', *Economic Journal*, **113**: 190–206.

Schils, T. (2007), 'Employment protection in Dutch collective agreements',

Amsterdam Institute for Advanced Labour Studies working paper no. 56, Amsterdam.

Streeck, W. and P.C. Schmitter (1985), 'Community, market, state – and associations? The prospective contribution of interest governance to social order', *European Sociological Review*, **1**(2): 119–38.

Wilthagen, T. (1998), 'Flexicurity: a new paradigm for labour market policy reform?,' Wissenschaftszentrum discussion paper no. 202, Berlin.

Wilthagen, T., F. Tros and H. van Lieshout (2003), 'Towards "flexicurity"? Balancing flexibility and security in EU member states', paper for the 13th World Congress of the International Industrial Relations Association, Berlin, September.

APPENDIX: REGRESSION DETAILS

Countries included in the analysis are Australia (AUS), Austria (AUT), Belgium (BEL), Canada (CAN), the Czech Republic (CZE), Denmark (DNK), Finland (FIN), France (FRA), Germany (DEU), Greece (GRC), Hungary (HUN), Ireland (IRE), Italy (ITA), Luxembourg (LUX), the Netherlands (NLD), New Zealand (NZL), Norway (NOR), Poland (POL), Portugal (PRT), Slovak Republic (SLK), Spain (ESP), Sweden (SWE), Switzerland (CHE), the United Kingdom (UK) and the United States (USA). Table 1A.1 shows data availability for these countries.

To estimate the effect of the policy instruments of interest on several labour market outcomes, the following three linear regression models are used:

1. Basic model

$$Y_{jt} = \alpha_j + \alpha_t + \beta_1 X_{1jt} + \beta_2 X_{2jt} + \beta_3 X_{3jt} + \eta_{jt}$$

2. Model with bilateral interactions

$$Y_{jt} = \alpha_j + \alpha_t + \beta_1 X_{1jt} + \beta_2 X_{2jt} + \beta_3 X_{3jt} + \beta_4 X_{1jt} X_{2jt} + \beta_5 X_{1jt} X_{3jt}$$
$$+ \beta_6 X_{2jt} X_{3jt} + \eta_{jt}$$

3. Model with trilateral interactions

$$Y_{jt} = \alpha_j + \alpha_t + \beta_1 X_{1jt} + \beta_2 X_{2jt} + \beta_3 X_{3jt} + \beta_4 X_{1jt} X_{2jt} + \beta_5 X_{1jt} X_{3jt}$$
$$+ \beta_6 X_{2jt} X_{3jt} + \beta_7 X_{1jt} X_{2jt} X_{3jt} + \eta_{jt}$$

where $j = 1, \ldots, 25$ is the number of the countries; $t = 1, \ldots, 4$ is the number of the time periods, α_j are the country fixed-effects, α_t are the period fixed-effects, Y_{jt} is a set of dependent variables, X_{jt} is a set of independent variables and η_{jt} is the error term. The set of dependent variables consists of the employment rate (employed population as a percentage of total population aged between 15 and 64), unemployment rate (number of unemployed as a percentage of the labour force), share of long-term unemployment (percentage of unemployed with unemployment spell longer than one year), inflow into unemployment (number of people with unemployment spell less than one month multiplied by 12, as a percentage of the labour force), inflow into employment (number of people with employment spell shorter than one year as a percentage of total employed) and the expected income

Table 1A.1   Data availability for regression analysis of the effectiveness of labour market policy

Employment rate	Available for 1985–2004, except for HUN (1992–2004) and SLK (1994–2004).
Unemployment rate	Available for 1985–2004, except for CZE (1990–2004), HUN (1992–2004), POL (1990–2004) and SLK (1994–2004).
Share of long-term unemployment	Available for 1985–2004, except for AUT (1994–2004), CHE (1991–2004), CZE (1993–2004), HUN (1992–2004), NZL (1986–2004), POL (1992–2004), POR (1986–2004) and SLK (1994–2004).
Inflow into unemployment	Available for 1985–2004, except for AUT (1994–2004), CHE (1991–2004), CZE (1993–2004), HUN (1992–2004), NZL (1986–2004), POL (1992–2004), POR (1986–2004) and SLK (1994–2004).
Inflow into employment	Available for 1993–2004, except for AUS (n.a.), AUT (n.a.), CHE (1996–2004), CZE (1997–2004), FIN (1995–2004), GRC (1992–2001), HUN (1997–2004), NZL (n.a.), NOR (1995–2004), POL (1997–2004), SLK (n.a.), SWE (1995–2004) and USA (n.a.).
Expected income loss due to unemployment	Available for 1985–2004, except for AUT (1990–2004), CZE (1993–2004), HUN (1995–2004), NZL (1986–2004), POL (1991–2004), POR (1989–2004) and SLK (1995–2004).
EPL indicator	Available for 1985–2003, except for AUT (n.a.), CZE (1993–2004), HUN (1990–2004), LUX (n.a.), NZL (1990–2004), POL (1990–2004) and SLK (1993–2004).
UB generosity	Available for 1985–2004, except for CZE (n.a.), HUN (n.a.), LUX (n.a.), POL (n.a.) and SLK (n.a.).
ALMP expenditures	Available for 1985–2004, except for CZE (1991–2004), HUN (1992–2004), ITA (1990–2004), POL (1992–2004) and SLK (1995–2003).

Sources: OECD (2004), *Employment Outlook*, OECD (2008), *Labour Force Statistics*, online database, Paris: OECD; OECD (2008), *Social Expenditure Database*, online database, Paris: OECD.

loss due to unemployment (the probability of being unemployed multiplied by the average replacement income during an unemployment spell – which is calculated as total expenditure on unemployment benefits divided by the number of unemployed – as a percentage of the average wage[1]).

The set of independent variables consists of the OECD employment protection indicator (measuring the strictness of EPL on 18 items, ranging

Table 1A.2   Summary statistics for dependent and independent variables

		1985–89	1990–94	1995–99	2000–2004
Employment rate	Mean	65.9	65.6	65.8	68.2
	Min	47.5 (ESP)	49.0 (ESP)	50.3 (ESP)	53.2 (POL)
	Max	80.1 (USA)	84.8 (CHE)	83.2 (LUX)	94.1 (LUX)
Unemployment rate	Mean	8.6	8.6	8.5	7.3
	Min	0.7 (CHE)	1.5 (LUX)	2.4 (LUX)	2.2 (LUX)
	Max	19.1 (ESP)	19.3 (ESP)	19.8 (ESP)	18.5 (ESP)
Share of long-term unemployment	Mean	36.2	33.5	37.3	32.8
	Min	7.3 (NOR)	9.3 (USA)	8.5 (USA)	6.4 (NOR)
	Max	72.3 (BEL)	62.7 (ITA)	62.6 (ITA)	57.9 (SLK)
Inflow into unemployment	Mean	9.1	11.5	10.4	13.6
	Min	1.0 (POR)	2.8 (LUX)	2.7 (NET)	2.3 (NET)
	Max	32.6 (USA)	35.6 (USA)	22.9 (USA)	22.6 (USA)
Inflow into employment	Mean		12.0	12.9	13.0
	Min	n.a.	4.8 (ITA)	6.2 (LUX)	6.3 (LUX)
	Max		21.2 (ESP)	23.9 (DEN)	20.6 (DEN)
Expected income loss due to unemployment	Mean	5.3	5.9	6.4	5.5
	Min	0.1 (LUX)	0.6 (LUX)	0.1 (DEN)	0.1 (DEN)
	Max	16.5 (ESP)	14.6 (ESP)	16.6 (ESP)	17.6 (POL)
EPL indicator	Mean	2.4	2.2	2.0	1.9
	Min	0.2 (USA)	0.2 (USA)	0.2 (USA)	0.2 (USA)
	Max	4.2 (POR)	3.9 (POR)	3.7 (POR)	3.6 (POR)
UB generosity	Mean	28.7	29.9	31.5	28.3
	Min	1.1 (ITA)	9.9 (ITA)	13.2 (USA)	5.9 (CZE)
	Max	55.7 (NET)	53.2 (NET)	62.8 (DEN)	52.7 (NET)
ALMP expenditure	Mean	0.75	0.82	0.81	0.70
	Min	0.20 (CHE)	0.19 (ITA)	0.17 (CZE)	0.20 (GRC)
	Max	1.81 (SWE)	2.52 (SWE)	2.01 (SWE)	1.72 (DEN)

Sources: OECD (2004), *Employment Outlook*, OECD (2008), *Labour Force Statistics*, online database, Paris: OECD; OECD (2008), *Social Expenditure Database*, online database, Paris: OECD.

from 1 to 6), unemployment benefit generosity (OECD gross summary replacement rate over four different family types and three different income levels), and active labour market policy (expenditure as a percentage of GDP). Table 1A.2 shows the summary statistics for the relevant time periods, including means, minimum and maximum level.

As mentioned, we used a two-step analysis for the active labour market policy variable to reduce the problem of bi-causality. We first regressed the following model:

The labour market triangle

$$ALMP_{jt} = \beta_0 + \beta_1(GDP_{jt} - GDP_{j,t-1}) + \mu_j + \upsilon_{jt}$$

where β_1 represents the cyclical part of expenditures on active labour market policy in country j, whereas μ_j is the country fixed-effect and υ_{jt} is the error term. From this regression we calculate the so-called policy part of expenditures on active labour market policy, taking only the country fixed effect and the error term, and we include this variable in our models explained before (also included in the summary statistics in Table 1A.2). Table 1A.3 presents the regression results.

Table 1A.3   *Regression results for the analysis of the effect of labour policy instruments*

	Employment rate			Unemployment rate		
	Model 1	Model 2	Model 3	Model 1	Model 2	Model 3
EPL	2.362	0.320	−0.260	−1.180	0.389	−0.134
	(1.604)	(1.584)	(1.786)	(1.155)	(1.062)	(1.192)
UB	0.121	0.095	0.125	−0.041	−0.026	0.001
	(0.117)	(0.113)	(0.121)	(0.085)	(0.076)	(0.081)
ALMP	−2.862	−2.981	−3.134	2.972*	3.604***	3.466**
	(2.137)	(1.968)	(1.990)	(1.538)	(1.320)	(1.328)
EPL*UB		−0.228**	−0.213**		0.127**	0.140**
		(0.094)	(0.096)		(0.063)	(0.064)
EPL*ALMP		6.638***	6.725***		−5.068***	−4.989***
		(1.765)	(1.779)		(1.184)	(1.187)
UB*ALMP		−0.077	−0.038		−0.104	−0.069
		(0.139)	(0.150)		(0.094)	(0.100)
EPL*UB*ALMP			0.101			0.091
			(0.140)			(0.094)

	Share of long-term unemployment			Inflow into unemployment		
	Model 1	Model 2	Model 3	Model 1	Model 2	Model 3
EPL	−1.793	3.283	0.407	−4.166**	−3.864*	−4.144*
	(3.359)	(3.263)	(3.467)	(1.709)	(1.974)	(2.189)
UB	−0.172	−0.067	0.123	0.037	0.025	0.043
	(0.252)	(0.245)	(0.255)	(0.128)	(0.148)	(0.161)
ALMP	6.776	7.647*	6.914*	3.173	2.608	2.536
	(4.441)	(3.911)	(3.803)	(2.260)	(2.366)	(2.402)
EPL*UB		0.467**	0.528***		0.126	0.132
		(0.198)	(0.194)		(0.120)	(0.123)
EPL*ALMP		−15.392***	−15.133***		−1.537	−1.511
		(3.573)	(3.461)		(2.162)	(2.185)
UB*ALMP		0.007	0.188		0.200	0.218
		(0.292)	(0.296)		(0.176)	(0.187)
EPL*UB*ALMP			0.544*			0.053
			(0.270)			(0.171)

Table 1A.3   (continued)

	Inflow into employment			Expected income loss unemployment		
	Model 1	Model 2	Model 3	Model 1	Model 2	Model 3
EPL	−0.689	0.238	0.472	−0.783	0.551	0.307
	(1.333)	(1.756)	(1.842)	(0.964)	(0.895)	(1.012)
UB	0.126*	0.182*	0.141	−0.040	−0.028	−0.015
	(0.067)	(0.095)	(0.124)	(0.071)	(0.064)	(0.069)
ALMP	−2.717	−2.747	−2.961	2.125	2.487**	2.422**
	(1.586)	(1.688)	(1.766)	(1.284)	(1.112)	(1.127)
EPL*UB		−0.009	−0.006		0.131**	0.138**
		(0.082)	(0.084)		(0.053)	(0.055)
EPL*ALMP		−2.441	−2.224		−4.382***	−4.345***
		(1.839)	(1.917)		(0.998)	(1.008)
UB*ALMP		−0.094	−0.091		−0.032	−0.016
		(0.150)	(0.153)		(0.079)	(0.085)
EPL*UB*ALMP			−0.060			0.042
			(0.112)			(0.079)

Notes: Standard errors in parentheses, *= $p < 0.10$, **=$p < 0.05$, ***=$p < 0.01$.
Country and time period fixed-effects and constant term included in the analysis but omitted here.
Number of observations ranging from 48 (inflow employment) to 78 (other models).

Sources: Authors' calculations using OECD (2004), *Employment Outlook*, Paris: OECD (2008), *Labour Force Statistics*, online database, Paris: OECD; OECD (2008), *Social Expenditure Database*, online database, Paris: OECD.

NOTE

1. In formula: $I = u (1 − (B/Nu)/(W/N(1−u))) = u − (1−u)B/W$, in which u is the unemployment rate, B is total expenditure on unemployment benefits, W is the total wage bill, and N is the labour force.

2. Sweden

Eskil Wadensjö

INTRODUCTION

Swedish labour market policy has a tradition of relying on collective agreements between employers' associations and trade unions and on active labour market policy. The work principle has guided the formulation of active labour market policies. Passive labour market policy – unemployment insurance – was introduced relatively late and was not very generous at the start. The trade unions and the employers' associations developed rapidly in the early twentieth century and reached an agreement on respecting collective agreements in 1938, known as Saltsjöbadsavtalet (Edlund et al. 1989).

In 1928, rules regarding collective agreements were legislated and a special court for conflicts regarding the interpretation of collective agreements was founded, the Arbetsdomstolen. During the Second World War the labour market was regulated in various ways as part of the mobilization efforts but the regulations were dismantled after the war. The state did not intervene to any major extent in the labour market up to the 1970s. In the 1970s various labour laws were introduced, however. The most important was the Job Security Law (LAS). This law stated rules for lay-offs. The principle of 'last in, first out' was established, but with the possibility for employers to reach agreements with the trade unions on exceptions to this rule. There have only been minor changes in labour legislation since the 1970s.

UNEMPLOYMENT INSURANCE

The first trade union unemployment insurance societies in Sweden emerged in the late nineteenth century. They were not supported by the state. For the unemployed who were not insured or covered in other ways, the municipalities could provide income- and wealth-tested income support. During the First World War unemployment became a political issue in Sweden. Structural unemployment developed in sectors that were highly dependent on international trade. A governmental investigation studied the possibilities of introducing an unemployment insurance system, but recommended instead public work (with low wages) as support for the unemployed. For those not placed in public work, cash support from the municipality was the settled policy. The trade union unemployment funds had severe problems in periods of high unemployment, especially in the early 1920s and the early 1930s.[1]

As the Social Democratic Party formed a government after the general election of 1932, it radically changed employment policies. Public work with market wages was preferred to the earlier form of public work with low wages. State support to the trade union-organized unemployment insurance schemes, a so-called Ghent system, was introduced in Sweden in 1935. At the start, the rules regarding compensation and financing were so strict that many unions did not apply for state support, however.[2] Gradually, as the rules changed, it became more attractive for the trade union unemployment funds to apply for state support and other unions were induced to set up new insurance schemes. All trade unions and also some organizations of the self-employed and business owners are now related to unemployment insurance societies.

At the start it was possible, but rather complicated, to be a member of the unemployment insurance fund of a union without being a member of that union. In the first decades few people made such a choice. However, it gradually became easier to be a member of the fund without being a union member and in 1997 a special unemployment insurance society was founded by the state which was not related to any trade union. It has gradually increased in membership but a large majority of the workers are still members of a union-related fund and members of the union. In 2005, 16 per cent of fund members were not members of a union. Irrespective of those changes, Sweden in practice still has a Ghent system, a system which has contributed to high union density (see Clasen and Viebrock 2008; Kjellberg 2006 and Viebrock 2006).

The change of government after the general elections of September 2006 meant lower compensation rates and higher membership fees for unemployment insurance. For the first time it has now become common to be a member of a union but not of the unemployment fund related to it.

The Main Reforms since the 1990s

Sweden went through a severe economic crisis in the early 1990s. The unemployment rate increased from 1.5 per cent to close to 10 per cent. In the years after the crisis the replacement rate was lowered, making it less attractive to be a member of an unemployment insurance fund, but on the other hand the risk of unemployment was higher, making it more attractive. Since 1988 the replacement rate had been 90 per cent up to a ceiling (lowered in that year from 91.7 per cent). The replacement rate was lowered to 80 per cent in 1993 and 75 per cent in 1996. In 1997 the replacement rate was increased again to 80 per cent. The number of compensation days was reduced in the 1990s. At the start of the crisis of the 1990s the number of compensation days was 300 (60 weeks if five days per week are compensated) for those under the age of 55 and 450 for those aged 55 and older. In 1998 this age was raised to 57 or older. Many other minor changes were made in the 1990s in the direction of a more restrictive policy (Olli-Segendorf 2003). In the election campaign of 2006, one of the main topics was strengthening work incentives. The new government that came into office after the elections of September 2006 has changed the labour market policy in some respects. Changes in the unemployment benefit insurance are discussed below.

In 2006, the ceiling of the unemployment insurance was increased by the Social Democratic government to a daily maximum benefit of SEK 730 (€76)[3] during the first 200 days and SEK 680 (€71) for the following 100 days. On 1 January 2007, the ceiling was set by the new government to SEK 680 (€71) for the whole unemployment benefit period. More than 75 per cent of all employees reach the ceiling of the unemployment insurance. The replacement rate was also lowered by the new government. In 2006 the replacement rate was 80 per cent during the whole benefit period but as from 2007 it is 70 per cent after 200 benefit days and 65 per cent after 300 benefit days.

In addition, the insurance has become more expensive for the individual members. From 1 January 2007, the unemployment funds have to cover a larger share of the costs[4] and consequently the fees were increased. In September 2007 the highest fee paid by an employed member was SEK 433 (€45) and by an unemployed member SEK 135 (€14) per month (the fees of most insurance funds are slightly lower for those who are members of the union related to the fund).[5] This increase led to a loss of members of the unemployment funds. Between 1 January 2007 and 31 July 2008 the number of members of the unemployment funds declined by 480 400, corresponding to 12.7 per cent of total membership.

In the budget for the present fiscal year (2009) put forward in September 2008, the government proposes a higher state subsidy to the unemployment insurance societies which will lead to lower fees for most funds. The fees will still be much higher than before 2007, however. As a response to the large drop in the number of members of the unemployment funds, the labour market minister announced that the government intended to make membership in an unemployment fund mandatory. A governmental investigation put forward a proposal in spring 2008, which was strongly criticized. In September 2008 the government declared that it will not put forward a proposition to parliament on mandatory membership in an unemployment insurance fund, at least not in the period up to the next elections.

The Current System: Main Characteristics

The Swedish unemployment insurance system consists of two components: a universal basic insurance and a voluntary loss of income insurance (income-related benefit).[6] None of the two components is means-tested. The universal basic insurance is available to a person who is no member of an unemployment fund, or has not been a member for a sufficiently long period to comply with the membership condition (which entails having been a member of a fund for at least a year without interruption). The applicant is further required to fulfil a basic condition and a work condition to obtain a benefit according to the basic insurance. The rules are the same for all unemployment insurance funds.

The basic condition means that the applicant is fully or partly unemployed, capable of working for at least three hours a day and at least 17 hours a week, prepared to accept work offered, registered with the employment office as a job seeker, actively looking for work and participating in drawing up an individual action plan in consultation with the employment office. The work condition means that the unemployed person must have worked during a period of 12 months immediately preceding unemployment for at least 80 hours per month for at least six months, or 480 hours during six uninterrupted calendar months and at least 50 hours in each of these months. Periods of time on parental benefit or being conscripted can be counted as work for at most two calendar months. Employment in work with a wage subsidy, sheltered work and periods with severance pay may be counted towards the work condition.

The basic insurance benefit is SEK 320 (€33) per benefit day for a person who worked full-time regardless of previous income. For a person who worked part-time, the daily benefit payment is reduced proportionally. The benefit is paid for at most 300 days (at most five days a week) with an exception for parents whose children are under 18 years of age who can receive benefits for 450 days. Before the benefit is paid, a qualifying period of one week must have elapsed.

To obtain income-related unemployment insurance, the membership condition, the basic condition and the work condition described above must be fulfilled. The income-related insurance is also paid for a maximum of 300 days (again 450 days for parents with children under the age of

18) at most the daily amount paid for work over five days a week, with a waiting period of one week. The income-related insurance is paid at 80 per cent of the previous daily earnings during the 200 first benefit days up to a ceiling of SEK 850 (€88) per day. This corresponds to a maximum daily amount of SEK 680 (€71). During the next 100 days (250 days for parents) the benefit is paid at 70 per cent of the previous daily wage. The maximum benefit is still SEK 680 (€71) per day. The daily income is equivalent to 1/22 of the monthly wage. For benefit days (Monday through Friday) between the 301st and 450th day (only available for parents with children under the age of 18) the replacement rate is 65 per cent. When an unemployed person refuses a job referral without a good reason, the insurance compensation can be reduced in steps, the first time by 25 per cent for 40 days, the second time by 50 per cent for 40 days, and it is discontinued the third time.

During 2007, 371 193 individuals received income-related unemployment insurance and 54 883 received compensation from the universal basic insurance at least one day during the year. This corresponds to 8.4 and 1.2 per cent, respectively, of the labour force. Of those who received unemployment insurance, 13.2 per cent received the universal basic insurance.

Unemployment Benefit According to Agreement or from an Agreement-Based Insurance[7]

The unemployment insurance from the unemployment funds is not the only benefit that can be received when unemployed. There are several supplementary benefits in the event of unemployment.[8] There are three basic types of solutions: agreements between trade unions and employer organizations, member insurance coverage (for those who are a member of a particular trade union) and individual insurance policies taken out through a trade union. Agreement-based solutions came into existence first. Although these insurances are negotiated by the trade union organizations, they cover everyone within the sphere of the agreement, not just trade union members. There are four main agreements that together cover 75 per cent of all employees in the labour market.

For employees in the central government sector who have been given notice due to shortage of work or who have decided not to move to the new location in the event of relocation and therefore give notice themselves, the agreement provides them with the right to receive an additional benefit – severance pay – in the event of unemployment, provided that they have been employed for at least a year. Severance pay is paid for the same period of time as the benefit from the unemployment insurance. For a person who receives an earnings-related benefit from the unemployment insurance, the severance pay together with the unemployment insurance benefit amounts to 80 per cent of the wage during the first 200 days and 70 per cent for the following 100 days.

Municipal and county council employees also can obtain severance pay when given notice because of shortage of work. To be eligible for the lump sum benefit, it is required that the employee has been employed until given notice and has been so for at least 36 calendar months, is aged 25 or above and has not reached the age of mandatory retirement.

Approximately 72 per cent of the employees meet these requirements. The lump sum benefit is equivalent to one-third of the employee's normal monthly earnings multiplied by the number of full employment years within the entire local government sector. The lump sum benefit can amount to at most six monthly wages. Entitlement to periodic severance pay is based on age and period of employment within the sector; the minimum age is 45 and the period of employment required for a person aged 45 is 17 years. The total period of employment within the sector counts. An employee cannot receive both a periodic and a lump sum benefit. During the period that the employee receives a benefit from the unemployment insurance, the periodic severance pay together with the earnings-related benefit amounts to 80 per cent of the employee's monthly earnings before unemployment during the first 200 unemployment days and 70 per cent during the following 100 days.

The severance pay insurance, AGB, is an agreement-based insurance that covers blue-collar workers within the sphere of the collective agreement of the Confederation of Swedish Enterprise and LO (the confederation of blue-collar unions). This insurance was introduced in 1967. To obtain AGB the employee must have been given notice due to shortage of work, the employee must be aged 40 or older at the time of termination of employment and must have been employed for at least 50 months for an uninterrupted five-year period at one or more companies covered by AGB insurance. AGB is paid in the form of a lump sum when employment terminates.

According to an agreement between the Confederation of Swedish Enterprise and PTK (an association of the major trade unions for white-collar workers in the private sector), an employee who is made redundant due to shortage of work can obtain a severance pay, AGE. To be entitled to AGE, the employee must have been dismissed due to shortage of work, have attained the age of 40, have worked for at least five hours per week during a five-year period, be looking for work and be registered at the employment office. Approximately 50 per cent of the employees in this sector qualify for agreement-based insurance. The benefit level of AGE is 70 per cent of the monthly wage together with the earnings-related unemployment benefit for the first six benefit months, after which it decreases to 50 per cent.[9]

Besides the benefits determined by statute or by agreement between employer and employee organizations, there are private group insurances arranged by trade union organizations. These consist of group insurances that cover all members of a trade union and insurance policies taken out by individual members through their trade union. Members of an unemployment insurance association who do not belong to a union can take out individual private income insurance. The design of the insurance schemes is similar in the various areas although there are some differences with respect to the ceiling of the compensation or the length of the benefit period. The group insurances that cover all members of a trade union usually compensate for 80 per cent of the monthly wage together with the earnings-related benefit up to between SEK 35000 (€3629) and SEK 100000 (€10368) during 120 to 200 days and end when the insured is between 61 and 65 years old. Some trade unions also offer individual insurances that extend beyond the benefit period or the wage ceiling of the member insurance. The insurances that the trade unions offer to their members or that can be taken out by individuals directly from insurance companies usually have a longer compensation period of 280 to 300 days. The income and age ceilings are similar for the individual and group insurances.

Administration and Responsibilities

There are 33 unemployment funds with 3.3 million members (September 2008). The Swedish labour force age amounts at present to 4.6 million individuals. About 1.3 million people aged between 16 and 64 are not in the labour force. The unemployment funds decide on and pay unemployment insurance. The employment offices provide information to job seekers and check that they comply with the conditions for receiving unemployment insurance, that they are actively looking for work and accept offers for suitable work or a place in a labour market programme. There are 300 employment offices. Up to 2008 these were organized by 20 County Labour Boards with the National Labour Market Board (AMS) as responsible authority. Until 2003, the AMS was also responsible for supervision of the unemployment funds. As from 2004, this role was taken over by the Swedish Unemployment Insurance Board (IAF). The labour market administration used to have tripartite boards on all levels of the organization. In 1991 the main association for private employers left all boards as part of a new policy. Later the same year a new liberal–conservative government made the administration of the labour market administration similar to that of other governmental authorities (see Nycander 2002).

The present government re-organized the National Labour Market Administration from 1 January 2008. The AMS and the 20 County Labour Boards were closed down and one new authority, Arbetsförmedlingen (Swedish Public Employment Service) was established instead. Unemployment insurance is financed mainly from the state budget, but also from membership fees to the unemployment funds. Employers pay a 'labour market fee', actually a tax, to the state. In 2005, this tax covered 87 per cent of the costs of the unemployment insurance, and the employees' membership fees to the unemployment funds covered 13 per cent of the costs. Since July 2008 the membership fees cover one-third of the costs.

EMPLOYMENT PROTECTION

Until the mid-1970s the Swedish labour market was less regulated by the state than in most other European countries. The social partners (unions and employers' associations) had a strong position and regulated the labour market through collective agreements. However, in the mid-1970s several laws were introduced that governed several aspects of the labour market. The most important of those laws is the Job Security Law (LAS) of 1974. The seniority principle became the rule as regards the selection of whom to keep when reducing the workforce and a minimum period of notice at dismissals was agreed upon. These changes gave older workers stronger employment protection as they usually have higher seniority.

The Main Reforms since the 1990s

The laws decided on in the 1970s are still in force. There have been some minor changes regarding trial periods for new employees and exemptions of a number of employees from the seniority rules in small businesses, but these changes are minor.

The Current System: Main Characteristics

The Swedish labour market strongly relies on collective agreements. These deal not only with wages, but also with a lot of other issues, such as collectively agreed insurances complementing the social insurances (as mentioned before), a minimum notice period in case of dismissals (exceeding those decided by law), work environment, vacation, working hours and so on. Many labour laws can be surpassed by collective agreements.

This means that the laws give basic levels on working hours, holiday days, minimum notice period, and so on, which are valid if no collective agreements are agreed upon, but many agreements more favourable for the employees are reached.

The Job Security Law (LAS) gives the employer the right to dismiss workers on the condition that they do this in a certain order, according to seniority. The seniority is calculated for different groups of workers (in practice different occupations). The seniority principle is to be applied to employees in each group separately. The division of the employees in groups is decided on in agreement with the unions; if an agreement is not reached all employees are considered to belong to the same group. The order of dismissals may be changed according to an agreement with the union. In practice, this means in most cases that those with high seniority who are laid off get economic compensation (a lump sum or a pension) from the employer as part of the agreement. If the employer does not comply with the law and does not reach an agreement with the union, the union may go to the Labour Court. The Labour Court decides on economic compensation to the employees and the union. The amounts that will be decided on are well known. In practice, there is a price list for employers who do not comply with the law and dismiss other employees than those who should have been laid off according to LAS. The unions usually accept compensation corresponding to what they would have been able to get in the Labour Court. The system is rather efficient in avoiding long judicial processes.

Administration and Responsibilities

The labour laws are determined by parliament but the industrial relations system is administered in all important details by the social partners through collective agreements and by negotiations in individual cases. This implies that it is important for employees to be union members and for employers to be members of an employers' association. The Labour Court has an important role in interpreting the labour laws and determining the compensation that should be paid for those breaking the law. In practice, however, only a few cases are handled by the Labour Court as the social partners know in most cases what the result will be and avoid taking conflicts to the Labour Court.

ACTIVE LABOUR MARKET POLICY

International comparisons of public expenditures on labour market programmes, as regularly published by the Organisation for Economic

Co-operation and Development (OECD), show that labour market expenditure in Sweden is high and more concentrated on active measures than in most other countries. This emphasis on active labour market programmes is part of a long tradition.

The earliest Swedish labour market programme was the establishment of the first municipal employment exchanges in 1902. These were granted state support a few years later and expanded rapidly. The next programme was public relief work, which was tried as a means to fight unemployment during the First World War. These works were greatly expanded during the economic depression of the early 1920s. Wages for these public works were set at a low level, so that no one would be tempted to stay on if another job was available. The public relief works were also used as a test of the willingness of the unemployed to work. The work principle was strongly emphasized.

During the 1930s the policy was partially changed due to the influence of Keynes, the contemporary (and in some respects earlier) Stockholm School, and the trade unions. A new form of public work was introduced in 1931. This form of public work – temporary job creation schemes (*beredskapsarbeten*) – was compensated according to the market wage. The Social Democratic Party, which came into office in 1932, strongly preferred this type of public work. The earlier form continued to exist but the new form soon came to dominate and in 1940 the old type of public work was disbanded. It was decided to increase the number of employment exchange offices to make it possible to check the willingness of those who received unemployment insurance benefits to accept work, after state support to the union unemployment insurance societies was granted as from 1935. During the Second World War the municipal employment exchanges and a strong central labour market authority were established. This system was made permanent after the war.

The early post-war period was characterized by high economic growth and low unemployment. A problem that confronted the trade union movement (LO) at the end of the 1940s was increased inflation and political pressure on the trade unions to hold wage demands down. LO economists, with Rudolf Meidner and Gösta Rehn as the leading figures, believed that it was unreasonable for the trade union movement to keep wages down. It would lead to conflicts within the organization and weaken the levelling of wages. Therefore they suggested a new policy composed of the following three features: (1) restrictive aggregate demand policy; (2) solidary wage policy (equal pay for equal work) with anticipated decreased wage differences; and (3) active labour market policy. The first two measures would result in higher unemployment compared with the – then current – expansionary policy. Therefore, a complementary requirement was an active, selective labour market policy helping the unemployed to move to job vacancies and to move jobs to the unemployed.

This policy, the Rehn–Meidner model, was accepted by the Social Democratic Party and thereby the government at the end of the 1950s. Labour market training and mobility grants were considered typical for the new policy. The period from the end of the 1950s until the middle of the 1960s may be seen as the high point for the Rehn–Meidner model. Labour market policy expanded quickly and the policy became generally accepted.

The development of the 1970s differed in some respects from the traditional Swedish labour market policy. Although the work principle was still dominant – in terms of both numbers and budget – the cash principle gained ground by way of changes in the income transfer systems. Another change was a shift in policy from 'employment security in the labour market' to 'job security in the enterprise'. The strong emphasis on market-strengthening measures decreased in relative terms. In the 1980s the labour market policy was increasingly geared towards groups with special problems in the labour market; young people and immigrant workers are two examples.

The Main Reforms since the 1990s

During the economic crisis of the early 1990s labour market policies differed from those of earlier recessions. First, the government waited much longer to increase the volume of labour market programmes. Second, at the start of the recession labour market training was very much favoured, compared to temporary job creation schemes. In the preceding downturns the use of temporary job creation schemes had been the main labour market programme to stabilize the business cycle. Later on in the crisis period the policy changed, however, and the temporary job creation schemes expanded. In 1993 a new temporary employment programme was introduced which paid lower wages, equal to the unemployment benefit.

A special programme, the activity guarantee, was introduced in August 2000. The activity guarantee assured placement in various programmes (in most cases shifting over time). The programme was open to those aged 20 years and older who were looking for a job at the employment offices and had been registered as a job applicant (unemployed or in active labour market programmes) for two years or more or who had a high risk of fulfilling that criterion in the near future. The activity guarantee gave the same compensation as the unemployment insurance. A person receiving unemployment insurance benefit could not refuse a placement in the activity guarantee without losing the right to unemployment benefit.

The programme thus followed the work principle tradition. As of 1 July 2007 the activity guarantee was replaced by a similar programme, activity support and development assistance, which combines job search, placement in different programmes and compensation corresponding to the unemployment insurance benefit.

In many countries active labour market programmes focus on younger workers. In Sweden, however, many older workers are placed in the ordinary business cycle-related programmes (Wadensjö 2003). The programme of Temporary Public Sector Jobs for Older Workers started in November 1996 and placed a large number of people shortly thereafter. It was intended for long-term unemployed workers aged between 55 and 64. The jobs were intended not to replace already existing jobs, but with the intention to enhance the quality of public services. No new placements were made after 1998 so the number of people in the programme gradually dropped, up to the end of 2001.

The Current System: Main Characteristics

Active labour market policies can be divided into different groups. The demand-side programmes used to be mainly programmes of employment in the public sector for the unemployed, but have gradually shifted to subsidized employment (often with training content) in both the public and the private sectors. The supply-side policies include mainly training programmes with vocational training in special training establishments, but also non-vocational education and training in companies. Of less importance, but much discussed, has been support to geographical mobility. In the last decades many of the programmes have been targeted to specific groups. Programmes for young people and for the disabled have been the most extensive.

As mentioned earlier, temporary jobs for the unemployed have existed as a policy since the 1910s. The rules for the programmes have changed. Initially, the compensation for those employed in such programmes was low, but it was raised during the 1930s to the market wage rate (or collective agreements). In the 1990s there has been a change back to lower pay and to an emphasis on the combination of work and training. This development continued in the 2000s.

Labour market training has gradually expanded since the 1950s. In the early stages of the recession of the 1990s, labour market training largely replaced temporary job creation schemes as a countercyclical measure. The two main arguments for labour market training have been that it facilitates mobility from unemployment-stricken occupations and regions to those with vacancies, and that it enhances the competence of the labour force. In general the allowance is the same as the compensation from unemployment insurance. For those who are not members of an unemployment insurance society, the compensation is set to a fixed, low amount. Quite a few evaluations have been made of labour market training programmes.[10] The oldest studies which cover the 1960s, 1970s and 1980s show in many instances positive results. However, the studies carried out in the 1990s regularly show that those who take part in a training programme lose economically (in terms of employment or wage rate) compared to those (with the same characteristics and labour market situation) who do not participate. It has led to a more sceptical attitude of many towards the labour market training programmes.

In July 1984 a new programme was introduced, which lent support to unemployed people who wanted to start their own business. After a trial period it became a standard programme as from July 1987. The maximum compensation period is six months with the possibility of an extension of six months, and the compensation is the same as for people in labour market training. The measure has been given a high priority and has rapidly expanded.

A large part of Swedish active labour market policy is targeted towards groups with special problems in the labour market. One of those groups is disabled people. In an international comparison, Sweden puts an especially strong emphasis on labour market policy programmes for the disabled (measured as share of participants or of costs).[11] The main programmes are: (1) employment in Samhall (a conglomerate of sheltered workshops); (2) sheltered jobs in the public sector (OSA); (3) work with a wage subsidy; (4) development employment; and (5) security development.

The sheltered workshops, which since 1980 have been organized as part of Samhall, are designed for workers who have disabilities that make it very difficult for them to be placed in the ordinary labour market. Many stay in sheltered workshops for very long periods, even if one of the goals of the programme is to rehabilitate people and place them in the ordinary labour market. At the end of 2007, 19,300 disabled workers were employed by Samhall. A special programme was introduced in 1986 – sheltered work in the public sector (OSA). The programme is mainly intended for people with socio-medical disabilities or long-term psychological occupational handicaps. In 2007 the average subsidy level was 75 per cent of the wage cost. The number of participants in OSA was on average 4900 in 2007.

Work with a wage subsidy also is a labour market programme for the disabled and has the most participants. As it is more integrative, it is given higher priority and is expanding compared to work in sheltered workshops. In 2007 close to 59 000 persons were in this programme on average. The average subsidy level was 62 per cent in 2007. The maximum period of placement is four years but many remain in work with wage subsidies for longer periods than that. The wage rate for a person in the work with wage subsidy programme follows the collective agreement for those with corresponding jobs at the workplace up to a ceiling (SEK 16 700 (€1731) per month in 2007). In that way income compensation may be 100 per cent for some employees, which gives low incentives to leave the programme.

The institutes for vocational rehabilitation (*arbetslivsinriktad rehabilitering*) are centres for extensive training and vocational guidance. The majority but not all of those who take part in this programme are disabled. The programme prepares workers for jobs (sheltered or otherwise) or training.

In September 2008, 70 009 persons were in various programmes supporting different labour market activities organized by the Swedish Public Employment Service, most of them in the programme for activity support and development assistance (40 416). In the same month 82 609 were in work supported by the Public Employment Service. Most of them, 70 948, were in programmes for disabled people. To this number could be added approximately 19 000 persons in Samhall.

Administration and Responsibilities

Active labour market policy is an integral part of Swedish economic policy. The main aims of Swedish labour market policies are to improve the functioning of the labour market and to raise the employment rate. The work principle is central to the Swedish model of economic and social policy. The active labour market measures are the centrepiece of Swedish labour market policy, and the employment offices are the centrepiece of active labour market policies. Labour market policy is carried out by Arbetsförmedlingen (Swedish Public Employment Service), a central state authority in charge of the employment offices. The primary work task of the employment offices is to match job seekers (the unemployed or people who want to change jobs) with vacancies. If the employment office is not able to find a job in the ordinary labour market in the short run for an unemployed person, placement in an active measure is the preferred option. The number of programmes is large and has gradually expanded.

THE TRIANGLE IN PRACTICE

Typical for Swedish labour market policies are the strong organizations, both unions and employers' associations, and the large scope of active labour market programmes. The labour market legislation is mainly from the 1970s. There have been a number of minor changes since then but the main features are the same now as when the legislation was introduced. Neither the present government nor the opposition parties have any plans to change the legal regulation of the labour market. The labour legislation is to some extent regulating and influencing the collective agreements between unions and employers, but the main regulation of the Swedish labour market is through collective agreements. They form a basis for the Swedish labour market model.

The work principle has been the guiding principle for Swedish labour market policies for many decades. Active labour market policy still dominates but passive labour market policy (or the unemployment benefit system) became more important from the 1970s. Since the early 1990s passive labour market policy has gradually become more restrictive at the same time as the compensation for those in active labour market programmes was reduced. This development has been strengthened since the change of government in 2006.

Output and Outcomes

The presentation above of the different policy areas shows that Swedish policy has been guided by the work principle for a very long period. The formulation of that policy and the relative importance of that policy have changed over time. In the 1960s, 1970s and 1980s people were expected to work until statutory retirement age, and if unemployed they were expected to return to work, in many cases after a period in an active labour market programme. But in the same period the social security schemes became more generous – the replacement rate increased and access to the system was made easier. The number of people leaving the labour market early increased, many of them on a disability pension. The number of people on sickness leave swelled. The costs increased, which led to proposals to reduce expenditure. The first steps were already taken in the 1980s, but many more steps were taken during the crisis of the 1990s. An impetus to those changes was increasing expenditure for unemployment benefits and active labour market programmes. The changes were all intended to increase employment, but the design differed between the various programmes.

One important change was the lowering of the compensation rate in the active labour market programmes. The dominant development has been from paying the going market rate to paying the same compensation as the unemployment insurance benefits. Other changes were the reduction of the period of unemployment compensation, more stringent requirements of active job search for those taking up unemployment benefits, and the

Table 2.1   Labour force participation of persons aged 55–64 years in Sweden, 1995, 2000 and 2006 (%)

Age	1995		2000		2006	
	Men	Women	Men	Women	Men	Women
55–9	82.2	77.3	83.9	79.1	84.9	79.9
60	71.6	65.7	73.7	67.1	78.9	70.2
61	64.9	59.5	66.5	58.7	71.6	65.8
62	55.9	48.6	57.4	52.1	67.1	59.7
63	51.3	37.7	43.6	35.1	58.0	51.1
64	41.9	31.2	38.0	25.2	52.1	40.7
16–64	80.2	76.1	80.2	75.5	81.2	78.2

Source: Statistics Sweden (2008), *Labour Force Surveys*, Stockholm: Statistics Sweden.

placement of more long-term unemployed in labour market programmes (which they have to accept in order to keep their benefit). All taken together, this boils down to putting more emphasis on the work principle.

Most of the policy changes are clearly targeted at an increase in labour force participation and employment among older people, or people aged 60 to 64 years. Table 2.1 shows the development of labour force participation among men and women aged 60 to 64 from 1995 to 2006, and the corresponding development for those aged 55–9 and those aged 16–64. The labour force participation has increased very strongly for those aged 60–64, while it has been stable for those aged 55–9 and 16–64. Since 2000, this development was particularly strong for those who are close to 65, the statutory retirement age. This is in line with the aims of the policy changes.

NOTES

1. See Edebalk (1975 and 1987) for the history of the trade union unemployment insurance funds.
2. See Edebalk (1990) and Erici and Roth (1981) for the development, and Olli-Segendorf (2003) for details regarding the rules.
3. All amounts in euros are based on the exchange rate of 2008 (€1 = SEK 9.65).
4. From July 2008 membership fees cover one-third of the costs of the income-related insurance. The state covers the rest and also all costs for the basic insurance.
5. The fees vary strongly between different funds.
6. The information on the unemployment insurance is taken from the webpage of the Swedish Unemployment Insurance Board, IAF, www.iaf.se; Sjögren Lindquist and Wadensjö (2006, 2007).

7. This section follows Sjögren Lindquist and Wadensjö (2006).
8. A related form of policy is fixed periods of notification for lay-offs determined by law. These periods are prolonged for many through collective agreements. See Danhard (2004) and Jans (2002).
9. For those who have yearly wages above 20 price base amounts (the price base amount is SEK 40 300 (£4176) in 2007) the replacement rate is 25 per cent above this ceiling. The social insurance schemes in Sweden use base amounts (the price base amount and the income base amount) for the calculation of benefits. The price base amount is revised yearly with the help of the consumer price index.
10. See Regnér (1997) for a study which also contains a survey of earlier studies.
11. See Bergeskog (2001), Skogman Thoursie (1999), Wadensjö (1984a, 1984b, 2001, 2002), Wadensjö and Sjögren (2000) and Wang (2001) for more information on the structure and the development of the Swedish labour market policy for disabled workers.

REFERENCES

Bergeskog, A. (2001), 'Labour market policies, strategies and statistics for people with disabilities: a cross-national comparison IFAU working paper 2001:13, Uppsala.
Clasen, J. and E. Viebrock (2008), 'Voluntary unemployment insurance and trade union membership: investigating the connections in Denmark and Sweden', *Journal of Social Policy*, **37**: 433–51.
Danhard, E. (2004), *Lön i konkurs med 2004 års regler om löneförmånsrätt och lönegaranti,* Uppsala: Lars Åhnberg AB.
Edebalk, P.G. (1975), *Arbetslöshetsförsäkringsdebatten. En studie i svensk socialpolitik 1892–1934*, doctoral dissertation, no. 17 in the series, Skrifter utgivna av Ekonomisk-historiska Föreningen i Lund.
Edebalk, P.G. (1987), 'Den fackliga arbetslöshetsförsäkringen i Sverige 1892–1934', *Arkiv*, no. 36–37.
Edebalk, P.G. (1990), 'Från motstånd till genombrott – den svenska arbetslöshetsförsäkringen 1935–1954', no. 45 in the series, *Arkiv*.
Edlund, S., A.L. Johansson, R. Meidner, K. Misgeld and S.W. Nilsson (1989), *Saltsjöbadsavtalet 50 år*, Stockholm: Arbetslivscentrum.
Erici, B. and N. Roth (1981), *Arbetslöshetsförsäkringen i Sverige 1935–1980*, Stockholm: Arbetslöshetskassornas Samorganization.
Jans, A. (2002), *Notifications and Job Losses on the Swedish Labour Market,* doctoral dissertations no. 54 in the series, Swedish Institute for Social Research, Stockholm University.
Kjellberg, A. (2006), 'The Swedish unemployment insurance – will the Ghent system survive?' *Transfer: European Review of Labour and Research*, **12**(1): 87–98.
Nycander, S. (2002), *Makten över arbetsmarknaden*, Stockholm: SNS förlag.
Olli-Segendorf, Å. (2003), 'Arbetsmarknadspolitiskt kalendarium II', IFAU Rapport 2003:9.
Regnér, H. (1997), Training at the job and training for a new job: two Swedish studies', PhD thesis, Swedish Institute for Social Research, Stockholm University.
Sjögren Lindquist, G. and E. Wadensjö (2006), 'National Social Insurance – not the whole picture: supplementary compensation in case of loss of income', report for ESS, Expert Group on Economic Studies 2006:5, Ministry of Finance.

Sjögren Lindquist, G. and E. Wadensjö (2007), 'Ett svårlagt pussel – kompletterande ersättningar vid inkomstbortfall', Rapport till ESS 2007:1.

Skogman Thoursie, P. (1999), 'Disability and work in Sweden', dissertation series 39 Swedish Institute for Social Research.

Viebrock, E. (2006), 'Reforming unemployment insurance in Denmark and Sweden', presentation to the 4th Annual ESPAnet Conference, 21–23 September, Bremen.

Wadensjö, E. (1984a), 'Labor market policy towards the disabled in Sweden', Wissenschaftszentrum discussion paper IIM/LMP 84-4C, Berlin.

Wadensjö, E. (1984b), 'Disability policy in Sweden', in R. Haveman, V. Halberstadt and R. Burkhauser (eds), *Public Policy Toward Disabled Workers*, Ithaca, NY: Cornell University Press, pp. 444–516.

Wadensjö, E. (2001), 'The employment status of disabled people in the EU. Country study: Sweden', supplement to *Employment of People with Disabilities*, Amsterdam: EIM.

Wadensjö, E. (2002), 'Labour market policy for disabled people in the EU. Country study: Sweden', supplement to *Labour Market Policy for People with Disabilities*, Amsterdam: EIM.

Wadensjö, E. (2003), 'Active strategies for older workers in Sweden', in Maria Jepsen, D. Foden and M. Hutsebaut (eds), *Active Strategies for Older Workers*, Brussels: ETUI, pp. 381–402.

Wadensjö, E. and G. Sjögren (2000), *Arbetslinjen för äldre i praktiken* [The Work Principle for Older in Practice], Stockholm: Swedish Institute for Social Research and Riksdagens revisorer (the Parliamentary Auditors).

Wang, Y.N. (2001), 'Promoting the rights to work of disabled people? A historical comparative analysis of Sweden, Great Britain and Taiwan', PhD thesis, School of Social Policy, Sociology and Social Research, University of Kent at Canterbury.

3. Denmark

Per Kongshøj Madsen

INTRODUCTION[1]

In recent years, Denmark has drawn a lot of international attention. The highest employment rate in the EU, the low level of unemployment and an overall positive macroeconomic performance have made Denmark stand out in Europe. Furthermore, Denmark shows some interesting traits when it comes to the country's combination of the well-known basic building blocks of a Nordic welfare state with some characteristics of more liberal market economies. Has the country found a third road between a flexible labour market on the one hand and security and welfare for its citizens on the other? Or in the words of the Organisation for Economic Co-operation and Development (OECD):

> Denmark provides an interesting combination of high labour market dyna-mism and relatively high social protection – the so-called flexicurity approach. Underlying the success of the Danish model is the combination of flexibility (a high degree of job mobility thanks to a low level of employment protection), social security (a generous system of unemployment benefits) and active labour market programmes. The Danish model of flexicurity thus points to a third way between the flexibility often attributed to deregulated Anglo-Saxon countries and strict job protection characterizing southern European countries. (OECD 2004, p. 97)

Under the heading of the Danish 'model of flexicurity' the story about Denmark is often cast in terms of a well-functioning relationship between unemployment insurance, employment protection legislation and active labour market policy in the following configuration:

- A flexible labour market with a high level of external numerical flex-ibility indicated by high levels of worker flows in and out of employ-ment and unemployment; and a low level of employment protection, allowing employers to adapt the workforce to changing economic conditions, makes the high degree of numerical flexibility possible.
- A generous system of income support for the unemployed.

- Active labour market policies aimed at upgrading the skills of those unemployed who are unable to return directly from unemployment to a new job.

In the following sections each of these elements of the Danish employment system are described in more detail before summing up the strengths and weaknesses of the model in the conclusion.

A FLEXIBLE LABOUR MARKET

Flexibility on the labour market can have many forms including:

- Numerical flexibility: the scope for adjusting the number of employees at the individual workplace through hiring and firing.
- Working time or temporary flexibility: the scope of adjusting the number of working hours (such as working overtime or part-time) and their placing (working shifts or weekends).
- Functional flexibility: the scope for transferring employees between job functions (horizontally or vertically) which is closely related to organizational flexibility, which is concerned with changes in the organization of operations and management.
- Wage flexibility: the rate at which nominal and real wages respond to changes in supply and demand for labour.

While all of the forms of flexibility can be found on the Danish labour market, attention is most often drawn to the high level of numerical flexibility. Between 25 and 30 per cent of the employees change their position on the labour market from one year to the next. Available register data yield the possibility to analyse such mobility patterns in a long-term perspective (1980–2003).

Looking at the level of job mobility on the Danish labour market from 1982–93 to 2002–3, shown in Table 3.1, the general picture is one of continuity over time. One year later, almost three-quarters of all employees are still employed at the same workplace across the three measurement periods (1982–3, 1992–3 and 2002–3). The remaining quarter of all employees change positions within one year. The majority of these changed to another firm, indicating numerical flexibility. This numerical flexibility increased slightly over the period (from 13 per cent in 1982–3 to 15.4 per cent in 2002–3), which corresponds to the economic upturn since the mid-1990s.

While around 6 per cent of all employees made a transition from

The labour market triangle

Table 3.1   Job mobility in Denmark (change of employment the year after, % of all employed)

	1982–3	1992–3	2002–3
Still employed at the same workplace	73.2	71.4	72.3
Change to another workplace in the same firm	3.3	4.2	3.8
Change to another firm	13.0	13.7	15.4
Change to unemployment	6.0	5.9	2.9
Change to outside the labour market (including early retirement)	3.9	4.1	4.8
Other change (such as job leave, emigration, death)	0.6	0.7	0.8
Total in employment	100	100	100
(Absolute number)	(2 004 212)	(2 087 764)	(2 284 315)

Note: The data are based on comparing the position of the persons in the last week of November from one year to the next. Multiple shifts during the 12 months from November to November are thus unobserved.

Source: Based on Bredgaard et al. (2007), Table 1.

employment to unemployment in 1982–3 and 1992–3, only 2.9 per cent made such a transition in 2002–3. In the same period, there was a slight increase in the number of persons who left the labour market (from 3.9 per cent exiting the labour market in 1982 to 4.8 per cent in 2002). This might be related to the increasing take-up of early retirement benefits. As for the people in employment in a given year, about 75 per cent were employees having been with the same employer the year before. Of the remainder, about two-thirds came from employment in another form in the previous year, while the remainder were evenly distributed between inflow from unemployment and from outside the labour market.

   From these data two findings emerge. First, there is a surprisingly high continuity over time in the share of employees who either remain employed at the same workplace, or change jobs. Second, the level of numerical flexibility (measured as a change to another firm) is at a relatively high level. This is observed for both skilled and unskilled workers, and for salaried workers and managerial staff, although the mobility at the higher levels of the job hierarchy or for the high-skilled is somewhat lower. For example, around 30 per cent of wage earners without qualifications or basic qualifications changed positions on the labour market within a year, while at the other end of the scale, only 17 per cent of senior managers was observed to do so. Studies also show that unskilled and semi-skilled workers are more mobile than high-skilled workers, indicating a relation between mobility and educational status (Bredgaard et al. 2007).

Despite these variations, the overall impression is one of rather high mobility for the largest part of the labour market, irrespective of occupational group, socio-economic group and educational groups and a high degree of continuity over time. It should be noted that there are no distinct gender differences in job mobility, and only minor differences by company size (where employees in firms with less than 50 employees are slightly more mobile than employees in medium-sized and large companies; Bredgaard et al. 2007).

These data do not show whether the Danish level of numerical flexibility is higher than in other countries. Available evidence concerning the average level of tenure in different countries does, however, point in this direction (Auer 2007). In 2005, the average Danish job tenure was between eight and nine years (as in the UK). By contrast, the average job tenure in Belgium and France was close to 12 years and that in Sweden, Germany and France was around 11 years (Auer 2007, Figure 1).

One reason for the relatively high level of numerical flexibility is probably the low level of job protection, also for persons with a standard work contract. In the recent exposure given to the Danish employment system, it is generally emphasized that the overall level of employment protection in Denmark is at a low level and comparable to liberal labour markets like that of the United Kingdom. The OECD index of employment protection legislation (EPL) for regular workers gives Denmark a score of 1.5, which is only a bit higher than that of the UK (score 1.1). By contrast France, Germany, Sweden and the Netherlands all have EPL scores above 2.5. Only Belgium comes close to Denmark having a score of 1.7 (OECD 2004).

While the general picture is that of a low level of employment protection, in reality the situation is somewhat more complex and implies different levels of protection for different groups. First of all, employment protection in Denmark is, to a large degree, an issue to be handled by the social partners as part of the general negotiations over work and pay conditions. Therefore, one will find only limited national legislation is this field (which is used for the calculation of the OECD index) and, on the other hand, different rules with respect to employment protection embedded in the various collective agreements.

One important exception, however, is the 'law on salaried workers', which regulates the employment conditions for large groups of white-collar workers. Within this law, a salaried worker is defined as a person

who conducts office work, clinical work or similar functions, or supervises the work of others. Furthermore, in many collective agreements it
is stipulated that those workers covered by the collective agreement have
the rights as defined by the 'law on salaried workers', even if they are not
covered by the definition in the law itself. It is the assessment that the
majority of public employees and about half of private sector employees
are covered by collective agreements or regulations that follow the 'law on
salaried workers'.

Among other things, this law stipulates a set of rules for dismissals,
whose main content is a definition of the employer's notice period in relation to the duration of employment. An increasing number of non-salaried
workers in the private sector have, as parts of the negotiations between the
social partners, been classified as 'quasi-salaried workers' and will therefore experience similar employment protection to those just described.
Part-time workers are covered by the same regulations as full-time workers
– a situation which is a general feature of the Danish labour market.
Furthermore, one should mention that legislation has been introduced to
ban the discrimination against pregnant women, when it comes to dismissals. Employers who dismiss pregnant women have to prove that the dismissal had nothing to do with the pregnancy, and face a fine and payment
of compensation to the former employee if this cannot be proved.

Apart from these groups, collective agreements state varying rules
concerning employment protection for different groups or sectors. For
example, the lowest employment protection level is found in the construction sector, where one can find dismissal periods down to one or a few
days. An interesting trait is that there are no special regulations for public
employees, which are in general subject to the same rules as employees in
the private sector. An exemption applies to a minority of public employees, which still have a special status as civil servants, although the tendency
over the last decades has been to phase out this category.

Table 3.2 shows some examples of the notice periods for different groups
of employees, as well as typical levels of severance pay, which are paid to
salaried workers with a high tenure, but rarely to blue-collar workers. As
explained earlier the rules for salaried workers are included in the 'law
on salaried workers', while the regulation of employment protection for
blue-collar workers is based on collective agreements.

Cases brought against employers for offending against the regulations
with respect to employment protection are handled by the separate legislative system that is established for the labour market. Employers offending
against the protection of their employees will have to pay compensation
to the former employee. However, the employer cannot be forced to rein-
stall the employee into employment. Unfortunately, it is difficult to get a

Table 3.2 Notice period and severance payment by tenure for different groups of workers in Denmark

Notice period	Tenure		
	1 year	5 years	10 years
Construction worker	3 days	5 days	5 days
Industrial worker	21 days	2 month	3 months
Salaried worker	3 months	4 months	6 months
Severance payment	12 years	15 years	18 years
Salaried workers	1 month's wage	2 months' wage	3 months' wage
Blue collar-workers	In collective agreement		

Source: Westerlund (2006), Tables 5 and 6.

statistical overview of the actual functioning of the system of employment protection as a whole, because most of the conflicts are solved through arbitration at the firm level, involving the local trade union representative and the local employer's organization. Only a few of the dismissal cases therefore reach the Court of Labour.

A final observation to be made is that the low level of employment protection is correlated with a relatively small share of employees having an employment contract of limited duration. According to the latest labour force survey for 2007, only 8.8 per cent of the employees have such a contract. For example, in Sweden and the Netherlands the share of temporary workers in 2007 was over 17 per cent (OECD 2008). The share is highest – about 20 per cent – for young persons aged 15–29 years among which are many students having some form of temporary job. For the EU-15 the average share of employees with fixed-term contracts was 14.8 per cent in 2007.

INCOME SUPPORT FOR THE UNEMPLOYED

When it comes to income support for the unemployed, the Danish organization of labour market policies is based on a division between those unemployed who are members of an unemployment insurance fund and those who are uninsured. In case of unemployment the latter group of workers have to apply for means-tested social assistance (cash benefits) that is administered by the municipalities. In addition, when it comes to active labour market policy, the municipalities also handle the group of uninsured unemployed people, while the insured unemployed are in the public employment system administered by central government. The vast majority (79 per cent in 2007) of the unemployed are members of an unemployment insurance fund.

While the two-tier character of both active and passive measures has been and still is an important feature of Danish labour market policy, the system has experienced a number of reforms since the early 1990s, having as their main characteristics:

- The introduction of a two-period benefit system for the insured unemployed with an initial passive and a subsequent activation period. Over the years, the passive period has been gradually shortened for older unemployed, and six months for the unemployed aged less than 30 years. The total duration of unemployment benefits is now four years, implying that the 'activation period' is now a little more than three years;
- A strong emphasis on rights and duties for the individual unemployed person, who has the right to get an individual 'job plan' spelling out the activities to be undertaken to get back to employment, but also a duty to take part in the different programmes of the employment service.
- A decentralization of policy implementation to regional and local authorities, which were to some degree empowered to adjust programme design to fit local needs.
- The removal of the connection between job training and the unemployment benefit system, implying that any employment with a wage subsidy no longer increases the duration of the period that an unemployed person is eligible for unemployment benefits.

As described in more detail below, from 2007 the two systems for the insured and the uninsured unemployed have been integrated in new local 'jobcentres'. However, the legal distinction between the insured and the uninsured unemployed remains, both when it comes to participation in activation programmes and to income support during unemployment. Accordingly, the insured unemployed still get their income support from the unemployment insurance funds, while the uninsured receive cash benefits from the municipalities.

The Danish Version of the Ghent-System

The Danish system of unemployment insurance is based on the so-called Ghent system (Clasen and Viebrock 2008). It consists of 31 state-recognized unemployment insurance funds. Four of them are unemployment funds for both employees and self-employed persons. One unemployment insurance fund only admits self-employed persons as members. When a person moves from one unemployment insurance fund to another, either due to a shift in occupation or because they decide to do so, the right to unemployment benefits is transferred at the same time.

Most of the unemployment insurance funds are affiliated with one or more trade unions, which is often taken as an explanation for the high union density of about 80 per cent in the Danish labour market. While membership of an unemployment insurance fund is independent of being a member of a trade union, most workers conceive the membership of the trade union and the affiliated unemployment insurance fund as a package. This is probably due to the long historical bonds between the two institutions, and the fact that trade unions do little to advertise the formal difference between the two sorts of membership. Moreover, membership of a trade union has additional advantages to employees, which are unrelated to receiving unemployment benefits, such as support in local wage negotiations and in conflicts with the employer.

The present version of the system for income support for the unemployed dates back to the last major reform of the unemployment benefit system in 1970, where the state took over the responsibility for financing the extra costs of unemployment benefits that were caused by increases in unemployment (the principle of public financing 'at the margin'). The members of the unemployment insurance funds will therefore only be obliged to pay a fixed membership contribution, independent of the actual level of unemployment.

This mechanism for financing unemployment insurance implies that the share of public funding depends on the total number of unemployed. In times of high unemployment, as in the early 1990s, the government's share rose to 80 per cent, while it falls to less than 50 per cent during economic upswings.

Apart from those having exhausted their right to unemployment benefits, the group of uninsured consists of those not being a member of an insurance fund in the first place. This group of people consists of those who voluntarily choose not to become a member of the insurance funds, or those who do not meet the membership conditions (see the list of criteria presented below). This group of unemployed must apply for cash benefits administered by the municipalities. As explained in more detail below, these cash benefits are means-tested and the amount depends on the family situation of the unemployed.

Membership Conditions

Membership of an unemployment insurance fund is voluntary. Members have to fulfil the following criteria:

- A member must stay and reside in Denmark. However, departures are made from this rule if the person resides in another EEA country.
- A person must be aged between 18 and 63 years when they join the unemployment insurance fund. They must have employment as an employee, a self-employed person or assisting spouse in a company owned by a self-employed person.
- A person can also be admitted as a member of an unemployment insurance fund if they have completed a vocational training course of at least 18 months' duration. The application for membership should not be later than two weeks after completion of the training course.

Both full-time and part-time employees can become members of an unemployment insurance fund. Part-time insurance is an option for persons working less than 30 hours per week. Both membership contribution and unemployment benefits are lower for this group. Thus benefits cannot be higher than two-thirds of the benefits for a full-time insured person.

Membership contribution includes:

- A flat-rate compulsory contribution to the unemployment insurance, which is the same for all members and in 2008 amounts to 3372 DKK per year (€453)[2];
- A flat-rate contribution to finance the Labour Market Supplementary Pension Scheme (the so-called ATP scheme).
- An administrative fee, which varies (considerably) between the individual unemployment insurance funds, as is shown later on.
- A voluntary contribution to the Voluntary Early Retirement Pensions (VERP). The yearly retirement contribution in 2008 amounted to DKK 4920 (€660) for full-time insured members.

All membership contributions are tax deductible, which implies that the net cost to the member is about two-thirds of the gross cost.

To be entitled to unemployment benefits, the unemployed must in general fulfil the following conditions:

- Have been a member of an unemployment insurance fund for at least one year;

- For persons insured on a full-time basis, the employment requirement means that they must have had employment to such an extent that in total it corresponds to employment during the full, normal working hours of the trade or profession for a minimum of 52 weeks within the past three years. If the full-time, normal working hours are 37 hours a week, the employment requirement for full-time insured members amounts to a total of 1924 hours of work within the past three years.

Furthermore, the unemployed must actively look for work and are subject to the rules and regulations of active labour market policy (see below). In principle, an unemployed person who has been unemployed for more than three months must accept any job offered by the Public Employment Service (PES) that the person could perform. For example, an unemployed academic must be willing to work as a postman. However, in practice the PES is not very strict in implementing this rule, because of the expected lack of motivation of the unemployed if actually employed in an undesired job.

Taking part in labour market training will not make the unemployed eligible for an extension of the benefit period. The benefit rate is individual and depends, among other things, on the size of the previously earned income. Unemployment benefits can, at a maximum, amount to 90 per cent of previous earnings. The maximum benefit rate in 2006 is 667 DKK (€90) per day for full-time insured members. Unemployment benefits are paid out for five days a week. The maximum yearly benefit therefore equals 173 420 DKK (€23 278).

Once being eligible for unemployment benefits, an unemployed person may collect them for a total period of four years, if they follow the directions concerning active job seeking and participation in activation programmes. After the end of the four-year period, the unemployed person loses the right to unemployment benefits and has to apply for cash benefits as an uninsured unemployed person, see below. Moreover, entitlement to unemployment benefits is automatically lost at the age of 65 years, at which age the person qualifies for an old-age pension.

Sanctions are imposed by the funds on individual members who receive unemployment benefits without being eligible, for example if they are not available for work or do not actively look for work. The standard sanction is withdrawal of benefits for a short period of time. Suspension can be for one week and up to 26 weeks. For 2006, statistics of the Directorate of Labour show that approximately 13 800 persons had their benefits suspended. Of those, 3200 were sanctioned with a suspension for more than three weeks. The number has been relatively stable over the last few years and can be compared to an annual number of cases handled by the job-centres of about 980 000 (Arbejdsdirektoraret 2007a, p. 6).

The Uninsured Unemployed

Apart from those having exhausted their right to unemployment benefits, the group of uninsured unemployed consists of those unemployed who do not fulfil the criteria for becoming eligible to unemployment benefits in the first place (see the list of criteria presented earlier). This group of unemployed must apply for cash benefits administered by the municipalities. These benefits are considered as a part of social policy and regulated by a separate law under the supervision of the Ministry of Employment. The financing is shared between the national government and the municipalities.

Cash benefits are means-tested and the amount depends on the family situation of the unemployed. For example, a person aged 25 or older with children will receive 139 500 DKK per year (€18 725), while a young person aged under 25 will receive 67 656 DKK per year (€9081). Like unemployment benefits, cash benefits are considered as taxable income. The duration of cash benefits is unlimited, but again the person has to accept the offers from the municipality to participate in activation programmes. If not, cash benefits may be reduced or abolished all together. In 2005, a total of 2700 unemployed recipients of cash benefits were sanctioned. This can be compared to an average number of unemployed recipients of cash benefits in 2005 of about 55 000 persons (Arbejdsdirektoratet 2007b, p. 6).

Replacement Rates

As presented in the description of the calculation of unemployment benefits, these can amount to 90 per cent of previous earnings (normally calculated over a three-month period before becoming unemployed). There is a maximum amount, at present equal to approximately 14 500 DKK (€1946) per month. This implies that the gross compensation rate declines rapidly with previous income, when the income reaches a limit of about 200 000 DKK (€26 846) per year. To give an impression, a wage earner in the private sector at the lowest income level would get about 175 000 DKK (€23 490) excluding pension contributions per year in 2005, while an average salesperson would get 235 000 DKK (€31 544) per year. A highly skilled white-collar worker would get 457 000 DKK (€6342) per year (Dansk Arbejdsgiverforening 2006, Table 5.28).

The OECD calculates net compensation rates for different family types

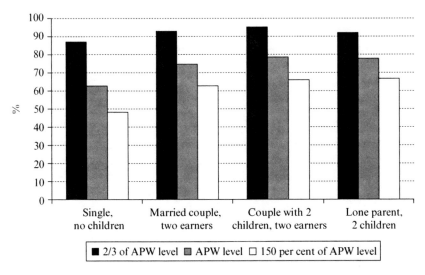

Source: OECD (2007), Table 3.1.

Figure 3.1   *Net replacement rates for three income levels and four family types in the first month of unemployment benefit receipt, Denmark 2002*

and income levels. As is evident from Figure 3.1, and a consequence of the ceiling on the unemployment insurance benefit, wage earners earning two-thirds of the average production wage (APW) experience a significantly higher rate of compensation than those earning 150 per cent of the APW. The family situation also plays a (limited) role, which is not due to the unemployment insurance system, but related to other benefits (like housing benefits), which are included in the OECD calculations.

Over the last few decades there has been a tendency for the compensation rates to decline, which has been the cause of some debate (LO 2006). The main reason for the decline is a special and rather complicated system for indexing the development of unemployment benefits (and other transfer incomes) to the increase in average wages. The main element of the indexation involves regulating unemployment benefits with the percentage increase in yearly wages (excluding pensions and paid absence) two years before, with a deduction of 0.3 percentage points. This deduction is used to finance targeted measures for special groups among the unemployed and other 'weak groups'. Furthermore, the introduction of collective pension schemes among blue-collar workers has led to a decline in the compensation rates, because contributions to such schemes are not included in the calculation of unemployment benefits. As a result, compensation rates (including pension contributions) have gradually declined since 1982. On average the reduction amounts to about 20 percentage points.

Costs and Financing

The major part of unemployment insurance (UI) is financed by the state. The total expenditure for unemployment benefits was 20 405 million DKK (€2743 million) in 2005. The other major payments from the unemployment insurance funds are for the voluntary early retirement pay, which amounted to 24 147 million DKK (€3246 million) in the same year. The costs are covered from three sources: the mandatory contributions to unemployment insurance from the members, the voluntary membership contributions to the VERP and the states.

In 2005 the total administrative costs of the UI funds were 3200 million DKK (€430 million), which was covered by the membership contributions. Accordingly, of the total membership contributions about 20 per cent covers the administrative costs of the funds, while 44 per cent is the mandatory membership contribution to the unemployment benefits and the remaining 36 per cent is VERP contributions.

Since the state covers all variations in the expenditure of benefits through the state budget, no special funds are accumulated. Membership contributions are unrelated to the general level of unemployment or the unemployment risks of the individual member or groups of members. The only factor that leads to differences in membership contributions between the funds is the variation in the administrative costs of each fund. This implies that the costs of membership (excluding the mandatory state contribution and the voluntary contributions to the VERP) will vary between around 600 DKK (€81) and 2750 DKK (€369) per year (Arbejdsdirektoratet 2005).

The PES employs approximately 2000 persons. To this number about 5000 employees in the unemployment insurance funds can be added. The total number of employees in the social services departments of the municipalities is about 6200 persons. Accordingly, the total number of full-time persons occupied in the administration of employment policy is about 13 000 persons. The number of full-time persons in the target groups for employment policy measures is estimated at 450 000 persons in 2002 (Finansministeriet 2004, Chapter 6).

Finally, it is worth mentioning that a small market for supplementary unemployment insurance has developed in recent years. These schemes are provided by private insurance companies on an actuarial basis and often marketed by trade unions as a service to their members. However, due to the high costs and limited benefits offered by such schemes, the number of persons taking them is rather small. In 2004, it was estimated that they covered about 50000 persons, which can be compared to the 2.1 million members of the traditional unemployment insurance funds (Forsikring and Pension 2004, p. 14).

ACTIVE LABOUR MARKET POLICY

As mentioned earlier, an important feature of the present system of labour market policy is its two-tier nature, which follows the dividing lines in the unemployment insurance system. At the individual level, the dividing line is therefore between those unemployed who are members of an unemployment insurance fund, and those who are not and therefore eligible for means-tested cash benefits.

In 2007, the so-called 'Structural Reform' implied major changes of the Danish public sector. The number of municipalities was reduced from 271 to 98. The 14 labour market regions (each headed by a director and a tripartite council) were replaced by four labour market regions, each still with a tripartite council. The councils, however, have less responsibilities than before and, most importantly, no longer have direct control over the allocation of funds for active measures. The reform thus implies two important changes:

- The role of local government in the implementation of labour market policy was increased.
- The influence of the social partners was reduced (probably as the outcome of some resistance from the present conservative–liberal government and the Ministry of Employment towards the more powerful role of the social partners under the previous system).

At the level of the municipalities, the reform implies the creation of new jobcentres, one for each municipality. These jobcentres are responsible for both the insured and the uninsured unemployed, and combine the tasks which are now solved by the PES and the social assistance branch of the municipalities. However, apart from 14 pilot jobcentres, the formal legal responsibility for the unemployed is still divided between a state branch and a municipality branch of each jobcentre. The new model is thus a hybrid between a one-tier and a two-tier system. In addition, the responsibility for the payment of benefits to the unemployed is still divided between the unemployment insurance funds and the social security office of the municipalities. Table 3.3 gives an overview of the tasks and responsibilities of the different actors in the employment system.

Table 3.3   Administrative and corporatist bodies at national, regional and local level in Denmark after the 2007 reform

Level	Name	Main responsibility
Administrative bodies		
National	National Labour Market Authority	Overall managing of active employment policy
	Labour Directorate	Supervising the unemployment insurance funds and the municipalities' administration of cash benefits
Regional	Employment region	Supervising the performance of the local jobcentres
	Regional PES administration	Managing the state branch of the jobcentres
Local	Jobcentres	Employment services to insured and uninsured unemployed
	Social security office of the municipality	Payment of cash benefits to non-insured unemployed
	Unemployment insurance fund	Payment of unemployment benefits to unemployed and control of availability for work
Corporatist bodies		
National	National employment council	Advisory body to the Minister of Employment in all matters related to labour market policy
Regional	Regional employment council	Advising the regional labour market director. Monitoring regional labour markets.
Local	Local employment council	Advising the municipality and the local jobcentre

Programmes and Participants

As shown in Figure 3.2, active programmes cover about 70 000 full-time persons per year, which corresponds to 2.4 per cent of the workforce (with a workforce of about 2.9 million persons). The figure does not include participants in the so-called flexi-jobs, which are jobs with a permanent wage subsidy for persons with lastingly reduced work capacity. Their number has been rapidly rising and at present (2007) amounts to 44 000 persons.

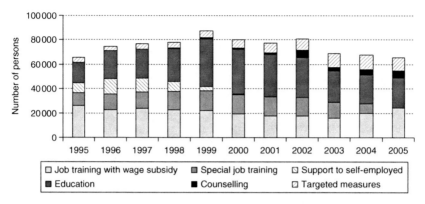

Source: Databanks of Statistics Denmark (1995–2005).

*Figure 3.2   Number of participants in ALMP measures, Denmark
1995–2005*

This figure includes information about the main programmes of Danish active labour market policy:

- Job training with a wage subsidy, implying that the unemployed person is paid a normal wage from a public or private employer for a limited time period (up to one year).
- Special job training for weaker groups of the unemployed, typically taking place in special projects in the public sector.
- Support to self-employment (a three-year subsidy equal to 50 per cent of benefits). The programme was phased out from 1998 and is now closed.
- Education, covering a wide range of education and labour market training with a duration up to one year.
- Counselling, including job search activities and so on.
- Targeted measures, or programmes targeted at special groups like immigrants or older workers.

Mainly as a reflection of the improved conditions in the Danish labour market, the number of participants has been falling in recent years. At the same time, and reflecting a deliberate policy shift of the present government, more emphasis has been put on job training with private employers and on counselling under the heading 'work first'. Lower priority is given to educational measures. Targeted measures have also grown in importance due to the increased emphasis on the integration of immigrants and their descendants.

Effects of Active Labour Market Policy

As in many other countries, the net effects on the participants in activation programmes are disputed. The reason is that such programmes have both positive and negative effects on the future employments prospects of the individual participants:

- The motivation effect implies that an unemployed person looks more actively for work in the period immediately before they have to participate in a mandatory activation programme. The strength of the motivation effect is indicated by the change in the probability of leaving unemployment in the period immediately before the person is obliged to take part in an activation programme.
- The 'locking-in' effect means that job search activities are reduced during the period that an individual takes part in a programme.
- The training or qualification effect stems from the rise in the level of qualifications during activation, which should improve the possibilities of job finding for those who have participated in one of the active programmes.

In a study published in 2000, the Ministry of Labour presented some of the first results based on a new database which it had developed (Ministry of Labour 2000). This database contains information on the labour market situation of all individuals, including their participation in activation programmes and their contacts with the social security system. Advanced statistical methods based on individual labour market histories can be applied (such as fixed effects methods and estimates of hazard rates) showing the effect of active labour market policies. First of all, the study revealed significant motivation effects, measured by an increased probability of taking up employment in the period immediately before having to take part in mandatory activation programmes. Such effects have been confirmed by later studies (such as Geerdsen 2003; Rosholm and Svarer 2004) and play an increasing role for the proponents of active programmes. However, the specific dilemma posed by such observations should be borne in mind. If it is wished to increase the motivation effect, there may be a temptation to change the content of activation programmes in order to make them less attractive to participants. However, this would probably also imply that the quality of the programmes themselves would be lowered in terms of their training content and other activities to improve the skills of the participants. As a result, the overall outcome might be less positive for those unemployed persons who are unable to find a job before entering activation.

The improvement in employability in terms of the qualification effect in the study of the Ministry of Labour is measured by the reduction in the proportion of the year for which the persons concerned receive any form of transfer income (such as unemployment benefit, cash benefits or sickness benefit). A reduction in this proportion is a reliable indicator of a genuine improvement in the employment situation of an individual, because they have either found ordinary employment or taken up some form of ordinary education. Such qualification effects of the various types of labour market programmes are of considerable interest. The largest improvement in the employment situation (measured by an increase in the economic self-dependency of the participant) was observed for participants in private job training. For public job training and labour market education the effects are positive, but smaller. These findings are in line with international experience (Martin 2000).

In the most recent study from the Ministry of Employment (Beskæftigelsesministeriet 2005) the following conclusions are made concerning the qualifications effects:

- Positive effects from participation in active programmes are found for both insured and uninsured unemployed and the estimated magnitudes of the effects are rather similar.
- Job training with a wage subsidy gives the largest effects, especially job training in the private sector.
- Positive effects are also found for educational programmes, especially when targeted towards job types with labour shortages.
- Especially for the uninsured unemployed, a larger effect of education is observed when measuring the effect one year after participation compared to measuring the effects after six months, thus pointing to the importance of longer-term effects.
- It is observed that combinations of different programmes (for instance education combined with job training) give larger effects than participating in single programmes, although this must be seen in the light of the longer duration of such combined programmes.

Some studies have been sceptical about the positive net effects of active programmes, often pointing to the existence of significant locking-in effects. For example, the chairmen of the Economic Council in their report from December 2002 ascribe about one-third of the reduction in unemployment since 1993 to improved structural performance of the Danish labour market and attributes part hereof to improved labour market policy (Det Økonomiske Råds Formandskab 2002). However, the report gives a rather critical account of the majority of the instruments applied within active labour market policy and especially points to the significant locking-in effects of several measures. Only job training in private firms seems to have large positive net effects and to be cost-effective. Job training in the public sector, and many forms of education, have dubious or negative net outcomes for the participants. Against this background the chairmen proposed improvements in the use of active measures, including giving higher priority to job search and private job training.

One barrier to getting reliable quantitative assessments of the effects of different activation programmes is the heterogeneity of the participants. While easily observable differences between participants with respect to age or education can be compensated for with statistical techniques, it is more difficult to take account of unobserved differences like work motivation and self-confidence. These problems are reinforced if those actors responsible for the programmes are able to discriminate between different participants based on their assessment of the degree to which they will benefit from the offers of the programme. Such effects are often referred to as 'creaming' (preferential treatment of the 'strong' unemployed) and 'parking' (giving the less resourceful unemployed only the minimum remedies).

Over the years, the existence of such effects has been documented in several Danish studies of active labour market policy. Given the increased emphasis in recent years on private service providers and economic incentives in the implementation of the programmes, there is a higher risk of such effects, which have been observed in other countries introducing similar systems. The results from a recent Danish study indicate that this is actually the case, although the use of private service providers in Denmark has some special traits including (Bredgaard and Larsen 2006):

- Not applying a full-scale outsourcing but the parallel use of public, private and semi-private providers, including also some trade unions and unemployment insurance funds.
- A decentralized scheme for tendering.
- A process characterized by dialogue and cooperation between the PES and the service providers.
- Inclusion of the social partners in the outsourcing process, in some cases having the trade unions as providers.

Concerning international comparisons, it is difficult to assess the efficiency of Danish activation policy in a comparative perspective. However, Denmark is among the best performers among the EU countries, when assessed by various aspects of unemployment. Also, when measured by other indicators of labour market performance like life-long learning, gender pay gaps and employment rates of older workers, Denmark is among the top performers of the EU member states although it would of course be dubious to attribute these positive traits solely to a successful activation policy.

FLEXICURITY IN DENMARK

First, it is important to emphasize that while the term 'flexicurity' has only recently been associated with the Danish employment system, its basic characteristics have a long history. While the current attention paid to the Danish model is caused by the significant reduction in unemployment since 1993 and the high employment rate, one should not confuse this recent success with the creation of a fundamentally new version of the Danish employment system since the 1990s. On the contrary, one of the fascinating elements of the story about the Danish labour market is the fact that the model has been able to survive since the founding of the modern Danish welfare state in the 1960s, in spite of the economic turmoil of the 1970s and 1980s. Furthermore, it has been successful in supporting the ongoing structural changes in the economy, which has kept Denmark in a position among the most affluent countries in the world.

The Danish labour market model is often described as a 'golden triangle', see Figure 3.3 (Madsen 2006). The model combines high mobility between jobs with a comprehensive social safety net for the unemployed and an active labour market policy. As mentioned earlier, job-to-job mobility (measured by average tenure) is remarkable high in an international comparison. This is largely related to the relatively modest level of job protection in the Danish labour market. Another reason could be the higher risk-willingness among workers due to the comprehensive social safety net, as well as the low stigmatizing effects of social security in Denmark. It is interesting to note that despite one of the lowest levels of job protection among OECD countries (OECD 2004, Chapter 2), Danish workers have a feeling of high job security among all subgroups of workers (Auer and Cazes 2003). Moreover, more than 70 per cent of the Danes found it a good thing to change jobs every few years (Eurobarometer 2006).

The arrows between the corners of the triangle in Figure 3.3 illustrate flows of people. Even if the unemployment rate is low in an international perspective, Denmark almost has a European record in the percentage of employed who are each year affected by unemployment and receive unemployment benefits or cash benefits (around 20 per cent). However, the majority of these unemployed persons manage to find their own way back into a new job. Those who become long-term unemployed end up in

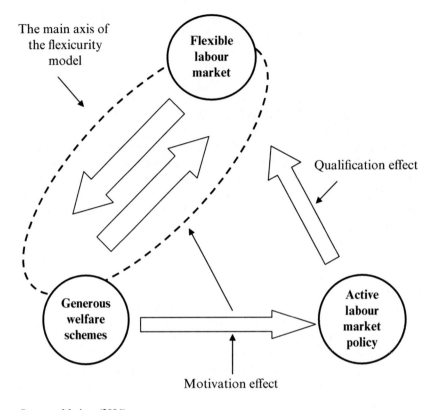

The main axis of the flexicurity model

Flexible labour market

Qualification effect

Generous welfare schemes

Active labour market policy

Motivation effect

Source: Madsen (2006).

Figure 3.3   The Danish flexicurity model

the target group for active labour market policy which, ideally, helps them to find employment again.

The model illustrates two of the most important effects in this connection. On the one hand, as a result of the active measures, the participants in various programmes (such as job training and education) are upgraded and therefore improve their chances of getting a job. As mentioned above, this reflects the qualification effect of activation policies.

On the other hand, the measures can have a motivational (or threat) effect in that unemployed persons, who are approaching the time when they are due for activation, may intensify their search for ordinary jobs in cases where they consider activation a negative prospect. Accordingly, one effect of labour market policy will be to influence the flow from unemployment benefits back to work for those unemployed who do not actually participate in the active measures. A recent study has in fact argued that this motivational effect accounts for the major part of the macro-effect of activation policies (Rosholm and Svarer 2004).

The social safety net in the shape of unemployment and cash benefits for the unemployed together with the high flexibility form the main axis of the model, in the sense that both elements have been characteristic for the Danish labour market for many years. Recognition of the employers' right to hire and fire at will dates back to the September Compromise of 1899. Danish labour market parties here entered into an agreement that focused on labour market disputes and how to solve them, as well as the appropriate role of organizations in the system. This established central-ized negotiations and mechanisms for resolving disputes and also laid the foundation for the practice of self-regulation by labour market parties in most matters of importance to the labour market.

The Danish development of the welfare state and labour market points towards an interesting hybrid between the flexible, liberal welfare states characterized by high numerical flexibility (liberal hiring and firing rules) and the generous Scandinavian welfare regimes of high benefit levels. The hybrid model manages to reconcile the dynamic forces of the free market economy with the social security system of the Scandinavian welfare states. This model is a result of a long evolution-ary development and is supported by relatively stable institutions and class compromises.

Both in the international as well as in the Danish debate there has been, from time to time, a tendency to jump to the conclusion that the macroeconomic success since the 1990s is a result of the specific flexi-curity model as just described. It is, however, essential to point out that the positive development in the Danish labour market since the early 1990s is not attributable exclusively to the Danish flexicurity model. Without a successful balancing of macroeconomic policy and the trends in the international business cycle, the growth in employment and the falling unemployment would not have been possible. The coinciding of low inflation and a halving of registered unemployment rates is also a by-product of a new agenda for collective bargaining and wage for-mation, which helped the labour market adjust to the shift from high unemployment to full employment while keeping wage increases at a moderate level and not departing from the international trend towards low inflation. This agenda developed gradually during the 1980s and was formalized by a joint declaration of the social partners in 1987, where they stated that they would take the international competitive-ness and macroeconomic balance of the Danish economy into account during wage negotiations.

CONCLUSION

Given its long history and development through an ongoing process of political compromises with strong elements of path-dependency, it is not surprising that the Danish system of social insurance and labour market policy has developed into a rather complex structure. However, its main traits can be summed up as follows.

First, the system still reflects a basic division between those workers who are members of the unemployment insurance funds and those who are not. The first group are under the auspices of a basically state-run system, while the latter are taken care of by the municipalities. With the latest reform from 2007, the borders between the two systems are weakening (especially with respect to active labour market policy), but will remain, especially when it comes to the benefit side.

For the insured unemployed the demand for insurances is individual in the sense that the choice to become a member of a fund is a voluntary choice made by each worker. Given the strong links between the unemployment insurance funds and the trade unions, there is however a solid element of collectiveness in the system due to the fact that the membership of the fund and the union are conceived as a package, although formally being independent of each other. For this reason, the position of the unemployment insurance funds close to the unions is often taken as an explanation of the high degree of unionization in the Danish labour market.

Moreover, the financing of unemployment benefits for the insured unemployed is mainly based on the state through general taxation, giving the benefits the character of a public transfer income, although distributed through private organizations (the unemployment insurance funds). Given that membership contributions are unrelated to the risk of becoming unemployed, there are no actuarial elements in the system.

For the uninsured unemployed who either do not fulfil the membership criteria for the unemployment insurance funds or have chosen not to become members, the means-tested cash benefits are financed through general taxation (central and local) and administered by the municipalities.

The provision of employment services is a public task, although private service providers can enter as subcontractors for the public agencies (central or local). The state-run public employment service is mainly responsible for the insured unemployed, while the group of uninsured unemployed is the responsibility of the municipalities. From 2007, a more integrated system has been implemented. However, as mentioned, the benefit side is still based on a two-tier system.

Furthermore, recent studies and policy discourses have put increasing emphasis on the interplay between the different elements of the system of social security and labour market policy, pointing to the manner in which it is characterized by an extending safety net provided by social security and active labour market policies on the one hand, and a low level of individual employment protection on the other.

Finally one may consider the issue of winners and losers in the much-admired Danish model of flexicurity (Madsen, forthcoming). Here, the main groups of winners appear to be large groups of salaried and skilled workers and also some unskilled groups. In general, the model provides easier access to a standard employment contract and thus plays a minor role for temporary workers and agencies. On the other hand, the main groups of losers on the Danish labour market are indicated by the general growth in the number of adults receiving transfer incomes. The people in this group may not all be at risk of absolute or relative poverty, but they will in many cases suffer from social exclusion due to the important role of working life as a road to social integration in Denmark. The groups mostly in risk of becoming marginalized are immigrants from non-Western countries, some unskilled groups, older workers and persons with health problems.

However, it is unclear whether the Danish version of flexicurity in itself is the cause of these exclusionary elements in the Danish employment system. One can argue that a lower level of employment protection has the role of also creating winners among the weaker groups on the labour market due to lower barriers to entering employment. With it being easier to dismiss their employees, the employers will also be less reluctant to hire workers who have had some troubles in their labour market career like long-term unemployment or health problems.

Furthermore, within the framework of the Danish model, active labour market policies and policies to support adult education and training have the role of improving employability for those groups who are in danger of becoming marginalized. One may also see these institutional arrangements as counterbalancing the risk of firms providing less continued education and training to their employees, due to the risk of losing their human capital investments with employees leaving their jobs.

Finally, looking briefly at the employer's side of the labour market, the main winners in the Danish model will be those firms that experience frequent fluctuations in demand (for example within the tourism industry), and the smaller firms, for whom less numerical flexibility could imply higher costs due to the fact that their possibility to apply other forms of flexibility will probably be less than for larger companies.

Taking a longer-term perspective, a number of problems may be identified which could increase the forces that are already causing a rise in the number of persons excluded from the Danish labour market (Bredgaard et al. 2006). These include: the demographic changes over the coming decades, which imply a growth in the number of older workers, with higher risks of becoming marginalized; the rising share of immigrants in the Danish population, with the proportion of persons from non-European countries rising from about 4 per cent in 2008 to about 8 per cent in 2020; and the increasing wage competition from low-wage countries, also within Europe, which has been amplified due to the entry of a number of Eastern European countries into the European Union. These challenges to the Danish model will place the need to reduce the upward trend in the numbers of persons left outside the flexicurity triangle high on the Danish political agenda in coming years.

To these challenges one can add the uncertain impacts of the present reforms of the model involving the mentioned new structure of governance with respect to labour market policy. While the major political parties and social partners still support the basic features of the model, a stronger liberal political ideology could gain momentum, which in the longer run might hamper the social balance behind the model.

NOTES

1. The chapter is an abridged and updated version of Madsen (2007).
2. Due to Denmark's membership of the European Exchange Rate Mechanism (ERM) the Danish currency is stable at the rate of 7.45 DKK to €1. This rate is therefore applied to all currency conversions in the chapter.

REFERENCES

Arbejdsdirektoratet (2005), *Benchmarking af arbejdsløshedskasserne 2005*, Copenhagen: Arbejdsdirektoratet.

Arbejdsdirektoratet (2007a), *Rådighedsstatistikken 2. halvår 2006. Rådigheden hos forsikrede ledige*, Copenhagen: Arbejdsdirektoratet.

Arbejdsdirektoratet (2007b), *Rådighedsstatistikken 1. halvår 2006. Rådigheden hos kontant- og starthjælpsmodtagere*, Copenhagen: Arbejdsdirektoratet.

Auer, P. (2007), 'In search of optimal labour market institutions: the relationship between stability, flexibility and security in labour markets', in H. Jørgensen and P.K. Madsen (eds), *Flexicurity and Beyond: Finding a New Agenda for the European Social Model*, Copenhagen: DJØF Publishing, pp. 67–98.

Auer, P. and S. Cazes (2003), *Employment Stability in an Age of Flexibility: Evidence from Industrialized Countries*, Geneva: International Labour Organization.

Beskæftigelsesministeriet (2005), *Effekter af aktiveringsindsatsen*, Beskæftigelsesministeriet working paper 6, Copenhagen.

Bredgaard, T. and F. Larsen (2006), *Udlicitering af beskæftigelsespolitikken*, Copenhagen: DJØF Forlaget.
Bredgaard, T., F. Larsen and P.K. Madsen (2006), 'Opportunities and challenges for flexicurity: the Danish example', *European Review of Labour and Research*, **12**(1): 61–82.
Bredgaard, T., F. Larsen and P.K. Madsen (2007), 'The challenges of identifying flexicurity in action: a case study on Denmark', in H. Jørgensen and P.K. Madsen (eds), *Flexicurity and Beyond: Finding a New Agenda for the European Social Model*, Copenhagen: DJØF Publishing, pp. 365–91.
Clasen, J. and E. Viebrock (2008), 'Voluntary unemployment insurance and trade union membership: investigating the connections in Denmark and Sweden', *Journal of Social Policy*, **37**: 433–51.
Dansk Arbejdsgiverforening (2006), *ArbejdsMarkedsRapport 2006*, Copenhagen: Dansk Arbejdsgiverforening.
Det Økonomiske Råds Formandskab (2002), *Dansk Økonomi, Efteråret 2002*, Copenhagen: Det Økonomiske Råd.
Eurobarometer (2006), *Survey on Europeans and Mobility*, Brussels: European Commission.
Finansministeriet (2004), *Finansredegørelse 2004*, Copenhagen: Finansministeriet.
Forsikring og Pension (2004), *Forsikring i velfærdssamfundet*, Copenhagen: Forsikring og Pension.
Geerdsen, L.P. (2003), *Marginalisation Processes in the Danish Labour Market*, Copenhagen: Socialforskningsinstituttet.
LO (Landsorganizationen i Sverige) (2006), 'Dagpengesystemet, En analyse af dagpengesystements dækning', København: LO.
Madsen, P.K. (2006), 'How can it possibly fly? The paradox of a dynamic labour market in a Scandinavian welfare state', in John A. Campbell, John A. Hall and Ove K. Pedersen (eds), *National Identity and the Varieties of Capitalism: The Danish Experience*, Montreal: McGill-Queen's University Press, pp. 321–55.
Madsen, P.K. (2007), 'Distribution of responsibility for social security and labour market policy: Country report: Denmark, Amsterdam Institute for Advanced Labour Studies working papers no. 07/51, Amsterdam.
Madsen, P.K. (forthcoming), 'Denmark: upstairs and downstairs in the Danish model of flexicurity', in: M. Jepsen and M. Keune (eds), *Europe on the Road to Flexicurity? Assessing the Weight of Flexibility and Security in the Reform of European Labour Markets*, Brussels: Peter Lang.
Martin, J.P. (2000), 'What works among active labour market policies: evidence from OECD countries' experience', *OECD Economic Studies*, **30**(1): 79–112.
Ministry of Labour (2000), *Effects of Danish Employability Enhancement Programs*, Copenhagen: Ministry of Labour.
OECD (Organization for Economic Co-operation and Development) (2004), *Employment Outlook*, Paris: OECD.
OECD (2007), 'Benefits and wages 2007', in *OECD Indicators*, Paris: OECD.
OECD (2008), 'Labour force statistics', online database.
Rosholm, M. and M. Svarer (2004), 'Estimating the threat effect of active labour market programmes', Institute of Labour Studies (IZA) discussion paper no. 1300, Bonn.
Westerlund, L. (2006), *Tryggare på andra sidan sundet? – Om flexicurity i Danmark*, Stockholm: Landsorganizationen i Sverige (LO).

4.   The United Kingdom

Jochen Clasen

INTRODUCTION: A DIFFERENT KIND OF TRIANGLE[1]

The type of, and the interaction between, employment protection, active labour market policy and unemployment benefit support in the UK bears little resemblance to other countries covered in this book. Despite a moderately expansionist trend since 1997, the current government is anxious to maintain a deregulated and flexible labour market. The UK has one of the lowest levels of individual employment protection in Europe, benefits for the unemployed continue to be rather modest and spending on active labour market policy remains relatively low, with longer training courses or subsidized employment playing a minor role, while job search, intensive counselling and individual case management have been emphasized. Also unchanged is the top-down centralized policy model. There is no institutional involvement of the social partners in policy making which goes beyond information and consultation in questions of employment law. Rather than established tripartite talks as elsewhere in Europe, employers are primarily seen as partners in policy implementation.

The architecture of and the interaction between the three policy domains reviewed in this chapter have to be understood within the context of a distinctive political economy. The fields of social insurance and industrial relations elsewhere in Europe might be regarded as 'tightly coupled' (Manow 1997; Hemerijck et al. 2000) with benefits functioning as a 'social wage', or wage replacement benefits rendered by employment-based contributions, complemented by a high level of employment protection. No such link exists in the UK where the term 'social wage' makes little sense. This 'deviant' British case can be traced back to policy paths taken in the 1920s and 1930s when trade union-run unemployment support schemes collapsed and the British labour movement began to lobby for improved state benefits. By the time of the major restructuring of the welfare state in the 1940s British trade unions had decided against an involvement in the administration of social insurance which became solidified as a 'weak' citizenship model (Crouch 1999, p. 448) with low contributions and low benefit levels. This divorce between the labour movement and social insurance has remained a characteristic feature. Exacerbated by a fractured and decentralized trade union and wage bargaining structure, the absence of a 'social wage' has arguably made it impossible to 'link advances in welfare provision with a medium- to long-term commitment to wages and price stability' (Rhodes 2000, p. 36). In short, while elsewhere in Europe social insurance-based 'deferred wages' and employment protection might be interlinked domains, debates about social protection have traditionally been disconnected from workers' 'economic security' or employment protection in the UK (Bonoli 2003), with industrial relations focusing exclusively on wages and employment conditions.

Today, the domains of industrial relations, employment protection and unemployment compensation remain separate and cannot be regarded as functionally complementary as in other countries. However, as is argued in this chapter, the erstwhile disconnection between cash support for the unemployed and active labour market policies has come to an end under the current Labour government. At the same time, the focus of active labour market policies has shifted from the unemployed as a narrow target group for labour market integration towards the much broader understanding of 'worklessness' amongst working-age persons, irrespective of the reason for benefit support. Accordingly, there has been an administrative amalgamation of benefit provision and employment integration for persons of working age. Finally, access to benefit support has become more conditional, most visible in a mandatory participation in some New Deal programmes. This aspect will be reviewed first before subsequent sections assess changes in the fields of active labour market policy and employment protection.

UNEMPLOYMENT PROTECTION

Historically British unemployment protection is rooted in poverty alleviation rather than maintaining living standards for industrial workers. Integrated in the single comprehensive National Insurance (NI) after the Second World War, unemployment insurance benefits were modest and flat-rate. Fiscal problems led contributions to become fully proportional to earnings in the 1970s while benefits had become partially proportional to wages with the introduction of earnings-related supplements in 1966. However, a restrictive access to the earnings-related part of unemployment insurance and the decline of its real value during the 1970s made it relatively easy for the Conservative government to terminate the experiment of wage replacement in unemployment (and sickness) in the early

1980s (Clasen 1994). Moreover, due to the modest generosity and small margin between the standard unemployment benefit and means-tested support it had become common for recipients of insurance benefits, particularly those with a non-working partner or dependants, to be claiming additional means-tested benefits such as housing benefit.

The Main Reforms since the 1990s

Rhetorically and administratively the policy direction during the 1990s remained similar to the late 1980s when unemployment benefit claimants were asked to be more active in their job search and to adapt their expectations to 'more realistic' wages. Having risen steadily during the 1980s, the dependence on means-tested transfers amongst the unemployed almost doubled between 1990 and 1993 (Evans 1998, p. 288), which was regarded as potentially undermining work incentives due to the interaction between benefits and wages at the lower end of the labour market. As a response, aiming to widen the gap between social security transfers and earnings, the Conservative government offered unemployed benefit claimants small-scale job subsidies such as 'back-to-work' bonuses (Meager 1997). This strategy can be regarded as the forerunner of subsequent policies aimed at connecting unemployment benefit policy more closely with labour market policy.

The most important change in unemployment support in the 1990s was the introduction of the Jobseeker's Allowance (JSA) in 1996. The reform implied both retrenchment and structural change in the wake of merging two previously separate schemes into a single programme which grants contributory support followed by means-tested support. With JSA the contributory benefit period was halved to six months and benefit eligibility became stricter (see Table 4.1).

The reform was expected to save expenditure, with about a quarter of a million people becoming worse off due to benefit exclusion or reduction. More generally, the JSA framework represented a further demotion of insurance-based support and a form of benefit homogenization for the unemployed. In other words, irrespective of the reasons for unemployment, needs-based income protection was beginning to become the norm and new mechanisms deemed to facilitate labour market integration were introduced for all benefit claimants, such as Jobseeker's Agreements and Jobseeker's Directions (more details to follow). Under the Labour government since 1997 the JSA benefit regime remained largely unchanged. However, the JSA programme was strongly, albeit indirectly, affected by significant changes in active labour market policies after 1998, which brought about a closer connection between benefit transfers and labour market schemes.

Table 4.1   JSA in the UK: eligibility criteria, benefit levels, entitlement (rates for 2008)

Criterion	Conditions
Membership	Compulsory
Waiting period	2 days
Qualifying condition	Contribution-based JSA (CB JSA): minimum 25 weekly contributions to National Insurance Fund paid and 100 credited within previous 2 years Income-based JSA (IB JSA): means-tested; savings over €7500 will affect the level of JSA, savings over €20 000 disqualifies; disqualified if partner works for 24 hours per week or more; earnings for work below 24 hours will affect the level of benefit
Level	Flat-rate benefit (weekly rates) 1. for single people: 16–24 year-olds: €60; 25 and over: €75.63; lone parents under 18: €60; older lone parents €75.63 2. additions (for IB JSA only): couple: depending on age of both partners and responsibility for children, between €60 and €118.67 Premiums: premiums (supplements) apply for families, disabled children, carers, disability; plus housing costs (where applicable); between €20.94 and €62.94
Maximum duration	CB JSA: 6 months IB JSA: in principle indefinite
Obligations	Availability, capability, actively seeking work; signing Jobseeker's Agreement specifying actions to find work and which type of employment; fortnightly interviews to re-establish benefit entitlement and review Jobseeker's Agreement; participation in New Deal programmes.

Note: All monetary values stated are based on an exchange rate of £1 equal to €1.25 (28 October 2008).

The Current System: Main Characteristics

Three main features distinguish British unemployment protection. First, both contributory and means-tested benefits are centralized, top-down and integrated. Second, although insurance-based benefits are funded differently and technically separate from non-contributory transfers,

*Table 4.2   Beneficiary rates in the UK (benefit recipients as share of
            registered unemployed)*

	1980	1981–4	1985–9	1991–3	1994–6	1997–2000	2001–6
UB or CB JSA	48	31	28	30	24	14	18
IS or IB JSA (means-tested)	40	53	60	60	69	73	82

Sources: Clasen, J. (2005), *Reforming European Welfare States. Germany and the United
Kingdom Compared*, Oxford: Oxford University Press; and Department for Work and
Pensions (DWP) (2004–2008), *Benefit Expenditure Tables*, London: DWP, Table C1 (for
1993–2000) – claimants divided by annual claimant unemployment; 2001 onwards: all
claimants with contribution (income) based JSA divided by all JSA claimants, (DWP
2008a), Table C1.

unemployment benefit support has a weak contributory basis and provides flat-rate benefits only. Third, there is no separate funding arrangement with earmarked contributions to unemployment insurance. Table
4.1 provides information about eligibility and entitlement criteria, as well
as other main features of Jobseeker's Allowance, which includes both
contribution-based unemployment insurance (CB JSA) as well as the
means-tested, or in government parlance 'income-based', JSA (IB JSA)
which is paid out of general taxation – and is by far the more important
source of income for unemployed persons.

Unemployment insurance (CB JSA) is paid out of the National Insurance
Fund (NIF), which is also the source for other contributory benefits, particularly the basic state pension. Employees contribute 11 per cent of
income between a lower and upper limit (€131 and €963 per week respectively in 2008[2]). Another 1 per cent (on all income) is paid by employees
with earnings above the upper limit. Employers pay 12.8 per cent of all
earnings above €131.

In 2006–7 the fund's total receipts were €85.25 billion and total expenditure amounted to €84.25 billion (National Audit Office 2008). By far the
largest single item of expenditure was the public retirement pension (86 per
cent). The next-largest contributory benefit was Incapacity Benefit (11 per
cent). By contrast, contribution-based JSA represented only 0.7 per cent
of total NIF spending, which is due to relatively low levels of unemployment, but also because of low benefit coverage (see Table 4.2) and short
maximum benefit entitlement.

Due to the modest generosity and small margin between standard unemployment benefit and means-tested support (in fact, both rates have been

identical for years) it has always been common to be claiming additional means-tested benefits, such as housing benefits. Moreover, the proportion of the unemployed who do not meet the contribution conditions or who have exhausted their entitlement, and are thus reliant on means-tested benefits, has traditionally been high. Thus, the scheme functions much less as a form of wage replacement than in other European countries.

Table 4.2 highlights the decline of the insurance element within British unemployment protection with respect to its coverage rate amongst the annual stock of the unemployed. Official statistics (DWP 2005) indicate 'contribution deficiency' as the most prevalent reason for non-receipt of the contribution-based JSA (59 per cent of all claimants without contribution-based JSA) and 'exhausted entitlement' as the second most important reason (13 per cent). In part this might indicate changes in the nature of employment (more part-time and short-term work), but it reflects the relatively tight eligibility criteria for contribution-based JSA too, as well as the relevance of unemployment spells longer than six months.

Administration and Responsibilities

The government determines the terms and conditions of both contribution-based and income-based JSA, with the Department for Work and Pension (DWP) as the responsible ministry for policy making and local Jobcentre Plus offices (see later) in charge of policy implementation. There is no role for local authorities in the delivery of JSA benefits. However, as part of the approach which links benefit payments and active labour market policy for the unemployed (and other groups), a large number of non-statutory agencies function as providers and local networks, including private companies, influence implementation and job reintegration programmes for JSA claimants (see the section on active labour market policy).

The National Insurance Fund, as a source for funding contribution-based JSA, is under direct government control, which is free to subsidize it or to use reserves for purposes outside of the National Insurance system. Social partners play no role in the administration or running of the fund. Unlike other social policy fields such as personal services or health care, social security is a so-called reserved policy domain, which means that it is governed by Westminster in London rather than by the Welsh Assembly or the Scottish Parliament.

The JSA was a step towards benefit and active labour market policy becoming more closely linked, also in terms of the cooperation between the previous public Benefit Agency and Employment Services staff at Jobcentres, or local offices of the Employment Services. In the new system, nationwide since 2006, Jobcentre Plus offices are charged with both functions.

Ever since the introduction of JSA unemployed claimants have been required to sign a Jobseeker's Agreement, specifying the detailed steps they intend to take to look for work. These actions are monitored fortnightly by JSA officials, who have received new discretionary powers enabling them to issue a Jobseeker's Direction, that is, requiring individuals to look for jobs in a particular way and to take certain steps to 'improve their employability'. The definition of 'actively seeking work' also changed under the JSA regime. Under the previous test the steps required were those which offered the 'best prospects of receiving offers of employment' (CPAG 1996, p. 10). By contrast, the JSA regime requires claimants to take such steps which have 'the best prospects of securing employment'. Claimants must be willing and able to take up any employment within 48 hours. Jobcentre Plus staff are required to check the steps to find work against the JSA agreement. More compulsory interviews were also introduced, at 13 weeks (at which point some voluntary schemes are made available), six months (restart interview), 12 months, 18 months and two years. At these stages different schemes became compulsory and different types of help available.

Finn et al. (2005) analysed the ways in which Jobcentres operate. New JSA claimants are seen first by a financial assessor (20 minutes) and then by an assigned personal adviser (40 minutes), exploring 'job goals' which are finally formalized into a Jobseeker's Agreement which has to be signed. A key feature is that most interviewed are given a 'better off in work' calculation, usually 'calculated in relation to the wage attached to a particular job vacancy' (Finn et al. 2005, p. 34). Benefit claimants have to attend the Jobcentre fortnightly for a ten-minute 'job search review', with a longer formal Restart interview after 26 weeks of unemployment. Persons under the age of 25 are allocated a New Deal personal adviser, and must participate in the New Deal. Older claimants must do the same after their third Restart interview after 78 weeks.

ACTIVE LABOUR MARKET POLICY

Leaving training mainly to employers, the UK does not have a strong record in active labour market policy. Nevertheless, in the light of steeply rising unemployment in the early 1980s a range of programmes including job creation schemes were put in place and subsequently expanded (see King 1995, p. 135; Meager 1997, p. 72). However, after Thatcher's third general election victory in 1987, labour market policy was scaled down and its focus shifted. There was less emphasis on training for the adult unemployed and more on low-cost schemes of job search, improving work incentives and subsidizing work placements for the long-term unemployed. There was also institutional reform which affected the Manpower Services Commission (MSC). Created in 1973, the MSC was a national tripartite forum for training policy intent on upgrading the skills of the workforce. Formally independent, it was given the responsibility of a network of public sector 'skillcentres' and worked closely with 23 sector-based Industrial Training Boards (ITBs), which had the 'power to levy from employers and distribute grants to pay for apprenticeships and other types of training' (Finn 2005). The ITBs themselves were corporatist bodies with equal representation from employers and relevant trade unions, while the MSC included minor representation also from local government, further education and the voluntary sector. While its training role eroded during the 1980s (King 1995, p. 185) the MSC itself was later abolished and its training role transferred to a network of employer-led Training and Enterprise Councils (TECs) (Local Enterprise Councils, LECs, in Scotland), which were established as private companies. The role of the trade unions in training was thus effectively marginalized.

The Main Reforms since the 1990s

Increasing unemployment in the early 1990s led Conservative governments to introduce some rather small-scale temporary job programmes and by the mid-1990s there was some experimentation with employment subsidies on a limited scale. By the mid-1990s a cross-party consensus around the problem of 'welfare dependency', as well as the emphasis on a stricter benefit regime and supply-side labour market policies had emerged (see Clasen 2005). This is evident in the light of the structural similarity between Labour's New Deal and the Conservative government's pilot Project Work, which was a compulsory (13-week) work experience scheme in 1996, aimed at people under the age of 50 who had been out of work for at least two years.

Having committed itself to maintaining the public spending limits of its Conservative predecessor the incoming Labour government in 1997 was keen to stress that employment programmes would be cost-neutral. Hence, although some more resources were channelled into help with job search and training, the gap between the share of national income devoted to active labour market programmes in the UK and the average spending across the EU has not narrowed (see Table 4.3).

Moreover, the Labour government not only maintained its predecessor's policy course but accelerated it, albeit augmented by more support for low-paid workers and by a more comprehensive and coherent policy regime. One of the influences which contributed to Labour's adoption of

Table 4.3   Spending on active labour market policy in the UK (% of GDP)

	1985	1986–90	1991–4	1995–7	2002	2005
UK	0.7	0.8	0.6	0.4	0.54	0.45
EU average[a]	0.9	0.9	1.1	1.1	1.0	1.0

Note: [a]Without Luxembourg and Greece.

Sources: OECD (2002, 2004, 2006, 2008).

a more prescriptive labour market policy and activation approach was economic theory which implied that the introduction of stricter work tests, more restricted benefit entitlement, mandatory training or other appropriate measures would improve the employability of particularly long-term job seekers and increase the actual supply of labour (Layard 2000). Any deadweight associated with these measures was expected to be compensated by employment-generating wage moderation effects due to an increase in the effective competition for jobs (Finn 1998). Indeed, increasing employability became seen as a way of not only improving employment chances but also combating systematic disadvantage among specific groups, and young people in particular.

As part of its much-heralded welfare reform, the Labour government introduced and subsequently modified a range of New Deal programmes which became a central component of its 'welfare-to-work' strategy (for details see Clasen 2007, Appendix A3). The programmes did not alter benefit rates, but considerably increased the conditionality attached to benefit receipt. Several schemes for different groups of working-age benefit claimants were devised, with different eligibility rules and degrees of obligations attached (Trickey and Walker 2001; Walker and Wiseman 2003).

The Current System: Main Characteristics

The New Deal programmes introduced a more explicit degree of obligation on the part of some job seekers, especially young people (the NDYP – for all people between 18 and 24 years) and long-term unemployed job seekers (the ND25+, which now applies to claimants aged 25 and over, out of work for 18 out of the past 21 months). Both the NDYP and the ND25+ involve the assignment of personal advisers and the drawing up of individual 'action plans'.

Programmes consist of three stages. First, within the NDYP a 'gateway period' of four months provides individual intensive job search assistance.

Table 4.4   NDYP and ND25+ participants during a particular month in the UK (June 2004), (thousands, rounded numbers)

	NDYP	ND25+
Total	83	53
On gateway	53	33
Options:		
Employment	3	Intensive activity period
Education and training	7	(IAP)
Voluntary sector	4	12
Environmental task force	3	
Follow through	13	9
All leavers June 2004	19	10
Leavers into jobs[a]	6	3

Note: [a]Sustained employment (13 weeks) or less.

Source: DWP (2004b).

A range of provision is available, including job search and careers advice, as well as short training courses (in basic skills or to help motivation and confidence), specialist support for the disadvantaged, or advice on self-employment. There is a target of 40 per cent of gateway participants who should find unsubsidized employment during this stage. Second, those who do not find work are transferred to one of four 'options' which last six months or more. These are subsidized employment, full-time education, or (for young people only) voluntary or environmental work. With the New Deal, the take-up of one of these four options has become mandatory, and non-compliance sanctioned by benefit reduction or withdrawal. All options involve some degree of training. Employers receive a weekly subsidy per participant and a flat-rate contribution towards training costs. Those on options receive an allowance which is equal to or slightly above benefit rates, except for subsidized work where a training wage is paid. Third, failing to enter unsubsidized work after completion of one of the options, further guidance and, if required, training follows (the 'follow through' stage).

The ND25+ consists of a shorter 'gateway' period (typically 13 weeks), which includes interviews, intensive job reorientation, identification of basic skill needs, followed by an 'intensive activity period' (IAP), offering 'basic employability training', work placements, work-focused training and so on. This period lasts 13 weeks but can be extended to 26 weeks. Table 4.4 illustrates the relevance of the gateway period as a phase where intensive local job search support takes place.

Other New Deals are voluntary, such as the New Deal for those aged over 50 years (ND50+) or and New Deal for lone parents (NDLP) which is aimed at lone parents whose youngest child is enrolled in primary school. In April 2001 the work-focused interview for lone-parent claimants (with children over five) became compulsory. Similarly, the New Deal for partners of unemployed is compulsory for those under 25 without children. It consists of personal advice and assistance with work for the potential second earner in an unemployed household. Finally the New Deal for disabled people (NDDP) is aimed at those who have claimed JSA or Incapacity Benefit for at least six months (Stafford 2003). There are training grants and employment credits, allowing participants to accept lower wages, which are paid directly to participants for a maximum of 52 weeks.

In recent years the mandatory New Deal programmes (NDYP and ND 25+) have been subjected to several revisions but the overall policy regime has remained unchanged. In brief, the aim continues to be the creation of a flexible and localized delivery system, as well as making more use of mandatory 'work-focused interviews' also for working-age benefit claimants who are not registered as unemployed (such as lone parents), to ease eligibility conditions for claimants with shorter unemployment duration, to allow greater local discretion and, more recently, to outsource service provision (Bruttel 2005).

As a whole, the New Deal programmes highlight Labour's embrace of a flexible and deregulated labour market, and its strategy aimed at integration into potentially low-paid employment which might thus require public subsidies. In this respect it should be noted that the New Deal is merely one element within Labour's welfare-to-work strategy. Other policies include the national minimum wage as well as several types of tax credits (see Walker and Wiseman 2003). Effectively subsidizing low-paid employment via a negative income tax the tax credit system has grown considerably under the Labour government. About 2.3 million families with children were in receipt of Working Families Tax Credit in 2004 compared with 1.4 million in 2002. In addition around 235000 households without children received tax credits in 2004 (DWP 2004c). This means that about 15 per cent of all households with income from paid work in the UK receive in-work benefits in the from of wage subsidies.

Administration and Responsibilities

Following examples in Australia and New Zealand (Clasen et al. 2001), in 2002 Jobcentre Plus became a single point of contact for all working age claimant groups. It brought together the previously separate Employment

Service (in charge of New Deal and other labour market programmes) and the Benefit Agency (responsible for the payment of unemployment and other cash transfers). Jobcentre Plus thus has a dual function: to help working-age people find employment and to pay out social security support. The British government defines its 'purpose' as contributing to the aim of 'tackling poverty' and 'reducing worklessness'. The terminology is deliberate, indicating a policy focus which has moved on from reducing 'unemployment' towards combating 'non-employment', that is unemployment and labour market inactivity (see also Clasen 2005). Moreover, the UK government distinguishes not so much between contributory and non-contributory (assistance) benefits, but between benefits for working-age people and other benefit groups.

Jobcentre Plus has 'significant operational autonomy' (Finn 2005) but is accountable to the Secretary of State and ministers at the DWP. The actual delivery of New Deal programmes involves various local organizations and a complex web of contractual relationships with Jobcentre Plus. The NDYP and ND25+ are provided through local partnerships in 144 'units of delivery' which are constructed in various models (Hasluck and Green 2006, p. 18). Which particular model applies where depends on existing partnerships, networks and local labour market conditions. Trade unions have varying degrees of incorporation in these partnerships, but 'little strategic involvement in the work of Jobcentre Plus' (Finn 2005). More generally, the role of social partners in labour market policy has become marginally more important in the past ten years, albeit restricted to local partnerships and policy implementation rather than policy formulation. Case study-based evaluations suggest that private sector led partnerships (PSL) seem the most effective delivery mechanisms due to a stronger emphasis on job search, more flexible management, participants remaining longer at the gateway stage and lower referrals to one of the four options (Hasluck and Green 2006).

EMPLOYMENT PROTECTION

Narrowly understood as laws relating to individual job protection, British governments first adopted relevant policies in the 1960s and early 1970s, with the implementation of notice periods (1963), the introduction of statutory redundancy compensation (1965) and the unfair dismissal law from 1971. Influenced by the perceived need to foster labour mobility at the time, but also by International Labour Organization (ILO) recommendations on enhancing employment security, these pieces of legislation were less interventionist than elsewhere, as illustrated by the exclusion of

part-time workers or employees on fixed-term contracts from unfair dismissal and redundancy pay legislation (Deakin and Morris 2005, p. 391).
Nevertheless, in the 1970s employment rights were seen as constituting a
statutory base upon which collective bargaining might build.

The subsequent period however was one of a 'decisive shift away from
voluntarism' (Dickens and Hall 2003, p. 127). Legislation was used not
to support collective bargaining but to reduce its relevance since it was
deemed to be hampering flexibility, imposing burdens on employers and
thus hindering economic and employment growth. Collective labour law
(employee representation, industrial action and so on) was weakened by
restriction of the legal basis for industrial action, the abolition of compulsory trade union membership (the 'closed shop') and the removal of
statutory floors to wages and intervention in internal trade union issues.

Individual employment rights, such as discipline and grievance procedures, unfair dismissal protection, redundancy payments and minimum
periods of notice, were curtailed too. The Employment Act 1980 weakened the protection against unfair dismissal and lengthened the qualifying period to two years for workers in small firms. Stipulating minimum
wage levels for some 2.5 million workers, the Wages Act 1986 reduced the
scope for the wages councils and in 1994 wages councils were abolished
altogether.

These restrictions had a clear impact. In the late 1980s more than half of
all part-time workers and 29 per cent of full-time workers were excluded
from unfair dismissal protection because of the tight hours of service
and length of service qualifications. Official tribunal statistics show that
individual employees made 'little use of their legal rights to seek redress,
with limited success and with limited redress for those who are successful'
(Dickens and Hall 1995, p. 269). Besides, the usual outcome of disputes
was then, and remains, compensation rather than reinstatement or re-
engagement within the company. In other words, redundancy legislation
is largely directed at monetary compensation for, rather than prevention
of, job loss or enhancing job security.

The Main Reforms during the 1990s

Within a context of emphasizing the responsibilities of workers and job
seekers, the Labour government improved basic employment rights after
1997. These applied to the introduction of a national minimum wage, the
rights of parents (family leave, parental leave, working time), the rights of
part-time workers, and the rights of those seeking to resolve disputes with
their employers over dismissal or redundancy matters (see Dickens 2002;
Deakin and Morris 2005). For example, the Employment Relations Act

1999 removed derogations from unfair dismissal protection for fixed-term contract workers and shorted the qualifying period for unfair dismissal protection from two years to one. It also raised the upper limit on unfair dismissal compensation awards and indexed it in line with inflation. The Employment Act 2002 required employers to institute an internal grievance procedure, and employees to pursue and complete this route prior to bringing a claim to an employment tribunal in respect of a wide range of statutory employment rights. Several other changes in legislation improved employment rights (for details see Clasen 2007, Appendix A1).

Although the Labour government ended the previous 'opt-out' from the EU Social Chapter, the adoption of EU law (for example on parental leave and working time) was introduced with some time lag and typically subscribed to at a level close to the minimum requirement so as not to place burdens on employers and to retain the 'most lightly regulated labour market of any leading economy of the world' (Cm 3968 1998). Thus, although expansionary, Labour's advances in employment protection have been pursued cautiously and in moderation. Moreover, there are examples of legislation which weakened employment rights, making it harder for employees to succeed in their claims for unfair dismissal, for example. Most notably in this respect, the Employment Act 2002 diminished the importance of procedural fairness, allowing tribunals to 'disregard procedural breach above basic standards where it was felt it would have made no difference to the outcome' (Dickens 2002, p. 627). Since 2004, redundancy dismissal cases have been subject to statutory dismissal and grievance procedures. This means that an employee who has been dismissed needs to have instituted the appropriate statutory grievance procedure prior to referring a claim for redundancy payment to a tribunal.

The Current System: Main Characteristics

The British system of individual employment rights continues to depend on minimum statutory provision which is often supplemented by voluntary payments in the case of redundancies or in lieu of notice. Employees who have lost their job might be entitled to statutory redundancy pay. This applies to dismissals due to reduction or closing down of the workplace. It is not redundancy if the employer takes on a direct replacement for the dismissed worker.

Eligibility for statutory redundancy payment requires a minimum of two years of service with the same employer. The actual amount depends on the length of service in relation to particular age bands. However, the maximum number of years which count towards redundancy is 20. Statutory redundancy pay in the UK is tax free but among the lowest-paid in the EU (Kaupinnen and Meixner 2005). It should be noted however that many employers pay employees with long service more than the statutory minimum (see below). If employers are unable to pay redundancy or pay in lieu of notice because of insolvency, the government will step in, granting only the legal minimum even if the contract of employment stipulates more.

Individual workers who consider themselves as having been unfairly dismissed and seek to enforce their statutory rights should first aim to resolve the dispute by mutual agreement with the employer, mainly through the company's own grievance or appeal procedure. Employees or employers might also seek advice from a conciliator of the Advisory, Conciliation and Arbitration Service (ACAS). If no agreement can be reached, employees have to apply to an employment tribunal (see below).

Statutory provisions require employers to inform and consult appropriate representatives of employees who may be affected by collective redundancies (at least 20 employees in one plant, over a 90-day period). Consultation must begin at least 30 days before the first dismissal (90 days if 100 or more redundancies are planned). Employers must disclose the reasons for redundancies, numbers and descriptions of employees affected, and method of carrying out the redundancies, including payments, as well as the method of selection. Employers must give reasonable time off for employees to look for another job. Agreement does not have to be reached but the employers should seek to reach it (DTI 2006).

Administration and Responsibilities

Unlike continental European countries, as a 'common law country' the UK relies less on substantive and procedural codification but rather on 'decision making by juries, independent judges, and the emphasis on judicial discretion' (Botero et al. 2004, p. 1344). In the area of individual employment rights, two bodies are important. First, established in 1964 and then known as industrial tribunals, employment tribunals (ETs) are responsible for the settlement of employment disputes and are decision makers in matters of dismissal, redundancy, discrimination and other forms of dispute (see ETS 2006). ETs are independent judicial bodies, with a qualified chair and two lay members.

In practical terms, the 'individualized, private law model characteristic of the UK remains the corner stone of enforcement' (Dickens 2002, p. 628). Individual workers can make applications to an ET. A copy of the completed form will be sent to ACAS and a conciliator will in most cases contact the employee or employer (or both) in order to establish whether a voluntary settlement can be reached without the need for a hearing. Legal

Aid is not available at ETs and the scheme does not cover legal representation at the hearing. Appeals against decisions by an ET are made to another specialist tripartite (the Employment Appeal Tribunal) and then to ordinary courts.

Unfair dismissal cases are by far the most prominent reason for employment disputes. In 2003–4 almost half of all 94 000 cases concerned unfair dismissals and only 4000 dealt with redundancy pay (Deakin and Morris 2005, p. 385). However, only about a quarter of all disputes are actually heard by a tribunal (Dickens and Hall 2003, p. 135) since most cases are settled through conciliation by ACAS, withdrawn and settled privately, or abandoned. In total, applicants succeed in about half of all cases, while about one-third of all applications against unfair dismissal are upheld. The normal outcome is compensation payment. Reinstatement or re-engagement is rarely sought by applicants and rarely awarded by tribunals (less than 1 per cent of all cases).

A number of collective agreements improve on statutory provision, including measures to avoid redundancies, longer consultation periods, more active redeployment policies, reducing overtime, the use of temporary staff or early retirement (Work Foundation 2004). Many employers, and most large companies, also exceed minimum statutory redundancy payments by removing the earnings cap on a week's pay, increasing the number of weeks paid per year of service or simply making additional lump-sum payments (Lloyd 2003). At times additional payments are fixed in collective agreements but in many other cases they are 'unilaterally determined by management or agreed with trade unions at the time of redundancies' (Lloyd 2003). Some employers might offer better terms than redundancy pay, or a lump sum severance payment, and in return staff might be asked to sign a legal document which will disallow any legal action against the employer in relation to the dismissal. Finally, in high-profile cases the government might provide support which goes beyond the usual statutory requirements. For example, in the case of the closure of the MG Rover plant at Longbridge in 2005 the government set up a regional task force, bringing together regional chambers of commerce, trade unions, community groups, industry bodies and Jobcentre Plus as well as the Learning and Skills Council (Armstrong 2006).

As for responsibilities, the relevant ministry in the area of employment legislation is the Department for Business, Enterprise and Regulatory Reform (BERR), the successor for the former Department of Trade and Industry (DTI). It has a significant role not only as a source of information for employers and employees, but also as commissioning body for employment-related research and workplace surveys. It is also the statutory agency which companies planning collective redundancies are required to notify. Finally, as the ministry responsible for the ET service, it appoints assessors, although the process of selection tends to be outsourced.

ACAS is a publicly funded independent body which has a major impact on the outcome of individual and collective employment disputes. Appointed by the Secretary of State, ACAS is governed by a council which consists of 13 'leading figures from business, unions, independent sectors and academics', mainly with a professional background in law (see http://www.acas.org.uk). The role of ACAS has become more important since 2001 when, supported by the Trades Union Congress (TUC) and the CBI (Confederation of British Industry), the 'arbitration' alternative to ETs came into force as a way of 'tackling undue legalism and the failure of tribunals to live up to their original remit to provide an accessible and informal way of resolving individual employment disputes' (Dickens and Hall 2003, p. 135).

THE 'TRIANGLE' IN PRACTICE

The Three Policy Instruments

The three domains of employment protection, unemployment insurance (UI) and active labour market policy (ALMP) are not part of some British corporatist arrangement delivering negotiated settlements between the government and social partners. Instead, despite devolution and the extensive use of employees and employers in partnership networks at a local level, policy formulation has remained firmly in the hands of central government. Moreover, there are no signs of a shift towards another settlement. Instead, given Labour's embrace of the comparative advantage of the British deregulated and flexible labour market, incremental adjustment is much more conceivable than restructuring.

It would be misleading to portray the domains of unemployment insurance, active labour market policy and employment protection as some sort of 'system' or even as complementary. The three policy fields are certainly less closely linked in the UK than in other European countries, and there has been little pressure to change this. Until 2008 the overall labour market development has been fairly positive, making it relatively easy for the Labour government to legitimate the current regime, keeping labour market policy expenditure low, focusing on job search and individual counselling ('work first') and refining existing programmes based on evaluative evidence. Pointing to deadweight effects, the Conservative opposition proposed the abolition of the New Deal programmes prior to the 2005 general election. However, under David Cameron as party leader a more cautious line has been adopted, advocating decentralization, privatization and localization instead of outright abolition.

In the field of unemployment protection, Labour's embrace of targeting and means-testing might make the abolition of contributory benefit support conceivable. Besides, the political emphasis is less on unemployment policies but rather on changing disability and incapacity benefit regulations with the aim of increasing labour market participation rates amongst working-age transfer claimants in general. Within individual employment protection a moderate expansionary trend can be observed. After Labour's signing of the Amsterdam Treaty this was partly due to the impact of EU Directives, but domestic motives were influential too. However, as discussed, the expansion of employment rights has been relatively modest and challenges neither the individualistic private law tradition of British employment relations, nor the cross-party consensus of maintaining a flexible and lightly regulated labour market perceived as a major asset in international economic competition.

All of this does not mean that there has been no change. ALMP and UI have become more closely linked than in the past. While unemployment support has become all but devoid of its contributory basis, it has become more tightly linked to ALMP as part of a more coherent 'welfare-to-work' approach linking previously fairly isolated policy domains. However, the broadening of erstwhile unemployment policies (benefits, labour market programmes) to all groups of working-age benefit claimants is ambitious and its success is likely to be dependent on labour market developments.

Output and Outcomes

It would go beyond the scope of this chapter to discuss the effects of the three policies covered (for some of these, see Clasen 2007). However, in order to put the review of current systems and trends into some perspective it seems appropriate to offer a few observations. Overall, a positive labour market trend has provided the backdrop to legislation in all three areas. From a peak of around 10 per cent of the workforce in 1993, unemployment declined steadily to below 5 per cent in the new century, and has remained around this mark until the first half of 2008, but rose steeply afterwards. The absolute and relative decline of long-term unemployment has been another positive feature of the British economy (Table 4.5). However, unemployment for younger groups has remained high, with rates for the under-25-year-olds three to four times the rates of those aged 25 to 54 (OECD 2006).

Even though used to highlight positive trends, the government is well

Table 4.5   Long-term unemployment in the UK

	000s	% of unemployed
1997	731	36
1999	482	28
2001	371	25
2003	305	21
2005	300	21
2006	351	21
2008	388	24

Note: Unemployed out of work for more than 12 months, May/July figures.

Source: Office for National Statistics (ONS) (1998–2008), *Labour Force Surveys*, London: ONS.

Table 4.6   Labour market participation of low-skilled men aged 25-64 in the UK

	1994	1996	1998	2000	2005	1994–2005
Unemployment rate	18.8	15.1	13.7	11.6	7.4	−11.4
Employment–population ratio	61.0	61.7	59.1	60.0	59.5	−0.5
Labour force participation	75.1	72.7	68.5	68.0	64.3	−10.8
Inactivity rate	24.9	27.3	31.5	32.0	35.7	+10.8

Note: Less than secondary education.

Source: OECD (1996–2007), *Employment Outlook*, Paris: OECD.

aware that unemployment rates are a rather partial reflection of the performance of the labour market. Table 4.6 illustrates that it is particularly low-skilled men who have not benefited from the benign economic development since the mid-1990s. On the contrary, declining unemployment for this group was the result not of a growth in employment rates but of a steady increase in labour market detachment, with more than one-third of this group outside of the labour force by 2005.

Table 4.6 illustrates that a focus on unemployment is an imperfect indicator of policy problems or policy outputs. Table 4.7 underlines the minor role of unemployment insurance (contribution-based JSA) within British unemployment support, and within the context of the total social security budget for working-age people. The table also demonstrates the relevance

*Table 4.7   Social security expenditure directed at people of working age in
the UK, (real terms, 2007/08 prices), £ billion*

	CB JSA	IB JSA	Incapacity Benefit	Housing Benefit
1996–7	1.3	2.2	9.1	10.0
2001–2	0.6	2.7	8.3	8.4
2004–5	0.5	1.8	7.4	9.1
2007–8	0.4	1.8	6.7	10.1

Source: DWP (2008a), Table 6 (rounded; JSA adult element only; figures for 2007/8 are
forecast).

Table 4.8   Working-age benefit claimant groups in the UK (millions)

	Total	JSA recipients	Incapacity	Lone parent	Carer
2000	5.49	1.15	2.68	0.92	0.31
2002	5.26	0.96	2.75	0.88	0.33
2004	5.43	0.87	2.78	0.83	0.36
2006	5.38	0.94	2.71	0.78	0.37
2008	5.17	0.81	2.62	0.74	0.38

Notes: Incapacity: in receipt of incapacity benefit or severe disablement allowance; lone
parent with children under 16; carer: in receipt of carer's allowance; others: receiving other
types of benefits.
Figures do not add up to total because of other benefits not listed here.

Source: DWP (2008b), February figures.

of benefit expenditure for those who are categorized as long-term sick, or
having some form of incapacity, compared with JSA claimants. It illustrates the importance of housing benefit too, exceeding the total of JSA
expenditure for adults. Table 4.8 underlines this point with respect to the
total size of working-age claimant groups and its components.

As far as the generosity of unemployment support is concerned, there
has been a considerable decline since the 1970s (DWP 2004c), and in the
late 1990s the UK unemployment insurance system became, as far as gross
benefit levels are concerned, the least generous across 16 European countries (OECD 2006). Much depends on particular circumstances, though.
Calculations by the OECD indicate that a single unemployed person
without children who previously earned 67 per cent of average wages in
the UK has a relatively high benefit level in European comparison (higher

than his or her German or Austrian counterpart), but the relative generosity is lower for somebody on the same wage who is married to an employed spouse. The UK is a good illustration that calculating the actual 'replacement rate' (degree by which benefit compensates for lost earnings) is not straightforward (Kvist 1998). For most of the unemployed, the standard level of JSA is typically supplemented by additional means-tested support such as Council Tax benefit and housing benefits. Indeed, once help with housing costs is included, UK replacement rates improve considerably in international comparisons since the receipt of housing benefits can have an even more important impact on post-transfer income than unemployment compensation or social assistance (Clasen 2007).

Turning to the impact of active labour market policy, in accordance with Labour's emphasis on 'evidence based' policy making, there have been numerous evaluations of the New Deal programmes. A New Deal Evaluation Database (NDED) was established which collects information recorded by front-line staff on interactions with job-seeking claimants. For example, there seems to be considerable area-based variation, with claimants moving out of benefits in areas where front-line caseworkers adopt strong 'work-first' practices, such as frequent and closely spaced repeat interviewing, the use of sanctions to enforce the mandatory nature of NDYP and the 'usage of short courses that helped clients choose work experience or educational options' (White 2004, p. 23).

Several other studies of the NDYP have been conducted which found positive, albeit mainly moderate, effects in terms of a reduction in benefit claiming and job entry rates (for an overview see Hasluck and Green 2006). There are indications that subsidized employment proved the most effective option in terms of job entry and securing unsubsidized work, and Blundell et al. (2003) found that the NDYP had a positive, albeit small, net employment creation effect. Apparently the NDYP has improved the chances of exit from unemployment, but a main effect has been a shift from unemployment into education and training. Indeed, while youth unemployment fell, the employment rate of 18–24-year-olds in the UK also declined. Thus, rather than raising employment, the main impact of the NDYP seems to have been in the area of reducing long-term unemployment (Blundell et al. 2003).

Not all employment is 'sustainable' however, defined by the government as jobs lasting at least 13 weeks, or more precisely, the non-return to JSA within this period. In 1998, just under half of all NDYP leavers moved into jobs which lasted at least 13 weeks. Cumulatively, between the start of the New Deal programmes in 1998 and May 2006, 45 per cent of leavers from the NDYP are known to have entered sustained employment, compared with about 31 per cent of leavers from the ND25+ and over 54 per cent of leavers from the voluntary programme for lone parents (DWP

2006). However, with falling numbers of NDYP participants (from about 140000 in March 1999 to about 80000 five years later), job entry rates have also declined.

Finally, as far as employment protection is concerned, OECD league tables confirm that the level of regulation regarding both regular and temporary jobs in the UK was the weakest in Europe in the mid-1980s, as well as 20 years later (OECD 2004). However, as discussed, regulations in the area of unfair dismissal, procedural inconvenience on the part of employers in dismissal processes, as well as notice and redundancy pay provisions have become somewhat more pronounced. Thus, while the scope of employment regulation in the UK continues to be considerably lower than in other European countries, there has been a trend of 'constrained expansion' (Dickens 2002).

As for some direct effects in the areas of redundancy, dismissal and employment disputes, many but certainly not all affected workers receive more than the statutory minimum compensation. In the absence of comprehensive data, a survey indicated that 41 per cent of those who had left a job because of a dismissal, redundancy or dispute received some kind of payment form their employer (Corbin 2004, p. 34). However, more than half of all respondents either already had another job to go to when they left, or left because they wanted another job, and a majority of the survey (65 per cent) reported that they had resigned from their job voluntarily while just 3 per cent had been dismissed. Thus, the low scope of employment protection in the UK does not necessarily imply high levels of involuntary job losses due to redundancy, dismissal or end of a temporary job. More generally, employment protection is less aimed at employment (and certainly not job) security, but more at procedural fairness which is individually enforced. Building on relatively low levels of statutory minima, the role of informal procedures and non-statutory payments has remained significant.

CONCLUSION

It would be easy to dismiss the British model of employment protection and unemployment support as one of the least generous and, potentially, least effective in Europe. As discussed, the scope of legal employment protection has remained relatively modest, statutory transfers in case of dismissal or redundancy are not expansive and, typically, they do not compensate for similarly low levels of unemployment insurance transfers. There is no space for collective agreements which could substitute for the residual income protection provided through either unemployment insurance or employment protection. In addition, expenditure on active labour market programmes has increased only relatively modestly under the Labour government.

However, a closer look reveals some 'functional equivalents' which raise the effectiveness of unemployment protection and narrow the gap between the UK and other European countries. This applies to better-paid and short-term unemployed persons in particular, who often rely on private unemployment insurance (as part of mortgage protection plans; see Clasen 2007) and non-statutory redundancy monies to top up meagre state support during shorter spells of unemployment. For those out of work for longer, or more frequently, these avenues are less applicable. Additional public support is therefore needed and common, such as housing benefits or help with local tax duties. The package of unemployment support thus consists of much more than unemployment benefits, and in monetary terms contribution-based JSA is rather marginal. Resulting disincentives, which a system heavily reliant on means-tested support implies, have been counteracted with the introduction and significant expansion of wage subsidies (tax credits) which have mushroomed under the Labour government. Thus, supported by a long period of job growth, at least until 2008 the British model has been relatively successful, albeit at the cost of significant disparities in earnings and a concentration of labour market disadvantages.

It remains to be seen how the downturn in the British economy in the second half of 2008 will affect each of the policy fields reviewed here, as well as their interaction. However, it seems likely for policy making to remain centralized, with no role for the social partners in the formation of policy in any of the three domains. Nevertheless, or perhaps partly because of this, the complex and targeted support system has become more coherent than it was during the 1980s and most of the 1990s, when active and passive labour market policies were devised and provided in isolation from each other. The integration of benefit and job search services in the UK, as well as the amalgamation of benefit support for all claimants of working age, has proved to be of interest to many other European countries. Of course, its relative success has benefited from a long period of economic and labour market expansion. If the recent steep rise in unemployment continues, the sustainability of the model will be seriously tested.

NOTES

1. I would like to thank Christian Jakubik for research assistance.
2. All monetary values stated are based on an exchange rate of £1 equal to €1.25 (28 October 2008).

REFERENCES

Armstrong, K. (2006), 'Life after MG Rover', a report prepared for BBC Radio 4, London: Work Foundation.

Blundell, R., H. Reed, J. van Reenen and A. Shephard (2003), 'The impact of the New Deal for Young People on the labour market: a four year assessment', in R. Dickens, P. Gregg and J. Wadsworth (eds) *The Labour Market under New Labour*, Houndsmills: Palgrave, pp. 17–31.

Bonoli, G. (2003), 'Social policy through labour markets: understanding national differences in the provision of economic security to wage earners', *Comparative Political Studies*, **36**(9): 1007–30.

Botero, J. C., S. Djankov, R. La Porta, F. Lopez-de-Silanes and A. Shleifer (2004), 'The regulation of labour', *Quarterly Journal of Economics*, November, 1339–82.

Bruttel, O. (2005), 'Are employment zones successful? Evidence from the first four years', *Local Economy*, **20**(4): 389–403.

Clasen, J. (1994), *Paying the Jobless: A Comparison of Unemployment Benefit Policies in Great Britain and Germany*, Aldershot: Avebury.

Clasen, J. (2005), *Reforming European Welfare States: Germany and the United Kingdom Compared*, Oxford: Oxford University Press

Clasen, J. (2007), 'Distribution of responsibility for social security and labour market policy. Country report: United Kingdom', Amsterdam Institute for Advanced Labour Studies working paper 07-50, Amsterdam.

Clasen, J., G. Duncan, T. Eardley, M. Evans, P. Ughetto, W. van Oorschot and S. Wright (2001), 'Towards "single gateways"? A cross-national review of the changing roles of employment offices in seven countries', *Zeitschrift für Ausländisches und Internationales Sozialrecht*, **15**(1): 43–63.

Cm 3968 (1998), *Fairness at Work*, May, London: The Stationery Office.

Corbin, T. (2004), 'Job separations: a survey of workers who have recently left an employer', *DTI Employment Relations Research Series*, **37**, Department of Trade and Industry, London.

CPAG (Child Poverty Action Group) (1996), *Welfare Rights Bulletin*, **134**(February), London: CPAG.

Crouch, C. (1999), 'Employment, industrial relations and social policy: new life in an old connection, *Social Policy and Administration*, **33**(4): 437–57.

Deakin, S. and G.S. Morris (2005), *Labour Law*, London: Hart Publishing.

Dickens, L. (2002), 'Individual statutory employment rights since 1997: constrained expansion', *Employee Relations*, **24**(6): 619–37.

Dickens, L. and M. Hall (1995), 'The state: labour law and industrial relations', in P. Edwards (ed.), *Industrial Relations*, Oxford: Blackwell, pp. 255–303.

Dickens, L. and M. Hall (2003), 'Labour law and industrial relations: a new settlement?' in P. Edwards (ed.), *Industrial Relations*, 2nd edn, Oxford: Blackwell, pp. 124–56.

DTI (Department of Trade and Industry) (2006), 'Redundancy Consultation and Notification', (PL833), DTI, accessed www.consumer.gov.uk/er/redundancy/consult-pl833a.htm.

DWP (Department for Work and Pensions) (2004a), 'Benefit expenditure tables', updated 9/1/2004.

DWP (2004b), *Work and Pensions Statistics*, London: DWP.

DWP (2004c), *The Abstract of Statistics: 2003 Edition*, IAD Information Centre, London: DWP.

DWP (2005), 'Job Seekers Allowance quarterly statistical enquiry', February, London.

DWP (2006), 'DWP quarterly statistical summary', DWP Information Directorate, London, 16 August.

DWP (2008a), 'Benefit expenditure and caseload tables', 1991/2 to 2010/11, London.

DWP (2008b), 'DWP quarterly statistical summary', DWP Information Directorate, Newcastle, 13 August 2008.

ETS (Employment Tribunal Service) (2006), *Annual Report and Accounts, 2005–06*, HC 1303, London: Stationery Office.

Evans, M. (1998), 'Social Security: dismantling the pyramids?' in H. Glennerster and J. Hills (eds), *The State of Welfare*, Oxford: Oxford University Press, pp. 257–303.

Finn, D. (1998), 'Labour's "New Deal" for the unemployed and the stricter benefit regime', in E. Brunsdon, H. Dean and R. Woods (eds), *Social Policy Review*, no. 10, London: Social Policy Association, pp. 105–22.

Finn, D. (2005), '"Contracting out" and contestability: modernising the British public employment service', in T. Bredgaard and F. Larsen (eds) *Employment Policy from Different Angles*, Copenhagen: DJØF Publishing, pp. 233–49.

Finn, D., M. Knuth, O. Schweer and W. Somerville (2005), 'Reinventing the public employment service: the changing role of employment assistance in Britain and Germany', Anglo-German Foundation research report, London.

Hasluck, C. and A.E. Green (2006), 'Building on New Deal: what works for whom? A review of evidence and meta-analysis for the Department for Work and Pensions', draft, Warwick Institute for Employment Research.

Hemerijck, A., P. Manow and van K. Kersbergen (2000), 'Welfare without work? Divergent experiences of reform in Germany and the Netherlands', in S. Kuhnle (ed.), *Survival of the European Welfare State*, London: Routledge, pp. 106–27.

Kauppinen, T. and M. Meixner (2005), 'Redundancies and redundancy costs', European Industrial Relations Observatory (EIRO) thematic feature, Dublin: European Foundation for the Improvement of Living and Working Conditions.

King, D. (1995), *Actively Seeking Work? The Politics of Unemployment and Welfare Policy in the United States and Great Britain*, London: University of Chicago Press.

Kvist, J. (1998), 'Complexities in assessing unemployment benefits and policies', *International Social Security Review*, 51(4): 33–55.

Layard, R. (2000), 'Welfare-to-work and the New Deal', *World Economics*, 1(2): 29–39.

Lloyd, C. (2003), 'Redundancies and redundancy costs', European Industrial Relations Observatory (EIRO) thematic feature, Dublin: European Foundation for the Improvement of Living and Working Conditions, accessed at www.eiro.eurofound.eu.int/2003/11/tfeature/uk0311104t.html.

Manow, P. (1997), 'Social insurance and the German political economy', Max-Planck-Institut für Gesellschaftsforschung discussion paper 97/2, Cologne.

Meager, N. (1997), 'United Kingdom. Active and passive labour market policies in the United Kingdom', *SYSDEM Trends*, 28, European Commission, DG Employment and Social Affairs; also published Berlin: IAS, pp. 69–75.

National Audit Office (2008), *National Insurance Account 2006/7*, London: National Audit Office.

OECD (Organisation for Economic Co-operation and Development) (2002), *Benefit and Wages*, Paris: OECD.

OECD (2004), 'Employment protection regulation and labour market performance', in *Employment Outlook*, Paris: OECD.

OECD (2006), 'Statistical annex', in *Employment Outlook*, Paris: OECD.

OECD (2008), 'Labour force statistics', online database.

Rhodes, M. (2000), 'Restructuring the British welfare state: between domestic constraints and global imperatives', in F.W. Scharpf and V. A. Schmidt (eds), *Welfare and Work in the Open Economy*, Vol 2, Oxford: Oxford University Press, pp. 19–68.

Stafford, B. (2003), 'Beyond lone parents: extending welfare-to-work to disabled people and the young unemployed', in R. Walker and M. Wiseman (eds), *The Welfare we Want? The British Challenge for American Reform*, Bristol: Policy Press, pp. 143–74.

Trickey, H. and R. Walker (2001), 'Steps to compulsion within British labour market policies', in I. Lødemel and H. Trickey (eds) *An Offer You can't Refuse: Workfare in International Perspective*, Bristol: Policy Press, pp. 181–214.

Walker, R. and M. Wiseman (eds) (2003), *The Welfare We Want? The British Challenge for American Reform*, Bristol: Policy Press.

White, M. (2004), 'Effective job search practice in the UK's mandatory welfare-to-work programme for youth', Policy Studies Institute research discussion paper 17, London.

Work Foundation (2004), 'Managing redundancy', *Managing Best Practice*, **104**, London.

5. The Netherlands

Trudie Schils

INTRODUCTION

The Netherlands is frequently praised for its low level of unemployment and good social protection of workers. At the same time, labour market flexibility is perceived as relatively low in the Netherlands. Since the 1990s, the share of flexible workers has increased and in 1999 the Flexibility and Security Act was introduced that creates more room for employers to use flexible workers and at the same time protects the workers on such contracts. In recent years, some aspects of the Dutch social policy triangle have been reformed, while other aspects have been left unchanged. The distribution of responsibilities and the organization of the administration of the social policy triangle are the main aspects that have been reformed.

Since the 1990s, the role of the social partners in the administration of social insurance has been reduced. Their role is now largely restricted to collective bargaining and advising the government. However, some elements of social policy can be put on the collective bargaining agenda, such as particular elements of employment protection legislation, supplementary unemployment insurance and on-the-job training facilities to increase workers' employability. In this way, the social partners can extend national policies, as in the three-pillar model that is already used in the Dutch pension system (Schils 2005). As mentioned in Chapter 1, social dialogue is an important requirement for the establishment of flexicurity policies. As de Beer et al. (2004) have stated, a shared responsibility for social security implies cooperation and negotiation between all relevant actors. This contributes to a broader support for social security reforms among the population and to a better tuning of economic targets (or flexibility) and social protection (or security). It might, however, also delay decision making. The most recent social dialogue in the Netherlands, on the reform of employment protection legislation, ended at a deadlock because the trade unions and employers' associations firmly disagreed on the direction of the reforms. Trust is thin at the moment, although the current economic crisis seems to encourage the social partners to resume the social dialogue.

While the organization of social policy has changed considerably since the 1990s, the system as such has not changed all that much. The main reforms were made in the field of unemployment insurance and active labour market policy with a shift towards more activation. Employment protection legislation, however, has remained the same. This chapter discusses the main reforms as well as the current characteristics of the three social policy fields in the Netherlands, and investigates the relations between these fields and the labour market outcomes.

UNEMPLOYMENT INSURANCE

The Main Reforms since the 1990s

Dutch law on unemployment insurance dates back to 1949, but has been changed repeatedly since then (van Gerven 2008, Chapter 4). In response to increasing unemployment rates in the early 1990s, a large number of unemployment beneficiaries and a relatively large share of long-term unemployed, a series of reforms were made to the Dutch system of unemployment insurance. These reforms were geared towards a more activating system of unemployment insurance. Two types of reforms can be distinguished: reforms on the conditions of unemployment insurance (such as benefit entitlement and benefit generosity) and reforms of the administration of unemployment insurance and the distribution of responsibilities between the different actors (such as the state and the social partners). This short historical review starts with the first type of reforms.

In 1995, a two-tiered unemployment benefit system was introduced distinguishing between a short-term flat-rate unemployment benefit for those with a minimum work record and a longer-term earnings-related unemployment benefit for people with a longer work record. In the years that followed, many reforms were made to promote faster reintegration into the labour market. In 2003, the flat-rate follow-up benefit after the expiration of the earnings-related benefit was abolished in order to limit the maximum duration of unemployment insurance. In addition, the definition of work record and therewith the entitlement to a benefit was changed. Up to 2005, a fictitious work record was used for the worker's employment history before the final five years, based on their age and assuming working life started at age 18. As from 2005 onwards, the actual work record is gradually replacing this fictitious work record, to reflect heterogeneity in working lives (that is, the age at which working life starts and possible breaks during the career) and to establish an actual relationship between unemployment benefit entitlement and work record. Finally,

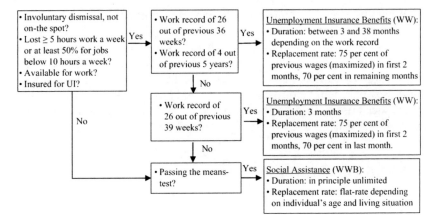

Sources: van Gerven (2008), UWV (2008).

Figure 5.1   *The Dutch unemployment benefit system in 2006*

in 2006 the two-tiered system was abolished and only the earnings-related benefit remained in place (see Figure 5.1). Furthermore, entitlement conditions have been tightened, replacement rates are increased in the first three months of unemployment, and the duration of unemployment benefits has been shortened. The new system, which grants higher benefits but for a shorter duration, is expected to increase the mobility in and out of unemployment (Buevink 2005). This should enhance the worker's probability of finding an optimal job match.

   The second type of reforms, those of the administration of unemployment insurance, were mainly made in response to the discontent with the role of the social partners. From the 1950s to the 1980s the employee insurances (including unemployment insurance) were administered by so-called trade associations at the sector level, to which all employers in the sector were associated by law. The board of these trade associations consisted of representatives of trade unions and employers' organizations. During the 1980s, as expenditure on social security rapidly increased, the system became increasingly criticized. Because of the low union density, serious doubts were raised about the representativeness of the trade unions in the administration of social insurance. As a consequence, in the early 1990s the trade associations were replaced by five administration offices (Uitvoeringsinstellingen, Uvi), that were responsible for the administration of social insurance. The social partners were now only part of the National Institute for Social Insurance (Landelijk Instituut Sociale Verzekeringen, Lisv), the principal for the administration of social insurance and manager of the social insurance funds. In addition, their role in monitoring social insurances was also reduced, with the replacement of the tripartite Social Insurance Council (Sociale Verzekeringsraad, SVr) with an independent monitoring institute, the Monitoring Board for Social Insurance (College van toezicht sociale verzekeringen, Ctsv).

With the second organizational reform in social insurance within a relatively short time, the SUWI II Act of 2000, the government wanted to establish 'less government and more market' in the administration of social insurance. While the assessment of unemployment benefit claims and the provision of benefits remained in public hands, reintegration was (partly) moved to the private sector. The five administration offices (uvi's) were replaced by two public bodies (the CWI and UWV, see below) in which the social partners no longer play any role. Their role is now merely advisory through their representation in the Social and Economic Council (SER), the Labour Foundation and the Council for Work and Income (Raad voor Werk en Inkomen, RWI). Furthermore, collective bargaining and the establishment of collective agreements is still one of their main activities.

The Current System: Main Characteristics

Benefit entitlement conditions, benefit duration and benefit replacement rates are determined by national law. Supplements on the level and duration of national benefits can, however, be arranged at the sector or company level in collective agreements. All employees below the age of 65 (85 per cent of the total number of insured) as well as persons on disability, sickness or unemployment benefit are insured (14 per cent of the total number of insured). In addition, the self-employed can voluntarily insure themselves for national unemployment insurance, but this group reflects less than 1 per cent of the total number of insured. Contributions are set on a yearly basis and determined by national law (by the Ministry of Social Affairs and Employment). The contributions for employees are paid by the employers, the contributions for people on benefits by the administration office paying the benefit, and the voluntary insured pay their own contributions. Employers' unemployment insurance contributions consist of two parts: (1) a general unemployment contribution consisting of a worker part of 3.45 per cent of wages and an employer part of 5.2 per cent of wages; and (2) a sector-specific unemployment contribution, depending on the sector's unemployment rate, paid by the employer and varying from 0.5 to 12.5 per cent of wages. These sector-specific unemployment contributions are used to finance the first six months of unemployment and shift some of the costs and responsibilities of unemployment to the sector level.

Entitlement to unemployment benefits is first conditional on not being blamefully unemployed (to reduce moral hazard). The law states that a worker is blamefully unemployed in cases of serious misbehaviour usually followed by dismissal on the spot (for example in cases of theft, violence or refusal to work) or in cases where the dismissal is based on unreasonable grounds. Voluntary resignation at the worker's initiative does not yield entitlement to unemployment benefits either. Figure 5.1 shows that entitlement to unemployment benefits further depends on the worker's work record. For workers with a short work record, unemployment benefits are only paid for three months, but for workers with a longer work record, unemployment benefits can be paid for a maximum of 38 months. About one-fifth of the people who become unemployed do not meet the years condition (mainly young workers and women) and receive the short-term unemployment benefit only (SER 2006). Benefit levels are set at 75 per cent of the worker's previous wage in the first two months of unemployment and 70 per cent thereafter. The higher benefit level in the first two months is expected to work as a 'search subsidy' and to encourage fast outflow out of unemployment (Buevink 2005). The daily wage on which benefits are based is maximized at €183.15.[1] In cases where the unemployment benefit is below the legal social minimum, a supplement is granted up to the level of the social minimum. To keep entitlement to unemployment benefits, the worker has to search actively for a job, with a minimum of four search activities within four weeks (more on this later). The sanction on not meeting the search activities is that benefits are cut or withdrawn fully.

For about 37 per cent of the workers covered by collective agreements a sector-specific unemployment insurance supplement exists (Schils 2007b). Such supplements are most common for workers in education and health care, where almost all workers are covered by such provisions, while no such benefits exist in utilities and hotels and catering. In most collective agreements the duration of these supplementary benefits is similar to that of national insurance and benefits are supplemented up to 95 per cent of previous earnings.

When unemployment benefits are exhausted, or in case of non-entitlement to unemployment benefits, the unemployed worker can apply for social assistance. Unlike unemployment benefits, social assistance is means-tested on household income and wealth. The individual is still expected to be available for work, yet monitoring is different from unemployment benefits, as is shown later in this chapter. Social assistance only provides a flat-rate minimum benefit. For a single person without children the benefit amounts to a maximum of 70 per cent of the legal minimum wage (including housing benefits).

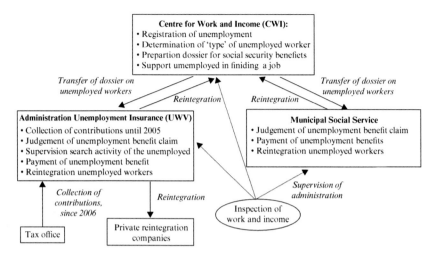

Figure 5.2   The Dutch chain of work and income in 2007

Social assistance benefits are tax-financed. Each year, the central government assigns a lump-sum budget to all municipalities for the administration of social assistance. The budget depends on previous years' budgets, the number of social assistance benefits paid, the size of the municipal labour force and the educational level of the labour force.

Administration and Responsibilities

The central government is responsible for determining the benefit entitlement conditions, benefit duration and benefit replacement rates. In case of reforms, usually first an advice is obtained from the SER, consisting of representatives of employers' associations, trade unions and independent Crown members (Schils 2007a, p. 14). The RWI, consisting of representatives of employers, workers and municipalities, also advises the government on work and income policies. While the SER mainly advises the government with respect to medium- and longer-term policies, the RWI advice focuses on the short term (Obbink 2002). Moreover, as mentioned, the social partners can bargain for supplementary unemployment insurance in collective agreements. Figure 5.2 shows the main institutions and their relation in the so-called chain of Work and Income, established with the 2002 SUWI Act. The Centre for Work and Income (Centrum voor Werk en Inkomen, CWI), the Social Security Agency (Uitvoeringsinstituut Werknemersverzekeringen, UWV) and the municipal Social Service are the main administrative bodies for unemployment benefits. In addition, the Tax Office collects the contributions for unemployment benefit. The Inspection for Work and Income (Inspectie Werk en Inkomen, IWI) monitors and supervises the administrative bodies for social security. It is an independent body with an indirect relation to the Minister of Social Affairs.

Both the CWI and the UWV are public bodies in which the social partners play no role. From 2009 the bodies were merged into one public body to increase further the efficiency of unemployment insurance administration. The CWI registers unemployed workers and determines the type of unemployment and the appropriate kind of benefit and activation programme (either unemployment insurance or social assistance). About 20 per cent of the registered unemployed workers find a job within eight days, without having to apply for benefits (CWI 2006). For those who remain unemployed, the CWI sends an application for unemployment benefits to the UWV or for social assistance to the municipal Social Service. These institutions are responsible for the payment of benefits (including the supplementary unemployment insurance) and reintegration activities. The IWI and the Minister of Social Affairs and Employment assess the legitimacy of granted claims and the efficiency of the administration by the CWI, the UWV and the municipalities. The UWV devotes about a quarter of its capacity to the prevention of fraud. The number of detected fraud cases has slightly declined since 2000 by about two percentage points to about 4 per cent of the total number of beneficiaries. The sanctions mainly concern full or partial deduction of benefits or a formal warning. The detected fraud cases have saved the UWV about €179 million on benefits (including other than unemployment benefits) in 2005 (UWV 2006).

EMPLOYMENT PROTECTION LEGISLATION

The Main Reforms since the 1990s

Dutch employment protection legislation was established in 1907 with the Employment Contracts Act (Wet op de Arbeidsovereenkomst) by which, among other things, a notice period was established to protect workers against instantaneous dismissal. During the Second World War a public route for dismissal was introduced under the German occupation to prevent mass unemployment and a corresponding increase in benefit claims. This created the current dual system with a public route for dismissal and an alternative dismissal route via the court system.

In 2000, an advisory committee established by the government concluded that the Dutch system of employment protection is not transparent, not in line with other EU systems of employment protection and that the state has a relatively large role in what according to the committee are private law issues such as the dismissal of workers (Adviescommissie Duaal Ontslagstelsel 2000). However, no changes were made to the system, since no agreement could be reached on the direction of the reforms.

In 2007, the discussion between the trade unions, employers and the government about reform of the dual system of employment protection flared up again. The employers argued that the high costs of dismissals have a negative impact on the economy (in particular on labour productivity and economic growth) because a company cannot adapt its workforce quickly to changing market circumstances. Right-wing and liberal political parties therefore want to relax the level of employment protection. The trade unions and left-wing parties, however, argue that a fair 'justification test' of dismissals and a reasonable severance pay are needed to protect workers against unreasonable dismissal. Moreover, they argue that state intervention is necessary to protect weaker groups of workers (STAR 2006). A political agreement on the reforms was out of reach. Consequently, only a few minor changes were made to the system of employment protection.

The 1999 Flexibility and Security Act enlarged the possibilities for the use of flexible working arrangements, while at the same time protecting the workers on such contracts. On the one hand, the law reduces the restrictions on the use of temporary agency workers and extends the (maximum) duration of fixed-term contracts, while on the other hand, it established a fairer pay system for temporary agency workers as well as the recognition of the temporary contract as a legal employment contract. Still, the law stipulates the maximum number and the total duration of a sequence of fixed-term contracts or temporary agency work, in order to prevent employers from using fixed-term contracts unlimitedly. Interestingly, this law is only semi-mandatory, allowing for deviations (both upward and downward, in contrast to unemployment insurance) in collective agreements (Schils 2007b).

In 2006 some changes were made with respect to the conditions for collective dismissal. The employer is no longer obliged to use the seniority or 'last in, first out' principle when choosing whom to dismiss. The mirror image or reflection principle should be the first selection criterion used instead. This principle is meant to prevent an uneven age distribution of dismissals by applying the seniority principle within each age group separately (Schils 2007a, pp. 26–7). In addition, the trade unions rather than a public body (the CWI) assess the economic conditions for collective dismissal.

The Current System: Main Characteristics

In order to dismiss a worker on a regular contract, an employer can follow
two routes in the Netherlands. First, the employer can file a request with the
lower court to dissolve the contract. About one-third of the dismissal cases
of regular workers are by mutual consent. This means that the worker and
the employer agree on the terms of contract termination. The terms include,
among others, severance pay, the end date of the contract, the payment of
non-claimed holidays and support in finding another job. However, such a
mutual agreement does not offer the worker a strong argument towards the
CWI which decides on the unemployment benefit entitlement. Therefore,
about 70–80 per cent of the mutually agreed dismissal cases are brought
to the lower court, to formalize the dismissal (van Zevenbergen and Oelen
2000). In addition, the cases in which the worker and employer disagree
on the dismissal are brought to court. The court decides on severance pay,
which amounts to a multiplier of monthly gross salary based on the worker's age, the duration of their labour contract, their earnings and a correc-
tion factor (Schils 2007a, p. 24). In about 83 per cent of the dismissal cases
via the court a severance payment is made, varying from €488 to €363 000.
It is on this point that the Dutch government and the social partners in
2008 agreed on some changes. As from 2009, the maximum severance pay is
€75 000 for employees below the age of 40 and €100 000 for employees older
than 40. When the contract is dissolved by the court, the worker is eligible
for unemployment benefits after a fictitious notice period that is similar to
that when using the second, public route for dismissal.

Second, the employer can ask for a dismissal permit at the CWI, as from
2009 part of the UWV. For collective dismissals only this public route is
available. The CWI judges the reasons for dismissal and decides whether
it grants the dismissal permit. At a hearing, the worker can oppose the
proposed dismissal. In 75 per cent of the cases, the worker only 'formally
objects' to the dismissal, mainly to keep their entitlement to unemployment benefits (van Zevenbergen and Oelen 2000). When the dismissal
permit is granted by the CWI, the worker still has legal grounds to contest
its validity in court. When the employer uses the public route for dismissal
no severance pay is obligatory, but instead a notice period applies. This
depends on worker's tenure (ranging from one month in the case of a
tenure of less than five years to four months in the case of a tenure of at
least 15 years). This period can be changed by collective agreement. For
example, a longer notice period applies for workers on a short-term contract in utilities, government and education, and a shorter notice period
for workers on a contract of more than ten years in construction and commercial services (Schils 2007b).

Although the court route is usually more expensive (because of the severance pay and court costs) it is quicker and administratively less burdensome. According to Declen et al. (2006), the average duration of dismissal procedures via court is 11 days for dismissal cases by mutual agreement (about 80 per cent of all court cases) and six to eight weeks for cases with objections. For the employer, the court route is even more attractive since the dismissal file for the court has to be less elaborate than the one in the CWI route. In addition, because of the high caseload of most courts, in many cases no further hearing is held, nor is an inquiry started on the details of the dismissal, increasing the success rate of court dismissal procedures. Although employers are reluctant to reveal the main reason for opting for the court route rather than the CWI route, the speed and the success rate of the procedure appears to be an important reason (van Zevenbergen and Oelen 2000).

In some cases different dismissal regulations apply. First, during the trial period, workers can be dismissed without a notice period and without severance payment. The trial period, however, is limited by law to a maximum of two months. Second, as mentioned before, the Flexibility and Security Act protects the workers on fixed-term contracts. A sequence of fixed-term contracts, in which such contracts follow each other within a period of three months, may only consist of a maximum of three contracts and can last no longer than 36 months in total. After this period, or with the fourth contract, the worker is entitled to a permanent contract. For workers in education and government a longer maximum duration and a larger number of contracts is observed in collective agreements (Schils 2007b).

Administration and Responsibilities

As with unemployment insurance, the government determines national legislation, such as dismissal procedural rules, notice periods, trial period, and the number and maximum duration of a sequence of fixed-term contracts. The tripartite SER has an advisory task. Severance pay is not determined by law but set by the lower court. At the sector level the social partners can bargain for different provisions in collective agreements. An important difference with the system of unemployment insurance is that the provisions on employment protection in collective agreements can deviate both upwardly and downwardly from national law. Thus, collective agreements on employment protection can be at the expense of the workers, while those on unemployment insurance can only be in favour of the workers as compared to national law.

As for the administration of dismissal law, either the CWI or the lower court tests whether national or sector-level regulations are correctly applied to the specific dismissal case and accordingly grants permission for the dismissal. Collective dismissals are handled solely by the CWI and the trade unions who judge the economic conditions for collective dismissals. In addition, the works councils are involved as an advisory bodies and the trade unions are involved in the establishment of the social plan (the conditions for the collective dismissal).

ACTIVE LABOUR MARKET POLICY

The Main Reforms since the 1990s

During the 1990s the emphasis in Dutch labour market policy changed from passive to active measures, or from merely paying unemployment benefits to activating benefit recipients (Rutte 2003). There has been a remarkable change in the role and position of the social partners. In 1991 a tripartite administration of the Public Employment Service (Arbeidsvoorziening, PES) was introduced in which the trade unions, the employers' associations and the municipalities shared responsibility for reintegration activities. It was expected that this would strengthen support for reintegration policy and a better match between labour supply and demand would be facilitated (Wielers and de Beer 2007). However, a few years later a governmental committee (the 'van Dijk' committee) published a report that showed the ineffectiveness of this tripartite responsibility: the three actors reached no consensus, resulting in a disappointing performance of the PES (Wielers and de Beer 2007). Another parliamentary report questioned the role of the social partners in relation to the large number of disability beneficiaries (the 'Buurmeijer' committee). Gradually the opinion grew that the market for reintegration services should be privatized to increase its efficiency, and that the social partners' role had to be reduced. This was established with the earlier-mentioned 2002 SUWI Act.

Among the (new) objectives are: more emphasis on active reintegration of the unemployed, more cooperation between local institutions that are responsible for reintegration and increased efficiency of reintegration programmes. The CWI and the UWV are collectively responsible for the reintegration of the unemployed who are on unemployment benefit, and the municipalities are responsible for the reintegration of the unemployed who are on social assistance benefit. A large part of the reintegration activities are outsourced to private reintegration companies, which specialize in a particular sector or occupational group. This new organizational structure of active labour market policy should reduce the inflow into unemployment insurance, increase the outflow out of unemployment benefits, both instantly and in the longer run, and balance the unequal distribution of unemployment over different population groups (Koning et al. 2004).

Apart from the organization and administration, the scope of active labour market policies has also changed since the 1990s. In the past, unemployed individuals were supported in their job search or received training to requalify them for the labour market. However, as Glebbeek (2005) points out, their willingness to work or their motivation for a fast return to the labour market is an important requirement for successful reintegration. The so-called 'Work First' programmes were designed to cover this second dimension of active labour market policy for the long-term unemployed, and especially for those on social assistance (Castonguay and Sol 2007). In 2008, the first evaluation studies were published, mainly showing a positive return to these Work First programmes in one of the large Dutch cities (Bunt et al. 2008).

The Current System: Main Characteristics

Unemployment benefit recipients are expected to actively search for a 'suitable job' to reduce the duration of benefit receipt. The definition of a 'suitable job' differs with the type and duration of unemployment. When the beneficiary is less than six months unemployed and receives unemployment benefits, a suitable job is 'a job which is in line with the qualifications and skills of the worker and which also fits the physical, emotional and psychological capabilities of the worker' (UWV 2008). A beneficiary who is more than six months unemployed, or who receives social assistance, also has to accept jobs that are below their qualifications and skills. As for the required search intensity, an unemployed worker on unemployment benefits is required to have a minimum of four search activities every four weeks. Search activities include applying for jobs, having interviews, taking assessment or other tests to find out one's capabilities and interests, and starting one's own business. As mentioned, benefits are (partly) withdrawn when the requirements are not met. A number of instruments are open to support the reintegration of the unemployed, including job mediation, either by public authorities or by private companies, wage subsidies, and training and education.

The type of reintegration support depends on the 'type' of unemployed. In the first six months, it is the worker's own responsibility to find a job. He is supervised in his job search by the UWV (which pays the benefits) and can request support from the CWI. The CWI divides the job seekers into two groups (CWI 2005). The first consists of job seekers who are 'ready' for the labour market and who can immediately start looking for a job. The main reintegration instrument for this group of workers is basic job mediation (such as vacancy overviews and assessment tests). The second group consists of job seekers who first need to be 'prepared' for the labour market. Due to personal problems, lack of qualifications or physical limitations these unemployed are not expected to start looking for a job immediately. This group, and the clients from the first group who are unsuccessful in finding a job within six months, are transferred to mandatory reintegration programmes. A 'reintegration coach' assesses the client (by using specially developed tests to assess what kind of support the client will benefit from most) and then supports them in finding a job by giving advice or encouraging participation in training programmes. The reintegration coach can also decide to enrol the unemployed worker in an individual reintegration programme with a (private) reintegration company. The unemployed beneficiary can also initiate their own private reintegration trajectory. In this case, he or she selects a reintegration company that fulfils the compliance conditions of the UWV, and signs an Individual Reintegration Contract (Individuele Re-integratie Overeenkomst, IRO) stating the reintegration objectives. It is believed that such individual reintegration trajectories are better suited to the individual's needs. However, a drawback is that the reintegration takes place outside the UWV's sight and, thus, control is weaker.

The municipal Social Service supervises and supports the job search of job seekers on social assistance benefits. Instruments commonly used are the reintegration by private companies, wage subsidies, and training activities such as vocational education or language courses, but also social activities and volunteer work. These latter are meant to introduce the long-term unemployed gradually into the labour market. Note that if the municipal Social Service offers reintegration assistance to the individual, they are obliged to accept this support. In refusing such support or work, the individual can expect a partial withdrawal of their social assistance benefit.

Administration and Responsibilities

In the new organization structure of social security administration (established with the Act SUWI in 2002), the CWI, UWV and municipalities are responsible for the reintegration of the unemployed, depending on the 'type' of unemployed, as explained above. All persons who become unemployed apply to the local CWI office and immediately receive some basic reintegration support (such as job mediation or career advice). In cases of entitlement to unemployment benefits they are transferred to the UWV, and in cases of entitlement to social assistance benefits they are transferred to the municipal Social Service. With the recent merger of the UWV and CWI, the unemployment beneficiary only has one office to turn to, which is expected to increase transparency and hence efficiency.

The UWV supervises and judges the search activities of the unemployed. The individual has to report every four weeks and has to show proof of relevant search activities. The UWV is also responsible for the mandatory reintegration programme after six months of unemployment, including those on the individual's initiative (IRO). Yet, the actual reintegration activities within this programme are outsourced by the UWV. The UWV contracts private reintegration companies, at least two per region. Currently, over 40 reintegration companies are contracted by the UWV (UWV 2006). The individual is able to choose between a number of reintegration companies, all specialized in a certain type of job or sector. The outsourcing of the UWV takes place by means of public tender, to ensure transparency of costs. The conditions for a contract are determined annually by the UWV and are available online.

To finance the reintegration activities, a special reintegration fund has been established. This fund is financed from the unemployment and the disability funds, since the reintegration activities concern both. In 2005 about a quarter of the reintegration fund was financed from the unemployment fund, representing the share of unemployed in the reintegration activities (UWV 2006). Remarkably, the UWV has no incentive to buy reintegration support as cheaply as possible; the only incentives in this respect are with the private reintegration companies, which have to operate as efficient as possible in re-employing their clients (Koning and Deelen 2003). The main objectives of the UWV are to start 80 per cent of the reintegration programmes within four weeks time and successfully to re-employ at least 40 per cent of the unemployed workers in a reintegration programme. No real efficiency incentives are applied.

The municipal Social Services are responsible for the reintegration of the unemployed on social assistance benefits. The municipalities are free to choose how to support the unemployed in finding a job. The municipalities receive a yearly budget from the central government, consisting of an 'income budget' to finance the payment of social assistance benefits and a 'work budget' to finance the reintegration activities. When a municipality exceeds its budget, 10 per cent of the budget is its own risk, to increase efficiency. In addition, there is a financial incentive to re-employ successfully job seekers. When the reintegration targets, set by the Ministry of Social Affairs and Employment, are reached, next year's work budget is increased as a kind of reward. If the targets are not reached, the budget is cut. In 2002, 89 per cent of the targets were reached (Peters and van Selm 2004).

The Inspection for Work and Income (IWI) evaluates the effectiveness and efficiency of the reintegration programmes of the various bodies and reports to the Minister of Social Affairs and Employment. Just as with respect to unemployment insurance, the role of the social partners, and in particular of the trade unions, in Dutch active labour market policies has been strongly reduced. In the period of the trade associations, the social partners had an important role in the reintegration of disabled and unemployed workers, but with the 2002 Act SUWI, this role has been abolished.

THE TRIANGLE IN PRACTICE

The Three Policy Instruments

Until the early 1990s, the three policy instruments of the Dutch triangle were not tuned to each other at all. As shown in Table 5.1, Dutch workers on regular contracts enjoyed a relatively strong protection against dismissal (compared to the Organisation for Economic Co-operation and Development (OECD) average), reducing the probability of (involuntary) unemployment. In cases where they were nevertheless dismissed, unemployment benefits were relatively generous and of a fairly long duration, while activation policies were rather weak. Consequently, the Dutch social policy instruments resulted in low flexibility but high security, with small labour mobility flows; or, the probability to stay in a certain labour market state (for example employment, unemployment) is large. However, this only applied to workers on regular contracts, the so-called insiders (prime-aged, full-time working men in particular). For other groups, such as workers on fixed-term contracts, employment protection was weaker and entitlement to unemployment benefits was limited to short-term benefits because of the work record condition. These outsiders, usually young workers, women and migrants, did not benefit from the above-mentioned advantages of the traditional social policy triangle. Instead, they had to rely on the less generous social assistance system, entitlement to which was restricted due to the household means test. This was one of the main points of criticism directed at the Dutch social policy triangle in the 1990s. One might say that flexicurity was very unevenly distributed, with inflexibility combined with a lot of security for the insiders, and flexibility but insecurity for the outsiders.

With the recent reforms this has changed somewhat. The maximum unemployment benefit duration has been reduced and active labour market policy has been intensified, in order to encourage a quick return to the labour market. The level of employment protection, has however been

Table 5.1 Input characteristics of the Dutch social policy triangle, 1990–2005

	The Netherlands				OECD average			
	1990	1995	2000	2005	1990	1995	2000	2005
Employment protection:								
Regular workers	3.08	3.08	3.05	3.05[a]	2.12	2.16	2.18	2.15[a]
Temporary workers	2.38	2.38	1.19	1.19[a]	2.30	1.97	1.69	1.61[a]
Unemployment insurance:								
Gross replacement rate	0.543	0.523	0.525	0.528[a]	0.291	0.311	0.323	0.323[a]
Benefit duration (max in mths)[b]	104	104	104	38	95	69	62	58
Active labour market policy:								
Expenditure % of GDP	1.043	1.052	1.116	1.330	0.733	0.826	0.653	0.707

Notes:
[a] Data referring to 2003.
[b] Data for OECD average only calculated for countries where unemployment insurance is limited in duration, thus excluding Australia, Belgium and New Zealand where benefits are in principle unlimited.

Sources: OECD (2008), *Labour Force Statistics*, online database. Paris: OECD; Scruggs. L. (2006), *Welfare State Entitlements Data Set: A Comparative Institutional Analysis of Eighteen Welfare States*, Version 1.2.

largely left unchanged. With the 1999 Flexibility and Security Act employment protection for fixed-term workers has decreased, due to the increased possibilities for employers to use flexible work arrangements. However, at the same time, workers on such contracts are protected in other ways by better pay, better working conditions and by a limited maximum number and duration of flexible labour contracts. The reforms of the unemployment benefit system have increased benefit generosity for those with only a short work record, although entitlement has been further restricted at the same time and the duration has been reduced from six to three months.

In sum, the reforms have focused on two corners of the triangle, unemployment insurance and active labour market policy, while employment protection for the vast majority of workers has been left unchanged. One could argue that the uneven distribution of flexicurity has been reduced somewhat by increasing the protection of flexible workers and lowering income security for regular workers, yet the gap still remains. In the near future, only minor changes will be made to the system of employment protection, by maximizing the amount of severance pay for dismissed workers. These reforms will not really increase the employer's flexibility with respect to dismissals. Along with the shift from passive to more active labour market policies in the Netherlands, the role of the social partners has been reduced. One point of criticism with respect to the former responsibility of the social partners for the administration of social policy was that it led to less consensus and decisiveness (Wielers and de Beer 2007). Ironically, the recent failure in reforming the system of employment protection was due to strong disagreements between the trade unions and the employers' organizations.

Output and Outcomes

Table 5.2 shows some indicators for the output related to the three policy fields. When looking at employment protection first, we find that despite a lack of reforms in this policy field, some small changes have occurred. Whereas the dismissal rate has not changed dramatically over time, and likely reflects the economic business cycle, in recent years a larger share of dismissals goes via court. In 1990 one out of three cases were brought to court, in 2005 half of the cases is brought to court. Apparently, the employers are willing to pay the higher price of dismissal in the form of severance payment in return for a higher success rate of the dismissal and a shorter procedure. As for the average job tenure, although it is often claimed that the current Dutch labour market is characterized by less long-term relations between employers and workers (so-called job-hopping behaviour of young workers), this is not supported by empirical

Table 5.2   Output characteristics of the Dutch social policy triangle,
1990–2005

	1990	1995	2000	2005
Employment protection:				
Number of dismissals through court (% of lab force)		0.44	0.32	0.68
Number of dismissals through public route (% of lab force)		0.66	0.41	0.61
Average job tenure	8.81	9.01	9.13	11.23
Unemployment insurance:				
New unemployment benefits (% of lab force)	3.23	5.49	2.55	3.43
Terminated unemployment benefits (% of lab force)	3.22	5.59	2.81	3.56
Stock unemployment benefits end of the year (% of lab force)	1.72	3.75	1.80	2.79
Average unemployment benefit duration (in mths)	6.7	8.7	11.6	10.9
Active labour market policy:[a]				
Net inflow into reintegration programme (% of unemployment beneficiaries)			6.86[b]	14.17
Outflow into jobs (% of net inflow)			34.52[b]	31.88
Outflow into other (% of net inflow)			33.03[b]	49.10

Notes:
[a] Data refer to the unemployed only, the disabled are excluded from this analysis.
[b] Data refer to the period before the outsourcing to private reintegration companies.

Source: UWV (2008), *Kroniek van de sociale verzekeringen 2007*, Amsterdam: UWV;
OECD (2008), *Labour Force Statistics*, online database, Paris: OECD.

evidence (de Beer 2004). The table shows that the average job tenure has increased from about eight to 11 years. Compared to the OECD average of ten years, it can be argued that the Dutch workers stay relatively long with the same employer.

As for unemployment insurance, currently just under 3 per cent of the labour force is on unemployment benefit (the stock of beneficiaries at the end of the year). Table 5.2 shows that apart from the cyclical fluctuations (explaining the peak in the mid-1990s), about 3 per cent of the labour force flows into unemployment benefits annually, yet outflow is about the same. In fact, outflow has become somewhat higher than inflow in recent years, while both were at the same level in 1990. Table 5.2 further shows that after an increase in the average duration of unemployment benefits from 6.7 months in 1990 to 11.6 months in 2000, it slightly declined to about ten months in 2005. In 2005, about one-fifth of the outflow took place within nine weeks, half of the outflow within six months and 75 per cent within one year. This can be partly attributed to the more activating labour market policy which currently applies to Dutch workers. Evidence on the number of participants in reintegration programmes is difficult to find, and it is often unclear which categories of people are included. The available data on the net inflow into active labour market policy suggest that the share of unemployed workers enrolled in a reintegration programme has increased since the beginning of the century, which is in line with the European Guidelines on the reintegration of inactive workers. The effective output rate, or the outflow into employment, is about one-third and has remained stable in recent years. The table also shows that in 2000 about one-third of the reintegration programmes lasted more than one year (no outflow into jobs or other destinations is observed), whereas in 2005 this was about one-fifth.

Finally, it is interesting to look at some labour market outcomes related to the social policy triangle. The Dutch labour market is characterized by relatively high levels of employment, high perceived job security and high job quality (Auer 2005). Table 5.3 shows that, compared to the OECD average, the employment rate in the Netherlands has indeed increased from just below to above average. This is mainly due to the increased labour participation of women in the Netherlands. It is not clear to what extent this can be attributed to the increased activation policies in recent years. Note that the average Dutch worker works fewer hours than the average OECD worker, which would lead to a lower employment rate expressed in full-time equivalents. Table 5.3 shows that flows into employment, including job-to-job transitions, are relatively large in the Netherlands. This is partly explained by employment growth and the above-average use of temporary workers.

Corresponding with the rather high employment rate is the below-average unemployment rate in the Netherlands. In 2005, the standardized unemployment rate was about 5 per cent and the corresponding inflow into unemployment 2 per cent. Note the difference between the percentage of new unemployment benefits shown in Table 5.3, and the inflow into unemployment. Reasons for this difference are the use of different data-sets, different definitions of unemployment (or reference group) and different calculation methods. Besides, the difference is partly due to the fact

Table 5.3   Characteristics of the Dutch labour market compared to the OECD average, 1990–2005

	The Netherlands				OECD Average			
	1990	1995	2000	2005	1990	1995	2000	2005
General stock indicators								
Employment rate	61.7	65.2	72.5	72.83	64.3	63.7	66.8	67.7
Unemployment rate	7.6	7.1	2.9	5.2	6.6	9.1	7.3	7.5
Flexibility indicators								
Inflow into employment	32.3[a]	29.1	57.9	n.a.	22.1[a]	19.0	27.3	25.5
Temporary employment (%)	7.6	10.9	14.0	15.2	10.3	8.4	13.0	10.1
Inflow into unemployment	2.1	3.4	1.1	1.9	7.2	7.8	7.1	7.6
Average unemployment duration	11.2	12.0	11.7	10.2	9.4	12.3	12.1	10.8
Share of long-term unemployment	48.7	43.6	37.7	39.4	35.3	38.6	34.7	34.1
Security indicators								
Expected income loss due to unemployment	3.8	3.2	1.4	2.3[a]	5.1	6.8	5.8	5.9[a]
Expected income loss due to inactivity	28.9	26.6	22.4	22.4[a]	30.2	30.8	29.4	29.0[a]

Notes:
[a] Data refer to 1992.
For the definition of the security indicators, see Chapter 1.

Source: OECD (2008), *Labour Force Statistics*, online database, Paris: OECD.

that new unemployment benefits can also refer to the revival of old unemployment entitlement without corresponding to a new inflow into unemployment. Unemployment spells last relatively long in the Netherlands, as is shown by the above-average duration of unemployment and the large share of long-term unemployed (those unemployed for longer than one year). This is especially true for the 'old' system, that prevailed in the previous century. In recent years the share of long-term unemployed has decreased, which is explained by the shortening of benefit duration and the more active reintegration of unemployed workers.

Social protection in the Netherlands is still on a relatively high level, as Table 5.3 shows. The expected income loss due to unemployment is about 2 per cent, compared to about 5 per cent for the average OECD worker. The difference between the expected income loss due to inactivity in the Netherlands and the OECD average is smaller, but still the Dutch worker who becomes inactive is relatively well protected. The expected income loss due to inactivity is about 20 per cent.

CONCLUDING REMARKS

The Dutch social policy triangle has changed considerably since the early 1990s. Both the unemployment insurance scheme and the active labour market policy programmes, and the administration and organization of the system, have been reformed. In recent years, the administration for unemployment insurance and activation programmes has been brought under the responsibility of a couple of public institutions, to increase efficiency and transparency. As from 2009 onwards, the unemployed claiming unemployment benefits fall under the responsibility of one public body (UWV/CWI) and the unemployed claiming social assistance fall under the responsibility of the municipalities. Employment protection remains a responsibility of the employers themselves, but the UWV/CWI acts as an important supervising institution, just as the labour courts do. The dual system of employment protection in the Netherlands has not been changed with the recent reforms in the social policy triangle. So, whereas the other two policy instruments have been tuned to each other, reforms in the third instrument are lagging behind.

The role of the social partners in social policy has been restricted to an advisory one. In the past the social partners played an important role in the administration of unemployment insurance and activation policies. However, strong criticism of their lack of consensus and their alleged responsibility for the extremely high inflow into disability benefits in the 1980s paved the way for a strong reduction in the responsibility of the social partners. Nevertheless, along with their advisory role, they still play an important role in the collective bargaining process. Collective agreements are of great importance in the Dutch system and provide supplementary unemployment insurance, additional employment protection clauses and agreements on training of the workforce to prevent unemployment. Social dialogue therefore remains an important cornerstone of the Dutch social policy triangle.

Since the beginning of the 1990s, the performance of the Dutch labour market has improved in a number of respects. The employment rate has risen, which is mainly explained by the increased female labour participation. Unemployment has decreased, which is surely related to the business cycle, but is probably also caused by stronger activation of labour market policy, the impact of which is, however, difficult to assess. However, the flexibility of the Dutch labour market has remained relatively low, which is primarily explained by the unchanged system of employment protection. As for social protection of Dutch workers, this has not changed much. One could argue that the increased activation of labour market policy and the reduction of unemployment have not been accompanied by a deterioration in the level of income protection for Dutch workers. Moreover, the reforms of the social policy triangle in recent years have not (yet) led to substantive changes in the labour market outcomes. The future will reveal whether the most recent reforms, with the establishment of one single authority in the field of unemployment insurance and active labour market policies, will lead to further improvement of Dutch labour market performance.

NOTE

1. This is the maximum daily wage as of 1 January 2009.

REFERENCES

Adviescommissie Duaal Ontslagstelsel (2000), 'Afscheid van het duale ontslagrecht', report for the Ministry of Social Affairs and Ministry of Justice during the symposium on The Future of the System of Employment Protection, Den Haag.
Auer, P. (2005), 'Protected mobility for employment and decent work: labour market security in a globalized world', International Labour Organization employment strategy paper no. 2005-01, Geneva.
Beer, P.T. de (2004), 'Flexibilisering maakt banengroei fragiel', *Economisch Statistische Berichten*, **89**(4442), pp. 434–6.
Beer, P.T. de, J. Bussemaker and P. Kalma (2005), *Keuzen in de Sociale Zekerheid*, Amsterdam: Wiardi Beckman Stichting.
Buevink, J. (2005), 'Minister de Geus over het curieuze proces van de WW-hervorming', *SER Bulletin*, **9**, published by the Social and Economic Council.
Bunt, S., M. Grootscholte, P.R. Kemper and C. van der Werf (2008), *Work First en arbeidsmarktperspectief: onderzoek naar de werking van Work First*, Den Haag: Raad voor Werk en Inkomen.
Castonguay, J. and E. Sol (2007), 'Is work working? An explorative study of the work first reintegration strategy in the Netherlands', conference report for the 5th International Research Conference on Social Security, Warsaw.

CWI (Centre for Work and Income) (2005), *Beschrijving intensive samenwerking CWI-UWV 'samen doen we het zo'*, Amsterdam: CWI/UWV.

CWI (2006), *Yearly Report 2005*, Amsterdam: CWI.

Deelen, A., E. Jongen and S. Visser (2006), 'Employment protection legislation: lessons from theoretical and empirical studies for the Dutch case', Netherlands Bureau for Economic Policy Analysis CPB document no. 135, Den Haag.

Gerven, M. van (2008), *Reform of Social Security Benefit Rights in European Countries: A Study of Path Dependent, but Not Predetermined Change*, Helsinki: Social Security Institution.

Glebbeek, A. (2005), 'De onrealistische evaluatie van het arbeidsmarktbeleid', *Tijdschrift voor Arbeidsvraagstukken*, **21**(1), pp. 38–48.

Koning, P. and A. Deelen (2003), 'Prikkels voor UWV', Netherlands Bureau for Economic Policy Analysis CPB document no. 32, Den Haag.

Koning, de J., A. Gelderblom, K. Zandvliet and R. Blanken (2004), 'Werkt scholing voor werklozen?' research report by SEOR commissioned for the Council for Work and Income, Rotterdam: SEOR.

Obbink, H. (2002), 'Raad voor Werk en Inkomen: Geen ideologische standpunten maar uitvoerbare adviezen', *SER Bulletin*, **2**, published by the Social and Economic Council.

Peters, M. and A. van Selm (2004), 'The active labour market policy reform – the second wave: statements and comments', peer review report.

Rutte, M. (2003), *Toespraak op het najaarscongres RWI Golfbreken of meedeinen*, Den Haag, RWI.

Schils, T. (2005), *Early Retirement Patterns in Europe*, Amsterdam: Dutch University Press.

Schils, T. (2007a), 'Distribution of responsibility for social security and active labour market policy: country study: the Netherlands', Amsterdam Institute of Advanced Labour Studies working paper no. 49, Amsterdam.

Schils, T. (2007b), 'Employment protection in Dutch collective agreements', Amsterdam Institute of Advanced Labour Studies working paper no. 56, Amsterdam.

Scruggs, L. (2007), 'Welfare state entitlements data set: a comparative institutional analysis of eighteen welfare states', version 1.2

SER (Social and Economic Council) (2006), *Ontwerpadvies: Welvaartsgroei door en voor iedereen*, Themadocument Arbeidsverhoudingen, 1 September, Den Haag: SER.

STAR (2006), *Actieprogramma gelijke behandeling en gelijke kansen mannen en vrouwen*, publication no. 06, Den Haag: STAR.

UWV (Social Security Agency) (2006), *Jaarverslag UWV 2005*, Amsterdam: UWV.

UWV (2008), *Kroniek van de sociale verzekeringen 2007*, Amsterdam: UWV.

Wielers, R. and P.T. de Beer (2007), 'Werkt de re-integratiemarkt? De gevolgen van de privatisering van de re-integratie', *Tijdschrift voor Arbeidsvraagstukken*, **23**(2), 90–93.

Zevenbergen, R.G. van and U.H. Oelen (2000), *Het duaal ontslagstelsel – beëindiging van arbeidsrelaties in de praktijk*, Leiden: Research voor Beleid.

6. Germany

Bernhard Ebbinghaus and Werner Eichhorst

INTRODUCTION: PARTIAL DEPARTURE FROM PASSIVE EMPLOYMENT POLICIES

High unemployment has been a central predicament of Germany since the mid-1970s, particularly intensified since unification in 1990. The persistent unemployment problem has been linked by critics to generous unemployment benefits, soaring labour costs and a rigidly regulated labour market. In fact, German statutory employment protection for regular employment contracts is relatively high and compulsory social insurance provides earnings-related unemployment benefits, given a sufficient contribution period. The 2005 reform that replaced the earnings-related long-term unemployment assistance with a means-tested flat-rate minimum income support scheme was a major break with Germany's long tradition of status maintenance. This reform was part of a broader policy shift towards activation also involving an overhaul of active labour market policies and organizational reforms of labour market administration. However, regarding employment protection only some liberalization measures at the margin of the labour market occurred.

In terms of governance, social security, labour market policies and employment protection are mainly based on national legislation, though leaving some role for the social partners. In the area of labour market policy, the employers and trade unions had a substantial role in the tripartite self-administration before the reorganization of the Federal Employment Agency (Bundesagentur für Arbeit or BA) which now restricts their responsibility to supervision only (Trampusch 2002; Bieber et al. 2005). German employment protection is legislation-driven and relatively universal, collective bargaining on employment regulation is not very important except for sector-wide agreements supplementing dismissal protection, firm-level employment pacts, and works council-negotiated social plans in the case of plant closure. Traditional German corporatism is still alive, yet it is declining at the sectoral level, while firm-level micro-corporatism is becoming decisive. This can be explained by declining membership of trade unions and employer associations and a weakening of collective bargaining, in particular a decline in coverage and an extension of opening clauses in sectoral agreements that allow firm-level deviation.

Since the late 1970s, German employment policies tended to be rather 'passive', seeking to take labour out of the market, particularly those with extensive employment protection through early retirement benefits and by hiding open unemployment through alternative benefits (Manow and Seils 2000). Until recent reforms, German active labour market policies had neither a clear priority on reintegrating inactive people into work, nor were these measures evaluated systematically.

Access to unemployment insurance benefits and certain active labour market policy measures are tied to previous standard employment contracts. Until recent reforms, passive unemployment benefits helped in maintaining previous earnings even during long-term unemployment, favourable suitability clauses allowed the refusal of lower-level job offers, and non-employment benefits facilitated bridges to early retirement for older workers. The passive orientation was also an indirect outcome of social partners' involvement; they favoured externalization strategies, or the use of social insurance benefits to reduce labour supply, mainly in order to provide a bridge to early retirement (Ebbinghaus 2006). Until recently, the German system provided ample protection against labour market risks for labour market insiders: strong employment protection, quite generous non-employment benefits (unemployment and early retirement), and access to active labour market policies. This employment-centred and status-maintaining protection helped stabilize the German model of production tailored to a high-skill, high-wage equilibrium with long-term employment relations (Estevez-Abe et al. 2001; Streeck 1997), though recent changes towards less externalization and more activation tend to undermine the old regime (Streeck and Trampusch 2005).

Germany's labour market institutions thus foster a dual labour market with, on the one hand, high security and stability at the core, and on the other, higher turnover and instability at the margin, making the situation of more vulnerable groups more precarious. In order to enhance labour market flexibility without threatening the stability of regular employment, gradual reforms fostered atypical employment. Thus the increasing numbers of temporary work agencies and fixed-term contracts, but also the increase in part-time work and marginal employment (so called 'mini-jobs'), go together with persistent long-term unemployment, slow increase in the labour force participation of women, and low employment levels of older workers. Hence, German labour market institutions favour a certain segmentation of the labour market, maintaining security for the core and slowly increasing flexibility at the margin.

Reform processes have been thorny due to the limited capacity of the federal government to intervene, the lack of tripartite (government–union–employer) concerted action and strategic coordination across policy fields (Ebbinghaus and Hassel 2000; Streeck 2003). Neither the tripartite talks of the Alliance for Jobs that occurred during the mid-1990s under the last Kohl government (1994–8), nor the talks under the first Schröder government (1998–2002), led to a consensus on labour market policy reforms. Although the Danish and the Dutch 'flexicurity' arrangements attracted considerable public attention, Germany lacked a negotiated recalibration of social security and labour market flexibilization that entails more flexible employment regulation in the core of the labour market, some re-regulation of the flexible segment and effective integration-oriented labour market policies.

Substantial labour market reforms since the 1990s were mainly initiated by the federal government, most prominently by the reforms following the recommendations by the Hartz Commission in August 2002, while the social partners could only lobby political actors with limited impact (Streeck and Trampusch 2005; Dyson 2005). The tripartite Alliance for Jobs, Vocational Training and Competitiveness was created in 1998 but was effectively deadlocked from its beginning. It could agree neither on reforms of labour market policies, nor on relaxing employment regulation; the moderate JobAqtiv Act for young job seekers was the only consensual policy initiative. The joint administration of active and passive labour market policies by the Federal Employment Agency (BA) contributed to the externalization strategy of the past, using passive policies to reduce labour supply. Theoretically, the joint responsibility in one agency could also facilitate an effective implementation of activation strategies by making passive benefits more contingent. However, there is no explicit link between labour market policies and employment protection beyond the 'social buffering' of mass redundancies through early retirement and other social plan measures. Moreover, given the importance of entitlement-based passive benefits and the limited state subsidies, the resources available for active labour market policies are limited and may be squeezed out in times of high unemployment when they are most needed.

The fourth Hartz reform package, legislated by the past red–green government after its re-election in 2002, aimed at activating the unemployed (and social assistance claimants) and strengthening the reintegration capacities of active labour market policies. It also sought job creation through a partial deregulation of the labour market. The increase in labour supply (due to activation) was to be absorbed by a more flexible labour market: 'new' flexible segments such as start-ups, part-time and minor jobs, but also temporary agency work. While the shift towards activation means a break with the past, further partial flexibilization steps followed the path of gradual reforms at the margin. Nevertheless, the Hartz reforms brought multiple changes in respect to passive and active labour market policies, employment protection, and an organizational reform of both the employment office and communal responsibility. Despite intense public debates and the Hartz reforms that are seen as a fundamental break from the past, German employment protection, unemployment insurance and active labour market policy still show considerable continuity and stability. Given the growing role of flexible employment contracts, the so far institutionally stabilized core of the labour market comes under increasing pressure, in particular with respect to growing wage dispersion in a system with stronger labour supply due to less attractive 'escape routes'. This, in turn, has triggered political pressure to restrengthen the principle of status protection, for example through longer insurance benefits for older workers, and by introducing binding minimum wages to limit inequality on the labour market.

EMPLOYMENT PROTECTION IN GERMANY

The Main Reforms since the 1990s

German employment protection has been characterized by relative stable dismissal rules for regular contracts. Through the workers' wing in the Social Democratic and Christian Democratic parties and due to the institutionalized role of trade unions in the industrial relations arena, the labour market insiders have been able to defend the status quo. Most reforms only addressed the firm size threshold for employment protection regulation (lifted from five to ten employees in 1996, lowered to five in 1999 and raised again to ten in 2004) and the social selection criteria in case of dismissals for business reasons. Although flexibility at the margin increased over time, there have also been some attempts at restricting 'atypical' employment conditions, some of which were revoked shortly after. Most prominent changes were more liberal options regarding renewal and the maximum duration of fixed-term contracts in 1997, followed by some tightening of fixed-term contracts without valid reason in 2000, a lowering of the upper age limit for unrestricted access to temporary contracts in 2000 and 2003, and a stepwise liberalization of agency work since the late 1990s (but also the introduction of 'equal treatment' and the negotiations of collective agreements for 'temporary' workers). There is a growing tendency to circumvent statutory employment protection through self-employment and freelancers as well as Minijobs and fixed-term contracts or by using temporary agency staff. This basically reflects employers' preferences, not necessarily those of employees.

The Current System: Main Characteristics

Germany's extensive employment regulation is based on a high degree of legal complexity and endorsed by specialized employment and social policy legislation, court-based law-making and collective agreements as well as works council accords. Legally, there is a fundamental difference between regular (open-ended) and atypical (fixed-term) employment contracts, the former guaranteeing substantial employment protection, while the latter give employers flexibility in terms of employment protection. There is no differentiation in employment protection and social contributions with respect to working time above the Minijob earnings limit.

Dismissal protection of regular contracts sets in after a probationary period of six months, thereafter individual dismissal by the employer is possible if certain conditions are met (minimum provisions based on legislation, supplemented by collective agreements or individual contracts). However, legal dismissal protection does not apply to small firms with less than ten employees. For larger firms, the legal minimum notice period is four weeks for both employer and employee. Minimum notice periods for employers increase with tenure (two months after five years, four months after ten years and six months after 15 years of service), though longer periods can be set by collective agreements or individual contracts, but shorter notice periods only by collective agreements. There is no legal obligation to severance pay, except for an option under mass dismissal rules and when collective agreements (mainly for older workers) exist, and legal disputes are decided by court-based law. Severance pay is increasingly taxed and is now partly taken into the calculation of means-tested unemployment benefits.

Employees can file a lawsuit against dismissal; however, this usually does not result in continued employment but in a bilateral agreement on severance pay. Since 2004, dismissed workers can opt for severance pay offered by the employer (half of monthly salary per year of service) or file a lawsuit in order to get higher severance pay (Jahn 2005). There are special provisions regarding collective dismissals according to firm size and the number of dismissals. When about 25 per cent of the staff in a smaller firm are concerned, or the number of terminations exceeds 30 employees, not only the works council, but also the local BA office has to be informed at least one month ahead. In recent cases in which firms met a difficult economic situation, trade unions and works councils agreed on concessions regarding working time and wages in exchange for the employer forgoing mass redundancies (firm-level 'alliances for jobs'; see Rehder 2003).

Fixed-term contracts are regulated by a special law (Teilzeit- und Befristungsgesetz), allowing temporary employment in cases of valid reasons such as temporary demand for additional labour, termination of vocational or academic training, replacement of permanent staff, the specific character of a task, extended trial period or availability of temporary funds only. Fixed-term employment without a valid reason is only possible for two years (four years in cases of enterprise creation) and cannot be prolonged without valid reasons, though deviations are possible through collective agreements. Fixed-term employment was unrestricted for older workers (aged 52 or older) but this provision was rejected as illegitimate age discrimination by the European Court of Justice in autumn 2005. New rules now limit it to newly hired older unemployed. Fixed-term employment terminates automatically without formal dismissal (or severance pay), but during the fixed-term contract period, employment stability is relatively high.

Jobs at temporary work agencies are mostly open-ended regular contracts between agencies and employees. In the past, agency work was restricted by a maximum duration of individual postings or a ban on the synchronization of employee and business contract. The posted work period was extended stepwise from three to six months in 1985, to nine months in 1994, to 12 months in 1997, to 24 months in 2002 and finally the limit was completely abolished in 2003. The most recent changes implemented with the Hartz reforms removed virtually all remaining restrictions, except the ban on 'temp' agency activities in the construction sector. However, agency workers are entitled to the same wages and working conditions as regular staff ('equal treatment'). Deviations are only allowed in the case of hiring unemployed people or if collective agreements exist, triggering several collective agreements between trade unions and 'temp' agencies on wages and working conditions.

In the German context, marginal part-time work (Minijobs) is a very important flexibility option. The most recent reform implemented in 2003 increased the maximum earnings of the Minijobs to €400 per month. While the employer has to pay full social security contributions and a lump-sum tax, amounting to 30 per cent of the gross wages, earnings from Minijobs are tax- and contribution-free on the employee's side. Exemption from employee social insurance contributions makes these jobs attractive, particularly for students, housewives and retired people, while allowing employers to offer relatively low gross hourly wages, thereby reducing labour costs. These marginal jobs are not an entirely new instrument but have grown in importance in private services such as cleaning, restaurants and retail. Until 1999, Minijobs were not covered by social insurance, but the employer was obliged to pay a lump-sum tax. Thereafter, social insurance coverage was introduced, but the lump-sum tax was lowered in return. As of 1999, a second Minijob could no longer benefit from the tax and contribution exemption, but the option of tax- and contribution-free second jobs was re-established in 2003, leading to an increase of 1 million secondary Minijobs within two years.

Self-employment is in general more flexible as it is not regulated by labour law and social insurance is not compulsory except for specific schemes in some professions. Given the relatively high burden of non-wage labour costs and regulations, 'outsourcing' of services to the self-employed is a cost-saving path for firms. The red–green government restricted 'bogus' self-employment in 1999, making social insurance coverage mandatory for those self-employed who are mainly dependent on one client and who are not searching for other clients, as well as working predefined hours and doing similar tasks as employees of the main client. However, to further labour market flexibility and business creation, most of these provisions were revoked in 2003. In addition, as a complement to stronger subsidization of business start-ups through active labour market policies, the requirement of a craftsman's diploma was abolished in some of the handicraft professions at the same time. The quasi-dependent employed are obliged to pay social security contributions.

Regulation and Responsibilities

Employment protection is mainly an issue of national legislation, though court decisions and collective agreements play some role in altering dismissal and severance pay rules. Court-made jurisprudence is relevant when it comes to defining the concrete substance of dismissal protection, the level of severance payments or the regulation of fixed-term employment. Dismissals can be challenged before the Labour Courts (Arbeitsgerichte), as mentioned before. Employees who are union members can be represented by trade union officials before the court; others rely on lawyers. Works councils have to be consulted in all cases of dismissals. Dismissals of disabled people need authorization by the BA, while mass collective dismissals require notification of the BA.

Additional provisions stem from collective agreements that frequently provide for additional employment protection favouring older employees on regular contracts with long tenure. Collective agreements can extend notice periods and severance payments, but also exempt employees with longer tenure. They can top up legislated protection, but cannot substitute for legal minimum standards. Hence, collective agreements provide even stronger dismissal protection than national legislation. Sectoral collective agreements and firm-level agreements to secure employment thus usually strengthen insider protection. Sectoral arrangements are most prominent in the public sector as a consequence of tenured positions, in tertiary education where academic qualifying periods are exempted, and in private sector 'job security' agreements (such as in the metal and chemical industry) that trade employment security for other concessions (see Ebbinghaus and Eichhorst 2007 for details). Many collective agreements include special clauses for employment protection of older workers and long-serving workers (Bispinck 2005).

UNEMPLOYMENT BENEFITS

The Main Reforms since the 1990s

Regarding unemployment benefits, there has been a dual tendency over time: while continuity characterizes the contributory, earnings-related unemployment insurance (Arbeitslosengeld I, ALG I), means-tested unemployment assistance was abolished as an earnings-related benefit and merged with social assistance to form a general flat-rate minimum income support benefit (Arbeitslosengeld II, ALG II) in 2005. A growing portion of the long-term unemployed now rely on ALG II income support. This marks a major departure from the Bismarckian social insurance principles. These changes are in line with an increased 'activation' orientation, although potentially activating provisions had been embodied in earlier legislation. New administrative structures were introduced in order to implement activating policies more effectively. Although the Hartz reforms from 2003 to 2005 can be seen as a 'big bang' of activation policies, the recent changes led to an 'awakening' of dormant principles (Eichhorst et al. 2008). There had already been some minor changes in this direction in the late 1990s, making access to unemployment benefits stricter and more selective. One major step was the withdrawal of occupational criteria for suitable jobs in 1997. Requalification for unemployment insurance benefits through participation in active schemes was abolished for training programmes in 1998 and for direct job creation and other schemes in 2004. More inconsistent are the changes affecting older workers: the duration of ALG I benefits was shortened from 32 to 18 months for older workers aged 55 as of early 2006, but was expanded again by the Grand Coalition to up to 24 months for those aged 58 in 2008 following pressures from trade unions and the workers' wings of both Christian Democrats and Social Democrats.

The Current System: Main Characteristics

In Germany, unemployment insurance is compulsory for nearly all employees in both the private and the public sector, except for tenured civil servants. Since 2006, some groups can opt for unemployment insurance if they were covered in the period immediately before, including people providing personal care, the self-employed (until 2010) and insured persons who migrate to non-EU countries. Voluntary unemployment insurance is ruled out. Entitlement to unemployment insurance benefits requires meeting the following two conditions: prior unemployment contributions of at least 12 months within the last 24 months, and the unemployed have to register with the Public Employment Service (PES) as early as possible. The unemployed are obliged to search for work on their own (albeit without further specification) and to be available for job placement by the PES and participation in activation schemes. Regarding individual search activities, the unemployed have to use all options of reintegration into the labour market, in particular all activities resulting from the reintegration agreement with the PES, services provided by third parties (such as private job placement agencies) and PES self-information services. The unemployed are considered to be available for PES activities if they are able to take up a job of 15 hours per week or more under usual conditions, if they follow all advice and recommendations by PES, and if they are willing to take up suitable jobs and participate in activation programmes.

Unsuitable are job offers that pay significantly less than the earnings in prior employment. During the first three months, the unemployed can reject jobs offering less than 80 per cent of prior earnings, thereafter less than 70 per cent, but after six months of unemployment all job seekers have to accept jobs providing net earnings equal to or higher than unemployment insurance benefits. Also long commuting time (up to 2.5 hours per day) is no valid objection and after four months of unemployment singles can be forced to move in order to take up a job offer. Until recently, the older unemployed (58+) did not have to be available for work or search for jobs in order to receive unemployment benefits, and the PES urges the older unemployed to apply for old-age pensions as soon as possible (at 60 until 2006, at 63 as of 2008). Those born after 1951 are not allowed to retire earlier.

Means-tested minimum income support (ALG II) is available to those jobless without any unemployment insurance, or after it has expired due to long-term unemployment or lack of sufficient contributions. Recipients have to be between 15 and 65 years of age, capable of working at least three hours a day, pass a means test, and have to be willing to accept any work (with few reasons to reject job offers) or public employment opportunities (relief work, 'One-Euro Jobs'). ALG II provides minimum income not only for the unemployed but also for the self-employed or people in dependent employment with low earnings; they can receive a supplement to their earnings up to a combined income equal to the subsistence minimum. ALG II thus provides a national minimum income for all without sufficient resources who are employable, though older beneficiaries (equivalent to the clause in unemployment insurance) and employable persons who take care of small children or elderly persons are exempt from the job search requirement.

Regarding sanctions, the unemployment insurance benefit (ALG I) can be suspended from one to 12 weeks in cases of voluntary quitting, insufficient job search, refusal of a suitable job, non-participation in activation policies or in cases of delayed registration. Concerning ALG I, in addition to sanctions, benefit cuts can be imposed in cases of refusal of job offers, non-participation in activation schemes or other infringements, non-acceptance of an integration contract or failure to meet the obligations agreed on, and concealing information on income or wealth. In contrast, ALG II assistance payments are reduced by 30 per cent (with the temporary supplement suspended) when meeting the sanctioning conditions. Repeated misconduct within one year results in further reductions of ALG II by 60 per cent or even a total suspension (or a replacement of cash transfers by benefits in kind). Sanctions last for three months. Benefits for young people can be restricted to housing and heating. Sanctions are implemented by the BA in cases of ALG I and by the bodies responsible for ALG II administration (joint bodies by the BA and municipalities or, in some districts, the municipality alone) and can be contested by filing an internal complaint or a lawsuit before a Social Court. In 2006, 17 per cent of all persons entering ALG I were sanctioned: 34 per cent of them due to voluntary terminations, 29 per cent for missing early registration with the PES, but sanctions for misconduct during unemployment was relatively rare. Regarding ALG II, merely 2.4 per cent of all recipients were sanctioned, half of them for missing early registration, but 18 per cent for not concluding an integration agreement and 22 per cent for refusing a suitable job offer (Eichhorst et al. 2008).

The unemployment benefit (ALG I) is related to prior earnings and household type, maintaining the standard of living during unemployment. It provides 67 per cent of insured net earnings (usually in the previous 12 months and after some minor adjustments) for the unemployed with children or 60 per cent in all other cases. Given the gross earnings ceiling relevant for the calculation of contributions of €5300 per month in the West and €4500 per month in the East, net maximum insurance benefits amount to €1604 per month in the West and €1432 in the East.

Recent calculations by the Organisation for Economic Co-operation and Development (OECD) for 2005 show a net replacement rate of single short-term unemployed receiving ALG I of 60 per cent both at two-thirds and 100 per cent of the average wage, while at 150 per cent of the average wage ALG I amounted to 58 per cent of the last net earnings. Until January 2006, the older unemployed (aged 55 and older) were entitled to unemployment benefits for a maximum period of 32 months, combined with a pension at age 60; older workers could leave employment at age 57 and four months. After a shortening of maximum duration effective as of February 2006, tax-free unemployment benefits last for six to 18 months, depending on age and prior work record. People below the age of 55 could obtain unemployment insurance benefits for a maximum period of 12 (6) months if they had a work record of at least 24 (12) months. People aged 55 and over could receive unemployment insurance benefits for 15 or 18 months if they had a work record of at least 30 months. This reform shortened the early retirement pathway of long-term unemployment benefit recipients which had become a popular early exit route since the late 1980s. As of January 2008, unemployment benefits are extended up to 24 months for workers aged 58 and older with 48 insured months.[1] Special unemployment schemes exist for temporary unemployment and short-time work in some sectors (construction) or under particular circumstances (demand slumps).[2]

Minimum income benefits are available for those without sufficient income from work, partners' earnings or income from wealth. These provide a basic allowance of €351 per month and appropriate housing (including heating) without any duration limit. The Hartz IV reform led to a major institutional change as the flat-rate ALG II replaced former earnings-related unemployment assistance in January 2005, thus leading to a major policy shift (see Table 6.1). However, if recipients of unemployment benefits are entitled to ALG I before moving to ALG II, they are entitled to a fixed-term supplement making up for two-thirds of the difference between unemployment insurance benefit and the flat-rate benefit in the first year, and one-third of this difference in the second year, smoothing the transition from insurance benefits to (lower) income support. If there are two employable recipients of ALG II within a household, the individual benefit is only 90 per cent of the normal rate. Younger recipients (below age 25) who live on their own receive only 80 per cent, while those living at home get only indirect child benefits through their parents. According to OECD calculations, the single long-term unemployed receive net income support of 48 per cent if they had earned two-thirds of the average wage in the past, 36 per cent if compared to the average wage and merely 26 per cent when they previously earned 1.5 times the average wage (OECD 2007).

Table 6.1   Inactivity benefits in Germany before and after Hartz IV reform

Old system (until 2004)	New system (2005–)
Arbeitslosengeld (unemployment insurance benefit): contribution-funded, earnings-related, limited duration	Arbeitslosengeld I (ALG I): (unemployment insurance benefit): contribution-funded, earnings-related, limited duration
Arbeitslosenhilfe (unemployment assistance): tax-funded, means-tested, earnings-related, infinite duration	Grundsicherung (minimum income): (1) Arbeitslosengeld II (ALG II) (minimum income support): tax-funded, means-tested, flat rate (but for former ALG I recipients: temporary supplement), infinite duration, stronger activation measures (2) Sozialgeld (social allowance) for children below working age (age 0–14) living in a household of a ALG II recipient
Sozialhilfe (social assistance): tax-funded, means-tested, flat rate, infinite duration, no activation	Sozialhilfe (social assistance): means-tested, tax-funded for those working age people not capable of working and for needy persons above 65 years (Grundsicherung im Alter)

Employed persons are also entitled to ALG II if their earnings are not sufficient to safeguard the social minimum income. This is particularly true for employees with low hourly earnings, but also for persons in marginal or part-time employment if there is no first earner in the household who provides substantial income. Given the fact that the social minimum threshold increases with household size (for example with the presence of a non-working partner or the number of children), the equivalent income from work required to pass this threshold also increases.

Since the 1990s, the number of transfer recipients has remained relatively stable in the case of unemployment insurance benefits (now ALG I) with only minor cyclical ups and downs in both West and East Germany, while the number of long-term unemployment assistance recipients increased substantially in Germany from below 0.5 million in 1991 to above 2 million in 2004. Due to the more comprehensive registration of former social assistance claimants as unemployed, the number of registered unemployed increased from 4.5 million to more than 5 million in early 2005. Receipt of minimum income support by working-age people capable of working (ALG II) skyrocketed to 5 million compared to less than 4 million in former unemployment assistance and the employable social assistance recipients. In 2007, about 5.3 million people relied on ALG II, and about 1.1 million received ALG I.

Alternative benefits available to inactive persons below the age of 65, such as partial or full disability pensions or early retirement through early pension drawing, have been or are being phased out for younger cohorts. These pathways to early retirement offered ample opportunities for labour shedding in Germany (Ebbinghaus 2006) until the pension reforms of the 1990s and 2000s and the Hartz reforms are increasingly limiting these passive reductions of labour. Social assistance (Sozialgeld) is only available for non-employable persons living in needy households with employable unemployed persons, or sick and disabled people incapable of working at least three hours a day within the foreseeable future or children below 15. With the exceptions of temporary leave for parents taking care of their children and for early retirement for the severely disabled, exit options for the working-age population have been closed.

ACTIVE LABOUR MARKET POLICY IN GERMANY

The Main Reforms since the 1990s

Since the late 1960s, Germany has a fully fledged system of active labour market policies funded through unemployment insurance contributions and state subsidies which balance the budget and support specific schemes. Regarding instruments of active labour market policies, there has been a strong tendency to regulate labour market policy schemes at the national level and change them frequently while leaving significant leeway for the BA, a public body governed by tripartite self-administration (the government, employers, trade unions), in the actual implementation of these schemes and allocating funds to different programmes. Regarding the overall orientation of active labour market policies, direct reintegration into the primary labour market was not the first and foremost objective. Instead, policies aimed at the stabilization of individual benefit claims and incomes, while a rather passive 'buffering' of unemployment was achieved through an expansion of placement schemes such as direct job creation or extended publicly funded training. This pattern was particularly dominant after the economic crises in the 1970s and 1980s and as a reaction to employment decline in Eastern Germany after reunification during the 1990s. This contributed to high non-wage labour costs and raised some criticism regarding BA's placement effectiveness and the cost-efficiency of active labour market programmes.

   Although there had been attempts at reforming the BA and active labour market policies in the 1990s, the 2002–5 Hartz reforms mark the departure from the established model of rather 'passive' policies. These reforms did not only reorganize instruments, but the governance of both active and passive labour market policy underwent a complete overhaul in order to facilitate a more 'activating' policy stance. This meant streamlining some of the instruments, stricter monitoring of cost-effectiveness and a more systematic evaluation, but also a general reorganization of the BA with the help of external consultants. After BA's restructuring, the social partners' influence is much smaller and indirect than in the past, while management by objectives and contracting-out of services has become a more prominent feature of active labour market policies in Germany.

The Current System: Main Characteristics

Germany now has a complex system of active labour market policies mainly regulated by federal law. The most important legislation addresses active schemes within the framework of the mostly contributory unemployment insurance (ALG I) and the tax-financed minimum income support for the uninsured or long-term unemployed (ALG II). Basically all types of active labour market policies are available to ALG I recipients such as training, employer subsidies, in-work benefits and supported self-employment. Part-time work for older workers (Altersteilzeit), originally conceived as gradual retirement, has been used as an early retirement pathway, blocking full working time and full retirement sequentially.[3] For ALG II recipients a similar repertoire of measures is defined, but it also allows for a more flexible and case-oriented application of activation with a stronger emphasis on in-work benefits. Active labour market policy is financed mainly through the unemployment insurance fund and tax-financed public subsidies in respect to the ALG II long-term unemployed.

   Regarding the relative importance of activation measures, recent data show a decline in inflow and stocks of active labour market policy in the contribution-financed ALG I framework. Further trends are a decrease in publicly funded training due to stricter criteria for the distribution of training vouchers, a decline in the use of wage subsidies, an enormous growth in inflow and stock of subsidized start-ups until 2006, a replacement of traditional direct job creation schemes which were oriented at wages set by collective agreements and allowed for requalification for unemployment insurance benefits by public employment opportunities that provide €1 to €2 per hour worked on the basis of 30 hours per week for six to nine months in addition to full benefits ('One-Euro Jobs'). The most 'innovative' instruments of active labour market policy addressing older workers are as rarely used as placement vouchers.[4]

However, there is no sectoral labour market policy in Germany except for agreements on active labour market policies for (former) employees in cases of mass redundancies (*Sozialpläne*) due to major business restructuring or plant closures (*Beschäftigungsgesellschaften* or temporary work agencies). The social plan is usually an agreement between the employer and the works council, but there is also the possibility of a firm-level collective agreement between the employer and a trade union. The agreement specifies the social criteria by which mass redundancies have to take place as well as severance pay for those discharged. However, if a temporary work agency is created, active labour market policies such as the job placement and retraining of redundant workers is undertaken by the new agency. For instance, redundancies at a privatized German telecom company (Telekom) were smoothed by creating a temporary work agency (Vivento) for those former employees. Specific legal provisions for active labour market schemes only exist for the construction sector (*Winterbauförderung*), in particular subsidized employment.

ADMINISTRATION OF LABOUR MARKET POLICIES IN GERMANY

In the past, German labour market policies have mainly been funded by social insurance contributions, although they also included means–tested benefits such as unemployment assistance and active labour market schemes. The federal government covered deficits through general taxation, whereas local social assistance was administered and financed through municipalities. Unemployment insurance is largely financed by social insurance contributions of both employees and employers: after unification, the contribution was increased to 6.8 per cent in April 1991, remaining at a stable 6.5 per cent from 1993 to 2006. As of 2007, the contribution was lowered by more than two percentage points to 4.2 per cent, thanks to subsidies from an increase in value added tax (VAT) and by efficiency gains from active labour market policies. Given declining unemployment, only a year later the contribution rate was further lowered to 3.3 per cent of gross wages.

ALG II and related active labour market policies are tax-funded mainly at the federal level, though federal government and municipalities jointly finance the housing and heating expenses of the long-term unemployed. In addition, municipalities pay for auxiliary reintegration services provided to the long-term unemployed (such as advice in cases of private debts or drug problems) and for the still existing social assistance for non-employable persons. Until December 2007, for each recipient of ALG I who became long-term unemployed and was transferred to ALG II, the BA had to pay about €10,000 to the federal government (Aussteuerungsbetrag). As of 2008 this was replaced by a lump-sum transfer payment covering half of the administrative burden and the active labour market policy expenditure for the long-term unemployed (Eingliederungsbeitrag) from BA to the government (€5 billion p.a.). According to OECD data, Germany spent about 3.0 per cent of gross domestic product (GDP) on active and passive labour market policies, of which nearly one-third (0.9 per cent of GDP) was devoted to active policies (0.27 per cent of GDP on PES administration and placement, 0.33 per cent on training, 0.12 per cent on start-up incentives), while two-thirds were passive income support. The overall expenditure needs to be disaggregated between the unemployment insurance scheme and tax-funded minimum income support, currently (2007) amounting to nearly half of the total €83 billion of German labour market policy expenditure.[5] Compared to 2005, the contribution-based BA budget declined by about €10 billion, whereas the tax-based ALG II funds remained approximately stable, indicating a shift from contribution-based to tax-based schemes over recent years. In a medium-term perspective, the structure of participation in active labour market policies also changed: between 2002 and 2007, average annual participant numbers in publicly funded training went down from 340,000 to 131,000 due to stricter targeting and shorter measures, while start-up subsidies expanded considerably from 56,000 to 217,000, and direct job creation (more than 200,000 in 2002) was virtually replaced by 'One-Euro Jobs' (322,000 in 2007).

German severance pay is a functional equivalent to experience rating in unemployment insurance as it is proportional to tenure and wage level (and the frequency of dismissals). Because there is no differentiation of contributions to unemployment insurance by sector or firm that would reflect the frequency of dismissals, sectors and firms with high employment protection and tenure (for example, in manufacturing) subsidize those sectors and firms with frequent unemployment spells through their unemployment insurance contributions. However, the opposite is the case with regard to early retirement, where unemployment and pension insurance provide benefits to redundant older workers in larger firms, particularly in manufacturing.

ALG I and ALG II are regulated by national legislation under a unified legal framework. Social partners can influence policy making and – to some extent – have a say in actual implementation of the benefit system through the BA. This influence was significantly curtailed with the Hartz reforms: the main body of social partner influence is the tripartite supervisory council (Verwaltungsrat), responsible for supervising the BA executive board with its three directors and for approving the annual report and budget. The supervisory board can also request additional information, internal audit reports or external review. Most importantly, the supervisory board has to approve the business objectives of the BA executive board. In this respect, the most recent shift towards effectiveness and cost-efficiency in BA resource allocation is also due to political support by the supervisory board. In contrast to other social insurances, there are no social elections for the BA; instead representatives are nominated by employer associations, trade unions and the government. There are no competing providers of unemployment insurance, though there are some licensed private employment services.

The structure of active labour market policies within unemployment insurance, but also minimum income support, is determined by national legislation. There can be some divergence at the regional or district level, in particular with respect to ALG II recipients, where there is no nationwide integrated administration. The BA provides an integrated organizational structure responsible for passive and active labour market policies for the short-term unemployed (ALG I), whereas responsibility for passive and active labour market policies for the long-term (or non-insured) unemployed is divided between the BA and municipalities. In most districts, joint agencies have been established (Arbeitsgemeinschaften or ArGe), while some municipalities have taken over these tasks in some districts (Optionskommunen). The BA management implements the activation programmes, though actual implementation takes place in regional and local BA agencies. Although active and passive schemes for the long-term unemployed are also defined by national legislation, there is more flexibility in legislation on activation programmes for the long-term unemployed. The two types of local offices thus have more leeway in actual implementation.

Major governance problems arise due to a lack of a clear responsibilities and ambiguous incentives for the different implementing actors. The BA focuses its own activation activities (funded by ALG I contributions) on better risks, or the potentially short-term unemployed, whereas the potentially long-term unemployed, identified through profiling, are neither provided with enabling active labour market policies, nor subject to 'demanding' activation during their initial period of ALG I benefits. Thus, the profiling of individuals as being expected to become long-term unemployed is a self-fulfilling prophecy. After expiry of ALG I, the long-term unemployed are transferred to tax-financed ALG II schemes administered by the local agencies (ArGe and Optionskommunen), while the federal government pays these benefits. However, the longer unemployment lasts the more difficult reintegration into the regular labour market becomes (Eichhorst and Zimmermann 2007). The financial responsibilities move between the two schemes for the short- and long-term unemployed, although the original reform aim was to establish a unified framework with 'one-stop' shops for all job seekers and increasing cost-saving efficiency. Expenditure on ALG I benefits and active labour market policies for the short-term unemployed tend to decline at the expense of higher expenditure on tax-based ALG II and active labour market programmes for the unemployed not entitled to unemployment insurance benefits, in particular the long-term unemployed, implying a shift towards tax-financed labour market policies. Increasing emphasis on cost–benefit calculations by the BA management is in stark contrast to the earlier situation. The Hartz reforms resulted in a complete overhaul of the BA's internal management and control. Applying stricter effectiveness and efficiency criteria in active labour market policy – in particular in active schemes for ALG I recipients that are administered by the BA – is also responsible for the relative decline of expenditure on and participation in active labour market policies.[6]

Regarding the evaluation of the employment effects of German activation schemes, there has traditionally been a neglect of systematic analysis before the Hartz reforms. However, research into the effectiveness of selected schemes carried out in the pre-Hartz period justified a sceptical assessment of active labour market policy (Caliendo and Steiner 2005), especially regarding the placement effects of publicly sponsored training and direct job creation schemes. These results created a general reluctance with respect to the future continuation of traditional active labour market policy. With the Hartz reforms bringing about a complete overhaul of the institutional repertoire of activation policies in Germany, they also triggered a comprehensive macro- and microeconomic evaluation exercise concerning the reorganization of the PES and active labour market policy within the framework of ALG I. Evaluation reports that became available in early 2007 show a mixed picture. Positive short-term effects were reported for employment subsidies and start-up grants as well as job search assistance and sanctioning, whereas direct job creation and some of the recently introduced instruments were judged more critically. Some of the available evaluation studies, however, suffer from short observation periods, and macro-evidence is less conclusive than micro-level findings (Jacobi and Kluve 2006; Kaltenborn et al. 2006; Eichhorst and Zimmermann 2007; Caliendo and Steiner 2006). Evaluation of the Hartz IV reform, in particular the shift towards activation of the ALG II long-term unemployed, has recently produced some comparable results.

The Hartz reforms reduced the influence of social partners as they had been criticized for not being interested in an efficient allocation of funds, and instead subsidizing training providers associated with either the trade unions or the employers' associations. More broadly speaking, the Hartz report made tripartism in operative decisions responsible for ineffective and bureaucratic procedures within the BA. After the reforms, BA management was strengthened and became more autonomous in respect of social partners' influence. While a general privatization of the BA was not considered, performance of the BA in job placement was to be improved through more intense competition with private providers of placement and contracting-out of some services. Private job placement had been liberalized in the mid-1990s but has not played a major role thus far. Quasi-market mechanisms only became more important in active labour market policy with the Hartz reforms, contracting-out of services using competitive tendering for services provided by external companies and for the use of training and placement vouchers that introduce more intense competition into the field of job placement. This led to the erosion of traditional close networks between the PES and providers of training and other services that were often affiliated with the social partners. In the old system, before the Hartz reforms, social partners involved in the implementation of active labour market policies could allocate resources to service providers under their control (with little transparency and supervision of quality and appropriateness of the services provided).

THE GERMAN POLICY ARRANGEMENT AND ITS PERFORMANCE

Germany has long been a country with a medium level of labour market participation; high long-term unemployment, particularly for the low skilled; widespread early retirement; and problems combining work and family duties for women. Germany fitted nicely into the stylized picture of a continental European 'welfare state without work' (Esping-Andersen 1996; Scharpf 2001). This, in turn, mirrored the German manufacturing-centred production model and the labour market institutions of dual (firm- and school-based) apprenticeship and stable long-term employment for male breadwinners who benefited from secure employment protection, status-oriented social benefits and rather passive labour market policies, as well as the virtual absence of child-related services, making it difficult for women with children to stay fully attached to employment. Since the 1980s, and increasingly so in the 1990s, flexibility was introduced at the margin of the labour market, in particular via part-time work, marginal jobs and – to a limited extent – also through an expansion of fixed-term contracts and temporary agency work.

Notwithstanding this long-term picture of medium-level employment performance in Germany, it is interesting to observe that during the most recent economic upswing both a historical peak in total employment and a revival of regular employment could be observed (see Table 6.2). In autumn 2007, employment reached 40 million people for the first time, indicating that there is no longer a crowding-out of employment covered by social insurance through marginal jobs. The German employment–population ratio is now close to 69 per cent, while female employment reached 63 per cent, and after the phasing out of early retirement pathways the employment rate of older workers (aged 55–64) increased significantly to over 50 per cent in 2007, the EU's target for 2010. Also, for the first time in decades, structural employment started to decline below levels observed in earlier boom periods. Registered unemployment declined to about 3 million people or 7.4 per cent of the labour force in the third quarter of 2008 – a massive decline compared to the 5 million jobless (10.6 per cent) in early 2005. It remains to be seen whether this positive employment performance will be maintained in the case of an economic downturn following the October 2008 financial market crisis.

Most observers argue that the labour market reforms, in particular the Hartz package and the Agenda 2010, led to higher flexibility in the labour market and set stronger incentives to leave unemployment. Both wage moderation and longer working times in collective agreements, and declining reservation wages of the unemployed job seekers (Kettner and Rebien 2007), resulted in stronger labour demand and higher employment-generating economic growth. In contrast to early boom periods and the recent phase of economic stagnation this has led to a revival of regular employment. The focus has now shifted towards the side-effects of this overall improvement of German labour market performance. First, long-term unemployment is still high, but due to the limited availability of alternative escape routes, more unemployed are now registered unemployed and can be activated. Nevertheless, the long-term unemployed find it more difficult to find work and move to stable employment despite the fact that changes in the incentive structures and stronger activation have helped improve labour market attachment for more vulnerable groups. In fact the re-employment of many short-term unemployed led to an increase in the share of long-term unemployed. About three-quarters of all German unemployed are now ALG II recipients, and the share of long-term unemployed (longer than 12 months) is almost 57 per cent now. This may have to do with a lack of tailored individual assistance, in particular services to stabilize and improve employability at early stages of unemployment or

Table 6.2 Indicators on employment and unemployment in Germany 1995–2007

	1995	1996	1997	1998	1999	2000	2001	2002	2003	2004	2005	2006	2007
Employment (1000s)*	37 546	37 434	37 390	37 834	38 339	39 038	39 209	38 994	38 633	38 794	38 749	39 006	39 659
Employment rate (%)													
Men	73.9	72.7	71.8	71.7	72.4	72.7	72.6	71.8	70.9	70.0	71.3	72.8	74.7
Women	55.3	55.4	55.2	55.6	57.1	57.8	58.7	58.8	58.9	58.5	60.6	62.2	64.0
15–24	48.0	45.5	44.4	45.1	46.2	46.1	46.5	45.4	44.0	41.3	42.2	43.4	45.3
25–54	76.9	76.7	76.6	76.9	78.3	79.3	79.4	78.8	78.1	77.2	78.2	79.4	80.9
55–64	37.8	37.9	38.2	37.7	37.8	37.4	37.7	38.4	39.4	41.4	45.4	48.4	51.5
Low-skilled	45.2	42.8	41.7	:	54.5	55.3	44.9	43.6	42.6	40.7	42.5	44.3	44.9
Employed with social insurance (1000s)	28 171	27 685	27 284	27 313	27 587	27 931	27 899	27 583	26 974	26 563	26 237	26 449	27 027
Minijobs (end of June, 1000s)	:	:	:	:	:	:	:	:	5 533	6 466	6 492	6 751	6 918
Fixed-term employment (%)	10.4	11.1	11.7	12.3	13.1	12.7	12.4	12.0	12.2	12.4	14.1	14.5	14.6
Part-time employment (%)	16.3	16.5	17.5	18.3	19.0	19.4	20.3	20.8	21.7	22.3	24.0	25.8	26.0

Table 6.2 (continued)

	1995	1996	1997	1998	1999	2000	2001	2002	2003	2004	2005	2006	2007
Self-employment (%)	10.0	10.0	10.2	10.2	10.0	10.0	10.1	10.2	10.5	10.9	11.2	11.2	:
Registered unemployed (1000s)*	3612	3965	4384	4281	4100	3890	3853	4061	4377	4381	4861	4487	3776
Recipients of insurance (1000s)*	1780	1989	2155	1987	1829	1695	1725	1899	1919	1845	1728	1445	1080
Recipients of assistance (1000s)*#	982	1104	1354	1504	1495	1457	1477	1692	1994	2194	4982	5392	5277
Standardized unemployment rate (%)	8.0	8.7	9.4	9.1	8.2	7.5	7.6	8.4	9.3	9.8	10.7	9.8	8.4
Share of long-term unemployed (%)	48.7	47.8	50.1	52.6	51.7	51.5	50.4	47.9	50.0	51.8	53.0	56.4	56.6
Average job tenure in years	10.00	10.00	10.10	10.40	10.30	10.30	10.20	10.80	11.00	11.30	11.00	11.10	11.20

Notes: * annual average; # unemployment assistance until 2004 or minimum income support (ALG II) since 2005.

Sources: Eurostat (2008); BA (2008); OECD.

inactivity. Education and training, but also human capital-oriented activation policy, has become a prominent topic in the public discourse.

On the other hand, employment growth is associated with wider wage
dispersion. This is partly due to the frequent use of Minijobs which allow
for low gross hourly wages – and some unemployed have also strong
incentives to adopt Minijobs only while continuing to receive ALG II
(Bruckmeier et al. 2007). There is growing inequality in full-time employment and only limited upward mobility from low-wage to medium-wage
jobs (Schank et al. 2008; Brenke 2007). Germany thus moved from a 'low
employment, low inequality' situation to higher employment, but also
higher inequality (Brenke 2007). This is not surprising as the additional
labour supply was mobilized by making out-of-work benefits less attractive, thus effectively activating people with relatively weak employability
who will receive low wages. This inequality trend has triggered political
pressure to limit wage dispersion by a renewal of direct public job creation
for the long-term unemployed or hard-to-place job seekers so that they
can be placed in 'surrogate jobs' and, even more important, the public calls
for introduction of a binding minimum wage. Since 1996 there has been
a binding minimum wage only in the construction sector, but recently the
Grand Coalition agreed to expand the number of sectors to be covered by
extension provisions. This will make collectively agreed minimum wages
binding for all employers, not only for those organized in employers' associations. So far, this has resulted in minimum wages for cleaning and postal
services, but temporary work agencies will also be covered eventually.

Taking a broader perspective on employment protection, unemployment benefits and active labour market policies, there have been major
cumulative changes over time. Employment protection for open-ended
contracts has only been modified marginally, but there has been a long-
standing trend towards liberalizing fixed-term employment, temporary
work agencies, self-employment and marginal jobs, although their subsequent expansion has led to some attempts at restricting or re-regulating
atypical jobs. As with standard dismissal protection, unemployment insurance benefits are still in place – however, they are now more activation-
oriented than in the past and less generous, in particular with respect
to older workers' long-term unemployment. But stricter activation has
focused on the long-term unemployed who rely on the means-tested flat-
rate ALG II income support scheme. Active labour market policies mirror
this trend towards 'work first' instead of more human capital-oriented
activation programmes. All in all, this has strengthened market forces and
weakened traditional social security. In a way, Germany has moved in the
liberal market-oriented direction.

In terms of policy making, most reforms have been initiated by the government with limited influence of the social partners. In fact, the role of trade unions and employers' associations has diminished in recent years, in particular in the field of active labour market policies. While employment protection and unemployment benefits are based on national legislation, there is some role for social partners in additional sectoral dismissal protection as well as in social plans to adjust firm restructuring. More recently, collective agreements on supplementary pensions and new old-age part-time work are compensating for the withdrawal of public social policies and subsidies. In contrast to other countries such as the Netherlands, Austria or Denmark, there is no explicit tripartite political exchange and therefore no systematic coordination across the relevant policy areas. As a consequence, there is no coherent 'flexicurity' policy bringing social security and employment flexibility in place. Policy reforms rather follow electoral considerations and party competition, although mediated by a complex federal system with some veto points. Given the fact that the German electorate expresses strong preferences for social justice and limited inequality, it comes as no surprise that after the activation and market-oriented reforms of Hartz and Agenda 2010 there is a widely shared tendency to restrict the realm of the market again. However, the electoral victory of the Conservatives and Liberals in September 2009 will swing the pendulum towards pro-market policies.

NOTES

1. With 30 insured months, the unemployed aged 50+ can draw insurance benefits for up to 15 months. If they have 36 (48) months of employment recorded and are 55+ (58+), the maximum duration is 18 (24) months.
2. Employees covered by unemployment insurance are also eligible for alternative benefits in cases of short-term unemployment if they meet specific criteria such as bad weather payment, additional benefits (and social insurance subsidies) for construction workers, short-time work (Kurzarbeit) benefit in cases of a temporary demand slump on request by employer and works council. The BA pays 67 per cent of reduced earnings up to the full 67 per cent of past wages in cases of no hours work to those who are de facto unemployed but fully eligible for unemployment benefits in cases of later dismissal. This was relatively common in the early 1990s.
3. However, public subsidization of old-age part-time work will be closed for new entrants in 2009, though a collective agreement was negotiated by the metal workers union IG Metall in September 2008 to fill in.
4. Some of these 'innovative', but rarely used, instruments have been abolished recently.
5. Regarding unemployment insurance (in 2007), the BA earned €43 billion, of which €32 billion was from employer and employee contributions and slightly more than €6 billion from the federal government for specific labour market schemes. BA expenditure (2007) amounted to €36 billion, of which €20 billion was for unemployment benefits and €10.5 billion for active schemes. With respect to minimum income support and related active schemes, expenditure reached €44 billion in 2007, of which two-thirds was spent on

monetary benefits, housing and heating, while 15 per cent was spent on social insurance for ALG II recipients and 10 per cent on active labour market policies.

6. In December 2007 the Federal Constitutional Court ruled that the joined administration of BA and municipalities embodied in the Arbeitsgemeinschaften is unconstitutional, calling for a revision of this practice. However, policy makers will most probably adjust the Basic Law (the German constitution) in order to facilitate the joint administration.

REFERENCES

Bieber, D., V. Hielscher, P. Ochs, C. Schwarz and S. Vaut (2005), *Organisatiorischer Umbau der Bundesagentur für Arbeit: Evaluation der Maßnahmen zur Umsetzung der Vorschläge der Hartz-Kommission*, Berlin: Institut für Sozialforschung und Sozialwirtschaft.

Bispinck, R. (2005), 'Altersbezogene Regelungen in Tarifverträgen – Bedingungen betrieblicher Personalpolitik', *WSI Mitteilungen*, **10**: 582–8.

Brenke, K. (2007), 'Zunehmende Lohnspreizung in Deutschland', *DIW Wochenbericht*, **74**(6): 73–9.

Bruckmeier, K., T. Graf and H. Rudolph (2007), 'Aufstocker – bedürftig trotz Arbeit', *IAB Kurzbericht*, **22**.

BA (Bundesagentur für Arbeit) (2008), 'Statistik', Nuremberg: BA, accessed at http://www.arbeitsagentur.de.

Caliendo, M. and V. Steiner (2005), 'Aktive Arbeitsmarktpolitik in Deutschland: Bestandsaufnahme und Bewertung der mikroökonomischen Evaluationsergebnisse', *Zeitschrift für Arbeitsmarktforschung*, **2–3**: 396–418.

Caliendo, M. and V. Steiner (eds) (2006), 'Evaluation aktiver Arbeitsmarktpolitik – Deutschland nach der Hartz-Reform im internationalen Vergleich', *DIW Vierteiljahrsheft zur Wirtschaftsforschung*, **75**(3).

Dyson, K. (2005), 'Authoritative and reflexive strategies for binding hands: Europeanization, government by commission, and economic reform', *German Politics*, **14**(2): 224–47.

Ebbinghaus, B. (2006), *Reforming Early Retirement in Europe, Japan and the USA*, Oxford: Oxford University Press.

Ebbinghaus, B. and W. Eichhorst (2007), 'Distribution of responsibility for social security and labour market policy – Country report: Germany', Amsterdam Institute of Advanced Labour Studies working paper 2007–52, Amsterdam.

Ebbinghaus, B. and A. Hassel (2000), 'Striking deals: the role of concertation in the reform of the welfare state', *Journal of European Public Policy*, **7**(1): 44–62.

Eichhorst, W., M. Grienberger-Zingerle and R. Konle-Seidl (2008), 'Activation policies in Germany: from status protection to basic income support', in W. Eichhorst, O. Kaufmann and R. Konle-Seidl (eds), *Bringing the Jobless into Work? Experiences with Activation Schemes in Europe and the US*, Berlin: Springer, pp. 17–67.

Eichhorst, W. and K.F. Zimmermann (2007), 'And then there were four . . . How many (and which) measures of active labour market policy do we still need?' *Applied Economics Quarterly*, **53**(3): 243–72.

Esping-Andersen, G. (1996), 'Welfare states without work: the impasse of labour shedding and familialism in continental European social policy', in

G. Esping-Andersen (ed.), *Welfare States in Transition. National Adaptations in Global Economies*, London: Sage, pp. 66–87.

Estevez-Abe, M., T. Iversen and D. Soskice (2001), 'Social protection and the formation of skills', in P.A. Hall and D. Soskice (eds), *Varieties of Capitalism: The Institutional Foundations of Comparative Advantage*, Oxford: Oxford University Press, pp. 145–83.

Jacobi, L. and J. Kluve (2006), 'Before and after the Hartz reforms: the performance of active labour market policy in Germany', Institute for the Study of Labour (IZA) discussion paper 2100, Bonn.

Jahn, E.J. (2005), 'Wie wirkt der Kündigungsschutz?' *Zeitschrift für Arbeitsmarktforschung*, **38**(2–3): 284–304.

Kaltenborn, B., P. Knerr and J. Schiwarov (2006), 'Hartz: Bilanz der Arbeitsmarkt- und Beschäftigungspolitik', *Blickpunkt Arbeit und Wirtschaft*, **3**.

Kettner, A. and M. Rebien (2007), 'Hartz-IV-Reform: Impulse für den Arbeitsmarkt', *IAB Kurzbericht*, **19**.

Manow, P. and E. Seils (2000), 'Adjusting badly: the German welfare state, structural change, and the open economy, in F.W. Scharpf and V.A. Schmidt (eds), *Welfare and Work in the Open Economy*, vol 2, Oxford: Oxford University Press, pp. 264–307.

OECD (Organization for Economic Co-operation and Development) (2007), *Benefits and Wages 2007*, Paris: OECD.

Rehder, B. (2003), *Betriebliche Bündnisse für Arbeit in Deutschland. Mitbestimmung und Flächentarif im Wandel*, Frankfurt am Main: Campus.

Schank, T., C. Schnabel, J. Stephani and S. Bonder (2008) 'Niedriglohnbeschäftigung: Sackgasse oder Chance zum Aufstieg?' *IAB Kurzbericht*, **8**.

Scharpf, F.W. (2001), 'Employment and the welfare state: a Continental dilemma', in B. Ebbinghaus and P. Manow (eds), *Comparing Welfare Capitalism: Social Policy and Political Economy in Europe, Japan and the USA*, London: Routledge, pp. 270–83.

Streeck, W. (1997), 'German capitalism: does it exist? Can it survive?' in C. Crouch and W. Streeck (eds), *Political Economy of Modern Capitalism: Mapping Convergence and Diversity*, London: Sage, pp. 33–54.

Streeck, W. (2003), 'No longer the century of corporatism. Das Ende des "Bündnisses für *Arbeit*"', MPIfG working paper 03/4, Cologne.

Streeck, W. and C. Trampusch (2005), 'Economic reform and the political economy of the German welfare state', *German Politics*, **14**(2): 174–95.

Trampusch, C. (2002), 'Die Bundesanstalt für Arbeit und das Zusammenwirken von Staat und Verbänden in der Arbeitsmarktpolitik von 1952 bis 2001', MPIfG working paper 02/5, Cologne.

7. Belgium

Johan De Deken

INTRODUCTION

Since the mid-1970s Belgium has been transformed from a unitary state into a federal state, in which a significant proportion of labour market policies have been devolved to the regional authorities. Not only was the responsibility over social security and labour market policies now distributed over various levels of government, but the different authorities also started to follow different policy pathways.

In order to provide a basis for understanding the division of responsibility, this chapter starts with a very cursory introduction to some of the peculiarities of Belgian federalism. There are two main complications in the devolved political structure that gradually developed after the constitutional reform of 1970. On the one hand, there has been devolution towards territorially defined jurisdictions. In this respect, Belgium is not that different from other countries with a federal structure: there is a federal jurisdiction and there are three regional jurisdictions. On the other hand, though, there has also been devolution towards three language communities. The main problem here is that the language communities and territorial entities do not correspond, and in some regions, in particular in the Brussels region but also in the German-speaking part of Wallonia, shared or parallel jurisdictions might exist. What further complicates the matter is that over time an asymmetric governance structure emerged, in which the governments of the Flanders region and the Flemish community have developed into one single body with its adjunct administration, whereas the Walloon regional government and the French community government have remained separate entities. All this has resulted in a very complicated system of government, and in a myriad of quasi-governmental institutions with responsibilities in the area of unemployment protection and labour market policies. Even though there are some consultative bodies at the level of the regions, employers' associations and trade unions remain largely organized on a national basis, and collective wage agreements are still conducted nationwide at industry or multi-industry level.

ADMINISTRATION AND DISTRIBUTION OF RESPONSIBILITIES

Because of the complicated federal structure of the Belgian political insti-tutions,[1] four Ministries are directly responsible for labour and employ-ment policies: one federal ministry and three regional ministries (in the Flanders region, in Wallonia and in the Brussels region). Without going into too much detail, employment regulation, social security and taxation are still almost exclusively the responsibility of the federal government; employment policy is both a federal and regional matter; job place-ment and re-employment are the responsibility of the regions (Flanders, Wallonia and Brussels). Finally, most aspects of training and activation of the unemployed are organized by the language communities, which in Flanders is the same governing authority, but in the regions of Wallonia and of Brussels are distinct governments; that is, the Walloon regional government and the Brussels regional government are distinct from the French-speaking community government (the latter has a special com-mission for the French-speaking part of the population of Brussels, the Commission Communautaire Française).

Before Belgium became a federal state, employment policy used to be implemented solely by the National Employment Office (RVA). The RVA is governed by a management committee under parity control by the social partners. In addition, there are also representatives of the Federal Employment Ministry and the Federal Ministry of Finance, as well as the general manager of the RVA and his adjunct, but they only have an advi-sory role and cannot vote when decisions have to be approved. In general, decision making in the committee is unanimous. Since the 1980s, the influ-ence of the management committee has declined because the representa-tives of the social partners disagreed on a number of fundamental issues (such as the termination of early retirement schemes). This has increased the power of the managing board, which normally only has to implement the decisions of the management committee. Formally, the members of this board are nominated by the management committee, but once in office they have the status of autonomous civil servants.

The main responsibility of the RVA is to implement unemployment insurance legislation: to decide upon the entitlement of claimants, to deter-mine their benefits and to issue payment orders to the so-called payment bodies. In addition, the RVA monitors unemployment legislation and sanctions the unemployed in case they to not comply with the rules. In 2005, the RVA administered a budget of about €8 billion, representing some 17 per cent of the total social security budget of the country.[2] The RVA operates via 30 District Unemployment Offices (RWBs) and some

600 Local Employment Agencies (PWAs). The regional offices process the files of the unemployed and decide on their entitlement to benefits in the event of complete unemployment, as well as in cases of temporary unemployment, interim pension, part-time work, career break or time credit[3].

The actual payment of benefits is made by the payment bodies. These include one public fund and three auxiliary funds that are linked to the three national trade union federations (the Christian, Socialist and Liberal federations). As a default, an unemployed person will receive their benefits from the public fund, but they can also opt to apply for and receive benefits via an auxiliary fund. The auxiliary funds can be compared with insurance brokers: they give advice, they help the unemployed with completing their dossiers and they also offer legal assistance should there emerge a conflict with the RVA administration. Most unemployed rely upon an auxiliary fund: in 2005, 44 per cent claimed their benefits via a fund linked to the Christian trade union federation, 38 per cent via a fund linked to the Socialist trade union federation, 6 per cent via a fund linked to the Liberal trade union federation and only 12 per cent via the public fund. The payment bodies receive a compensation for their administration costs based on a formula that takes into account the number of cases they process. In addition, the two smaller funds receive an additional subsidy to compensate for the lack of economies of scale. The unions and their auxiliary funds have no influence whatsoever on the decision of granting unemployment benefits. This decision is solely made by the RVA administration. For this, the RVA partly depends upon information provided by the regional employment offices: the Flemish Employment Service and Vocational Training Agency (Vlaamse Dienst voor Arbeidsbemiddeling or VDAB) in Flanders; the Walloon Vocational Training and Employment Office (Office Communautaire et Régional de la Formation et de l'Emploi or FOREM) in Wallonia; the Brussels Employment Office (Brusselse Gewestelijke Dienst voor Arbeidsbemiddeling – Office Régional Bruxellois de l'Emploi or BGDA-ORBEM) in Brussels; and the Employment Office of the German Community (Arbeitsamt der Deutschsprachigen Gemeinschaft or ADG) in the German-speaking municipalities in the eastern part of the Walloon region.

These regional offices were established as a part of the devolution process. They all have a bipartite governance structure that is similar to that of the RVA. The RVA continues to be responsible for the financial management of employment policies, while the VDAB and the FOREM are responsible for job placement, vocational training and the reintegration of the unemployed in, respectively, the Flemish and the Walloon regions. This covers about 90 per cent of the population. For the remaining 10 per cent, the inhabitants of the Brussels region, things are more complicated: the VDAB is in charge of the vocational training of the Dutch-speaking ('Flemish') inhabitants of that region (via its district office, the Regionale Dienst Beroepsopleiding Brussel or RDBB); while the French-speaking inhabitants of the capital result under yet another institution called Bruxelles Formation. The reintegration of the unemployed and active labour market policies of all inhabitants of Brussels, irrespective of the language community they belong to, is administered by the BGDA-ORBEM.[4]

The VDAB has 13 district-level agencies responsible for assisting the unemployed in the Flanders region to find a job and to retrain them, plus one for the Brussels region (RDBB), which is responsible for Dutch language training programmes in the Brussels region. The FOREM has 11 district-level agencies responsible for assisting the unemployed in finding a job and nine regional agencies offering training programmes and reintegration programmes. Figure 7.1 gives an overview of the various statutory institutions and actors responsible for the implementation of unemployment insurance policies and labour market policies in Belgium.

The upper part of the figure contains the institutions resulting under regional authorities, whereas the lower part contains the federal institutions. In the lower corner on the right the local government institutions (that have been established under federal legislation) are represented. The dotted lines refer to information exchange channels. This is particularly relevant for the district agencies of the regional employment offices on the one hand, and the RVA on the other hand. The information exchange is crucial for determining the entitlement to unemployment benefits, as only the regional offices assist the unemployed in finding a job and organize the training and activation programmes (failing to take a job offer or to participate in such a programme can be a reason for suspending unemployment insurance benefits). Finally, the broken line between the regional employment offices and the High Council for Employment (Hoge Raad voor de Werkgelegenheid or HRW) indicates a link of representation in consultation procedures. The HRW was established in 1995 as an advisory body, which coordinates the activities of the federal and regional institutions.

UNEMPLOYMENT PROTECTION

Even though the Belgian unemployment benefit scheme is often categorized as contributory, and does have an element of earnings-relatedness to it, it hardly qualifies as a genuine insurance system. It is only since the 1970s that its benefit structure became mildly earnings-related (Palsterman 2003). However, even after that reform, the Belgian scheme remained

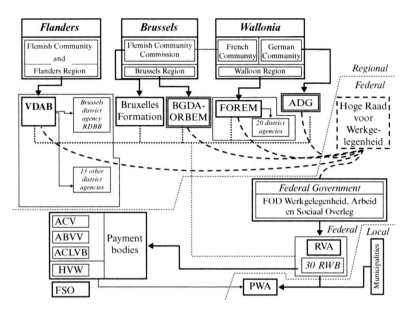

Note:
VDAB: Flemish Employment Service and Vocational Training Agency
RDBB: Regional Vocational Training Agency, Brussels
Bruxelles Formation: institution overseeing vocational training of French-speaking
    inhabitants of Brussels
BGDA-ORBEM: Brussels Employment Office
FOREM: Walloon Vocational Training and Employment Office
ADG: employment office for the German Community, Belgium
Hoge Raad voor Werkgelegenheid: advisory institution coordinating the regional
    employment offices
FOD Werkgelegenheid, Arbeid en Sociaal Overleg: federal public service responsible for
    labour affairs
RVA: National Employment Office
RWB: District Unemployment Office
PWA: local employment agency
ACV: Christian trade unions (auxiliary payment body)
ABVV: Socialist Trade Union (auxiliary payment body)
ACLVB: Liberal trade unions (auxiliary payment body)
HVW: public unemployment benefits payment body
FSO: Redundancy Payments Fund

*Figure 7.1   Institutions and actors in statutory employment and
            unemployment policies in Belgium*

quite unique, in that hardly any other unemployment benefit scheme in
the world relies so much on needs-based criteria in its benefit structure (De
Lathouwer 1997). The determination of these needs, though, is not based
on some form of means-testing, but is inferred indirectly from the family

Table 7.1   Work record and eligibility to unemployment benefit in Belgium

Age	Minimum insured days and referring period
< 36 years	312 days during the last 18 months *or* 468 days during the last 27 months *or* 624 days during the last 36 months
36–49 years	468 days during the last 27 months *or* 624 days during the last 36 months *or* 234 days during the last 27 months plus 1560 days during the 10 years before those 27 months *or* 312 days during the last 27 months plus for each day that lacks to get to 468 days, 8 days during the 10 years prior to those 27 months
> 50 years	624 days during the last 36 months *or* 312 days during the last 36 months plus 1560 days during the 10 years before those 36 months *or* 416 days during the last 36 months plus for each day that lacks to get to 624 days, 8 days during the 10 years prior to those 36 months

status and the age of the unemployed claiming a benefit, and the labour market status of the other members of the household in which he or she lives.

Benefit Entitlement

In order to be eligible, someone must have been working in an employment relationship liable to social security contributions for a certain number of days in the period prior to becoming unemployed. The minimally required number of days varies with the age of the claimant, as depicted in Table 7.1.

The gross daily unemployment benefit is obtained by multiplying the gross daily salary which was previously earned by a percentage rate ranging from 40 to 60 per cent. The system makes a distinction between three periods, with decreasing replacement ratios over time. The first period comprises the first 12 months of unemployment; the second period the subsequent six months and the third period starts as of the eighteenth month of unemployment.

Moreover, benefits vary according to the family situation: bread-winners are eligible for the most generous benefits, while those cohabiting with an earning partner get the lowest benefits. Singles are entitled to a benefit somewhere in between these two poles. The third period, which only offers a low flat rate benefit, is only relevant for those unemployed who live with a partner who has their own income. For breadwinners and singles, the benefits in the third period are as generous as in the second period. Finally there are, compared to other countries such as Denmark, the Netherlands or Germany, quite low maximum ceilings: the gross wages on the basis of which benefits are calculated are limited to 1.4 times the minimum wage (little under 60 per cent of the average production wage – APW).

Unemployed persons without work experience but upon completing their formal education are also entitled to a benefit, the so-called interim benefit. In order to be eligible for this benefit, they must have been enrolled in higher secondary education (participated but not necessarily succeeded in passing the final exams). The benefit is only granted after a waiting period, the length of which depends upon the age of the claimant: six months for those aged less than 18 years, nine months for those between 18 and 26 years, and 12 months for those between 18 and 30. Persons older than 30 years are no longer eligible for the interim benefit. The amount of the benefit is similar to that of social assistance, but is unlimited in time (until the claimant reaches the age of 30), and in contrast to social assistance benefits, it is not conditional upon a means-test. The amount does, though, again depend upon age and family status.

The older unemployed (aged 50 or over) are entitled to a seniority supplement, provided that they have worked for at least 20 years as a wage earner and have been unemployed for at least one year. These supplements again vary according to family status. The law foresees 13 different categories, each with a different benefit formula (in particular the group of cohabiting beneficiaries consists of a multitude of subcategories depending upon when the person became unemployed, and upon their age; in particular the category of the unemployed aged 58–64 enjoys substantially higher benefits).

Because of the importance of family status and age in the Belgian unemployment benefit system, it does not make any sense to cite only one replacement rate. Table 7.2 reports the net replacement rates for the unemployed under the age of 50, calculated for three wage groups (half the APW, the full APW and twice the APW).[5]

In assessing the comparative generosity of some of these replacement rates, one must bear in mind that in contrast to many other countries, Belgian unemployment benefits are rarely supplemented with social assistance. In a 2002 Organization for Economic Co-operation and Development (OECD) study, Belgium came out on top in terms of the replacement rates of its unemployment benefit scheme offered during the

Table 7.2   Net replacement rates of statutory unemployment benefits for households without children and recipients aged below 50 in Belgium, 2005

Family status	First 12 months (%)	13th–17th month (%)	As of 18th month (%)
Half the APW			
Single	70	70	70
Breadwinner	77	77	77
Cohabiting partner on minimum wage	63	46	40
APW			
Single	57	57	57
Breadwinner	60	57	57
Cohabiting partner on minimum wage	56	42	26
Twice the APW			
Single	37	34	34
Breadwinner	37	37	37
Cohabiting partner on minimum wage	25	25	15

first five years of unemployment. However, once social assistance supplements were taken into account, Belgium only occupied a middle position (OECD 2004).

The benefits as of the third period are in principle unlimited in time. This is one of the main reasons why the Belgian system, in comparison with other OECD countries, scores very high in overall benefit generosity: during the period 1973–89, the average expenditure on benefits per unemployed person as a percentage of per capita GDP amounted to 99 per cent – the highest share in the whole OECD area.[6]

Formally, the unemployment benefit system expects beneficiaries to be available for the labour market. In practice, however, this rule is rarely enforced. Many long-term unemployed are simply considered to be incapable of performing a job and would have ended up in a disability scheme in other countries. There is however one clause in the unemployment benefit code that often does lead to a suspension of benefits. This so-called Article 80 suspends the eligibility for a benefit for those unemployed who cohabit with an earning partner, and who have been unemployed for an 'abnormal' length of time (which since 1996 has been defined as 150 per cent of the average duration in the district where the unemployed person is living). Unemployed persons above the age of 50 with a work history of more than 20 years are exempted from possible suspension. In case, where the unemployed person enrols in a training or another active labour programme, the suspension can be postponed.

In essence Article 80 has introduced a form of means-testing for a particular category of unemployed. An unemployed person can appeal before the director of the district level employment office against their suspension. The most common reason for cancelling the suspension is that the family income of the family unit in which the unemployed person lives is below a certain threshold. This means-test is far more generous than the means-test that applies to social assistance, because partners can earn up to 140 per cent of the minimum wage before the unemployed spouse is subject to suspension (De Lathouwer et al. 2003, p. 9). On average about 3 to 4 per cent of the unemployed are suspended in this way. More than 80 per cent of the suspended unemployed are women. According to calculations based on data of the social security administration, the reintegration rate of the suspended unemployed is hardly any better than that of the non-suspended unemployed, which suggests that many of them end up in the silent reserve.

Those who do not qualify for any of the benefits discussed so far have to fall back on the social assistance scheme, administered by the municipal authorities. These benefits are means-tested for the incomes of other members of the household unit and depend upon the household status. In addition, social assistance beneficiaries are also eligible for family allowances. None of these benefits are subject to taxation.

Up to 1995, the various social security programmes in Belgium were administered separately, with each having its own financing based on legally prescribed contribution rates for employers and employees that were topped up by subsidies from the central government. If one programme ran a deficit, funds were transferred from programmes running a surplus, on an ad hoc basis. Later on, these transfers were formalized by establishing a fund for reapportioning via the so-called Fund for Financial Balance in Social Security (FFESZ).

Financing

Since the late 1960s one can observe important shifts in the burden of financing unemployment benefits. Up to the 1970s, when the unemployment insurance scheme only provided flat-rate benefits, financing was on a tripartite basis. The employees, the employers and the state were each responsible for providing about a third of the necessary funds. When in 1971 an earnings-related benefit system was introduced, the social partners' share of financing increased and the state's share decreased. But with the economic crisis that followed the first oil price shock of 1973, the unemployment insurance budget rose by more than 500 per cent, and the state had to assume most of this increased burden. State subsidies peaked during the early 1980s, providing close to 80 per cent of the necessary means. From that period onwards the financing burden was again shifted towards the social partners, as the central state needed to reduce its budget deficit as a part of its European Monetary Union (EMU) effort. From the 1990s most of the financing originated in the so-called wage moderation contributions. In addition, this period saw the introduction of various other sources of finance, such as a special levy paid by civil servants, the so-called *solidariteitsbijdrage* (introduced in 1981, but phased out a decade later); a special contribution for high-income groups (those with an annual income above €75 000 – at the time, this was more than three times the APW – introduced in 1983, but also phased out a decade later); and the establishment of the Redundancy Payments Fund (FSO, Fonds Sluiting Ondernemingen), established in 1982 to reduce the moral hazard of dumping the costs of enterprise rationalization on the unemployment benefit system (RVA 1997). Figure 7.2 gives an overview of the main sources of financing unemployment benefits up to 1994.

In 1995 the government introduced the so-called global management system (*globaal beheer*), whereby all social security contributions were collected by the National Office for Social Security (Rijksdienst voor Sociale Zekerheid or RSZ) and accumulated into a single fund.[7] The RSZ subsequently redistributed these funds on the basis of the needs of each branch of the social security system. The past ad hoc transfers between the different branches was now completely institutionalized. Since the introduction of this system the distribution of the financial burden for the entire social security system between the state, the employers and the insured has remained relatively stable at the 1993 level: employers' contributions account for about 43 per cent, employee contributions 22 per cent, the wage moderation levy 7 per cent, the state's subsidies 19 per cent and other sources the remaining 3 per cent. Ten years later this distribution was still about the same: only the share of VAT has seen a slow but steady increase from 9 per cent in 2000 to 13.5 per cent in 2004 (NAR 2005).

The social partners are involved in this new global management system via a tripartite management committee. Table 7.3 shows the 2006 contribution rates for the wage earner schemes. Because salaried employees and manual workers still have a slightly different social security and employment protection status, they also are subject to slightly different contribution rates. In cases, where the wage earner is exempted from participating in some programmes, there are also separate contribution rates for the

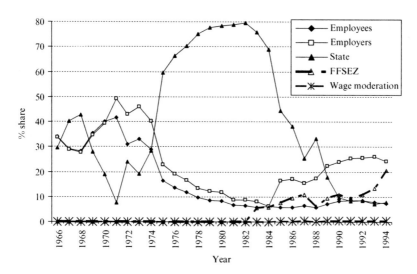

Note: Percentage share refers to the percentage of the total financing of the scheme.

Source: own calculations based on the annual social security reports of the Ministry of
Social Security.

Figure 7.2   The financing of unemployment insurance in Belgium, 1966–94

*Table 7.3   Social security contribution rates for wage earners in Belgium,
2006*

	Manual workers as a percentage of gross wages at 108%[a]		Salaried employees as a percentage of gross wages at 100%	
	Employees	Employers	Employees	Employers
Global contribution	13.07	24.79	13.07	24.79
Annual holidays	16.27	–	–	–
Wage moderation levy	–	7.48	–	7.48
Paid educational leave	–	0.04	–	0.04
Child care	–	0.05	–	0.05

Note: [a] Contribution rates for manual workers are calculated taking into account their
annual holiday payments that, in contrast to salaried employees, are financed via a social
security scheme.

unemployment benefit only: 0.87 per cent for the employee and 1.46 per cent for his employer.

In addition to this contribution rate, there is a special unemployment insurance contribution of 1.60 per cent (which, because of the added-on wage moderation levy, actually amounts to 1.64 per cent) for employers who, on 30 June of the previous year, employed at least ten persons. Contributions are levied on the entire wage; there are no contribution ceilings. Benefits, on the other hand, do have quite low maximum ceilings. The lack of ceilings in terms of contributions combined with the relative low ceilings in terms of benefits makes the wage earner scheme very redistributive amongst its participants.

The relative costs of administrating the entire social security system are average compared to other European countries. In 2004, Belgium spent about 3.4 per cent of its social security budget on administration, which was more than Denmark (2.9 per cent), and about the same as Germany (3.4 per cent), but significantly less than the Netherlands (4.8 per cent) (ESSPROS 2007, Tables B2 and B2.2). If one only looks at the unemployment benefit system, the costs are even smaller: in 2005 they amounted to 2.5 per cent (with the larger union-run schemes being more cost-effective: for example the payment body run by the socialist union ABVV spent only 2.3 per cent on administration, while the small public payment body HVW spend 3.1 per cent) (RVA 2005, Tables 7.3.II and 7.3.V).

EMPLOYMENT PROTECTION

Individual Dismissals

Statutory individual employment protection makes a distinction between manual workers and salaried employees, with the latter enjoying more protection. Towards the end of 2003, about 38 per cent of the dependent workforce benefited from the status of manual worker, 48 per cent had the status of salaried employee, with the remaining 14 per cent enjoying the status of civil servant.[8]

For manual workers the statutory notice period depends upon tenure, as can be seen in Table 7.4. For workers with tenure of less than five years, the rules are embedded in legislation. For workers with tenure of more than five years, a national collective agreement makes the employment protection more advantageous for the employee (increasing the notice period the employer has to observe, and reducing the period the employee has to respect).

Table 7.4   Statutory notice periods for manual workers and salaried employees in Belgium

	Period of notice	
	Employer	Employee
Manual workers with a tenure of:		
Less than 6 months	1 week	3 days (law)
6 months–5 years	5 weeks	2/3 weeks (age < 20/ age > 20, law)
5–10 years	6 weeks	2 weeks (CAO No. 75)
10–15 years	8 weeks	2 weeks (CAO No. 75)
15–20 years	12 weeks	2 weeks (CAO No. 75)
More than 20 years	16 weeks	4 weeks (CAO No. 75)
Salaried workers with a tenure of:		
Less than 5 years	3 months	6 weeks
5–10 years	6 months	3 months
10–15 years	9 months	3 months
15–20 years	12 months	3 months
20–25 years	15 months	3 months
25–30 years	18 months	3 months
30–35 years	21 months	3 months
35–40 years	24 months	3 months

For salaried employees with an annual income of less than 75 per cent of the APW, the statutory notice period is three months plus three months for every five years of tenure. Salaried employees who earn more than this annual income threshold have to conclude an individual arrangement with their employer, which has to be at least as advantageous as the statutory arrangement for the lower income category. If the employer and employee fail to come to such an agreement, a labour court decides the case. In determining the notice period, the court takes into account the age, tenure and wage of the employee. In cases, where the notice periods are not observed, both manual workers and salaried employees are entitled to a severance payment that normally equals the wage that they would have received during the notice period.

Neither the RWB nor the works council need to consent to individual dismissals. After being fired, employees can bring their case before the labour courts. It is up to the employer to provide proof that the dismissal was not arbitrary. When the court judges that the dismissal has been arbitrary, a worker is entitled to a severance pay amounting to six months of gross wages. Certain categories of workers (such as pregnant women, sick employees, union delegates and employee representatives) benefit from special employment protection.

During a probation period, manual workers cannot be dismissed during the first seven days, but can be dismissed without notice during the second seven days. For salaried employees the probation period lasts at least one month, and the notice period is seven days for both employers and employees. Fixed-term contracts cannot be terminated before the end of the term. They can only be renewed three times, and the total accumulated length of employment under such contracts may not exceed 30 months. In 2005, about 8.5 per cent of the dependent workforce was employed under such contracts.

Collective Dismissal

Collective dismissal in Belgian labour law is defined as all forms of notice that are unrelated to the individual employee, and that concern at least ten employees within a period of 60 days (for enterprises with 20 to 100 employees), 10 per cent of the workforce (for enterprises with 100 to 300 employees), or 30 employees (for firms with more than 300 employees). If an employer wants to resort to a collective dismissal, he has to comply with an information and consultation procedure involving workers' representatives (the works council or the trade union delegation in the firm; or, in absence of either, the workers themselves) and the director of the regional employment office.

Re-employment is in principle arranged on a voluntary basis, but in 2002 a national collective agreement was established that obliges employers to arrange outplacement for all dismissed workers aged over 45 with at least one year of service. Branch-level agreements can further extend this right.

Since the devolution of labour market policies, different practices have emerged in the three regions. The four employment offices of the regions and language communities have each set up a so-called regional re-employment unit with varying roles. In the Flanders region such a re-employment unit is presided over by the director of the district-level employment agency. It includes representatives of the employers, the employees, the industry-wide training fund, the redeployment fund,[9] the outplacement office, and of the SER (a parity-based advisory council at the regional level). The re-employment units are financed by a special employers' contribution. In a case of collective dismissal, the redundancy payment amount to half of the difference between the net wage (ceiled at about 90 per cent of the gross APW), and the statutory unemployment benefit that the employee is entitled to. There is a maximum ceiling for the net wage that is taken into account. Employers have to pay this extra benefit for a period of up to four months.

In the event of the closure of an enterprise and the employer defaults, the Redundancy Payments Fund (FSO) pays the employees who are dismissed. This fund was set up under the auspices of the RVA and is financed from levies payable by employers. The levies vary from to year to year, and according to industry branch and the size of the enterprise. In general they amount to some 0.25 per cent of gross wages. In addition, the FSO sometimes pays temporary unemployment benefits (benefits paid to employees whose employment contract is temporarily suspended), and so-called bridging benefits (benefits that bridge the period between a defaulting employer and the new employer after the bankrupt firm undergoes a restart).

ACTIVE LABOUR MARKET POLICIES

As mentioned before, since the devolution was implemented in the area of labour market policies, the regions became the main actors in the area of reintegration and activation policies. In what follows, the primary focus is on the policy developments in Flanders, as this region often took the lead in reforms.

Job Placement Service after Devolution

Job placement services have been subject to devolution and have become a regional competence. In 1997, the Flanders region decided to abolish the state monopoly on employment exchange and job placement, and the VDAB had to start competing with commercial employment agencies. Large commercial temporary employment agencies entered the market of training and recruitment. More than 250 organizations applied to become recognized as employment exchanges. This policy initiative has been related to the new International Labour Organization (ILO) guidelines issued on employment placement services.

Job Creation Programmes

Until a few years ago, active labour market policies in Belgium were largely limited to various forms of subsidized employment in the non-profit sector. With the devolution of labour market policies, the administration of these programmes was largely shifted to the regional governments. The regions carry the burden of the wage costs, but obtain for every job a federal subsidy that corresponds to an unemployment benefit.

The main problem with these schemes is that they create a parallel labour market in the public and the non-profit sector, with very few transitions to the regular labour market. According to an econometric study on the Walloon region, these programmes even reduce the transition to the regular labour market (Mahy et al. 1996). In part this poor performance is the paradoxical consequence of making the employment contracts, granted by these job creation schemes, less precarious. By offering contracts of indeterminate duration, the schemes soon tend to become saturated. After an initial reduction of unemployment these programmes do little to improve the employment situation. Only when additional funds are made available to create additional jobs can a net effect be expected. In the Flanders region, this sort of criticism has led to policy reforms, which have included a complete conversion of these special programmes into normal contracts in the semi-public non-profit sector.

Local Services and Local Jobs

In 1987, the so-called Local Employment Agencies (PWAs) were established. They allow unemployed workers to supplement their benefits by working in the local community. The scheme was initially run on a voluntary basis with three goals in mind: to relieve the labour shortages in the so-called social economy (in particular in areas such as nursing and care); to limit the growth of the clandestine economy, in which many long-term unemployed were suspected to make a living supplementing their unemployment benefits; and to activate the long-term unemployed and to facilitate their transition towards the regular labour market. The PWAs were to operate like a special kind of temporary employment agency. In 1987 a framework was created for municipal authorities that facilitated the establishment of non-profit associations that were to offer temporary job contracts to the long-term unemployed. These associations were governed by representatives of local political parties. It was encouraged, but not required, to have representatives of the trade unions on the boards as well. Like earlier types of subsidized employment, the programme was targeted at the long-term unemployed. Those working under the PWA system received a supplement to their unemployment benefits for part-time work. The PWA employed did not have a formal employment relation with the PWA, and kept their status of an unemployment beneficiary.

Whereas earlier programmes had been limited to employment in public organizations (such as schools and local public services) or non-profit organizations (cultural associations), the PWA system also opened up to a whole series of domestic services (such as ironing, cleaning or laundry work). Since 1994, federal law mandates every municipality to set up a

PWA service. They are also required to take representatives of the social partners onto the governing boards of these agencies. The unions use this leverage to change the status of those employed by the PWAs, making their position less precarious. Still, the nature of this contract continues to be far more insecure than a normal employment contract, as the supplement to the unemployment benefit is only paid out for hours actually performed, and as in case of sickness, the PWA employee only receives his or her unemployment benefit.

PWA jobs can be clearly contrasted with more integrative programmes such as the jobs provided by the so-called reintegration enterprises. Under these schemes the regional governments endow enterprises that employ unemployed persons who are difficult to mediate, with a subsidy of 80 per cent of the wage costs during the first year of employment, which in the course of the subsequent years is progressively reduced. Other schemes that encourage regular enterprises to employ the long-term unemployed include the Activa Plan (primarily aimed at employing the older long-term unemployed) and the Rosetta Plan (targeted at the young unemployed, to get a job or an apprenticeship). Both plans exempt employers from certain social security contributions. The Activa Plan, in addition, offers a wage subsidy. By 2003, some 48 051 people in the Flanders region were employed by this so-called 'social economy' (GOM West Vlaanderen 2005).

The Service Vouchers Scheme

The service voucher scheme was introduced in 2000 in order to promote further the provision of local services. The main idea behind the scheme was to allow both non-governmental organizations and for-profit enterprises to provide services at prices that could compete with the clandestine and underground economy. The service voucher system allows households to purchase special subsidized vouchers, which they can use to pay for 'local community services' such as childcare, care for the elderly and the sick, and household tasks such as cleaning.

Initially, the service voucher jobs were only provided by the local employment agencies (PWAs), but later on the scheme was extended to include profit-based providers. The scheme aims to create 'proper' jobs in the local services area (with normal wage contracts with social security benefits), and to combat the clandestine work in this sector. The original legislation allocated the organization to the regions, but in 2004 the management was put under federal control. By 2005, some 30 000 people were employed under the new scheme, but many of these jobs were on a part-time basis. The gross job creation because of the scheme was estimated to amount to some 17 350 full-time jobs (Gevers 2006, p. 146).

The problem with the voucher system is that a lot of substitution effects occurred: many of the newly created jobs replaced existing jobs – and not only, as the scheme intended, jobs in the clandestine sector. The substitution effects occurred in particular during the first year of the scheme's existence, when more than four out of ten service voucher workers had already had a job before they started to work under the scheme. But by 2005 substitution declined to a mere 3.4 per cent.

European Employment Strategy Activation Measures

In the advent of the European Employment Strategy (EES), that was launched in 1997, labour market policies refocused to the supply side. Even though the job creation programmes of the past and local service initiatives such as the PWA and the service vouchers had in part been set up with the intent to improve the labour market skills of low-skilled unemployed, it is only during the 1990s that one can observe a trend towards more individual career guidance arrangements and a more strict monitoring of the job search behaviour of the unemployed.

In 1991, the Flemish employment agency (VDAB) introduced a system of career guidance in order to facilitate the unemployed to find a job. During the first months of being without a job, the unemployed person is to be supported by a set of basic self-service provisions that have to allow them to manage their own job search; by means of a 'personal file' (a file that they can create and manage themself); by a training guide of various programmes offered by the VDAB; by a vacancy database and by an applications database onto which the unemployed person can upload their curriculum vitae. If an unemployed person fails to find a job within the first months, they are inserted into a compulsory career guidance system.

Active Monitoring of Unemployed

In July 2004, the federal RVA started a new nationwide activation scheme. Because eligibility to unemployment benefits was now more conditional upon participation in activation programmes, the new system required better coordination between the various governance levels and agencies that had evolved after the devolution of labour market policies. For that purpose the federal and regional governments concluded a cooperation agreement in 2004, in which they agreed to use the KSZ (Kruispuntbank van de Sociale Zekerheid) information database for social security as the platform for exchanging information between the various federal and regional institutions.

The regional employment offices inform the RVA about the participation

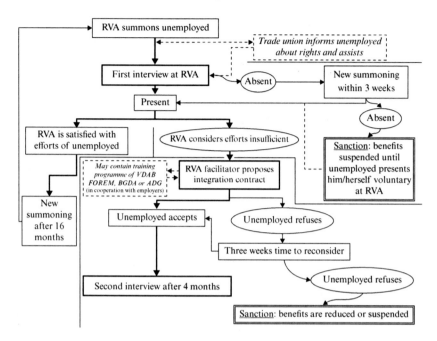

Figure 7.3   First phase of the monitoring procedure for controlling the unemployed in Belgium

of the unemployment beneficiaries in activation schemes such as the career guidance system in the Flanders region. In cases where it considers the efforts of an unemployed person in terms of job seeking or enrolment in a training programme to be insufficient, it can instruct the payment body to suspend the paying out of the unemployment benefit.

The new monitoring procedure is implemented by officers of the district-level branch offices of the RVA. As in the past, in the end they decide whether or not the unemployment benefit has to be suspended, and then instruct the payment bodies. The unions simply put this decision into practice, but as the trade union-based payment bodies also operate as a kind of insurance broker, they also offer their members legal advice and support if they want to contest the sanction of suspension imposed by the RVA.

Figure 7.3 gives an overview of the different steps of the new monitoring procedure. All those who have been unemployed for more than 21 months (for those under 25 years, 15 months) are invited for a personal interview at the district branch office (RWB) of the RVA. During this first interview, the employment officer assesses the efforts that the unemployed person has made to find a job, taking into account the information provided by the regional employment offices (about training programmes and activation schemes that the unemployed person might have been participating in). When the RVA summons an unemployed person, their trade union immediately invites them for a meeting to inform them about their rights and to assist them in defending their case. Sometimes trade union officials accompany the unemployed person to their interviews at the RVA. If the efforts of the unemployed are deemed insufficient, an individual action plan for the coming four months is proposed, in the form of a reintegration contract (that can contain enrolment in one of the activation schemes operated by one of the four regional employment offices). Four months later a second interview is scheduled, where the RVA assesses whether the unemployed person has complied with the action plan. If this is the case, they will only have to start the procedure again in 12 months and no sanctions are applied. If the unemployed person did not comply with the action plan, a temporary sanction is imposed (a reduction or suspension of the benefit) and a more strict reinsertion contract is proposed. Non-compliance with the second reintegration contract can lead to a permanent suspension of unemployment benefits.

Output and outcomes

In 2007, about 604 000 unemployed persons were contacted by the RVA and informed about the new monitoring procedure. About one in two was summoned for a first interview. Table 7.5 gives an overview of the regional differences with respect to the implementation of the procedure that year. If during the early years the Walloon region lagged behind the Brussels and the Flanders regions (De Deken 2007), this now no longer seems to be the case. If one relates the number of unemployed contacted for a first interview to the number of registered unemployed that are expected to look for a job, Wallonia even scores markedly better than the Flanders region.

   Even though the three regions are often claimed to differ in the extent to which they have embraced the supply-side policy agenda of the EES, labour market trends have been remarkably similar since the late 1990s, as illustrated in Figure 7.4. There are very important and persistent regional differences in the country: whereas in Flanders the unemployment rate hovers around 5 per cent, it is more than double that figure in Wallonia, and almost three times as high in Brussels. One should bear in mind though that the Flanders region embarked earlier (1991) on EES-type activation measures, which during the middle of the 1990s had contributed to widening the gulf with the other regions, disparities that in the subsequent decade have remained relatively stable. In the Flanders region the absolute

Table 7.5   The active monitoring of unemployed in Belgium, by region

	Brussels	Flanders	Wallonia
Number of registered job seeking unemployed	311011	287401	92251
Number of registered unemployed exempted from job seeking	149515	107896	18865
Number first step (information letter)	183000	320000	101000
– as a percentage of job seeking unemployed	59	111	108
Number second step (first interview)	77000	158000	47000
– as a percentage of first step	42	49	47
– as a percentage of job seeking unemployed	25	55	51
Percentage unemployed judged to have made insufficient efforts	53	61	57
Number of unemployed sanctioned	14000	24000	9000
– as percentage of first step	7.0	7.5	8.9

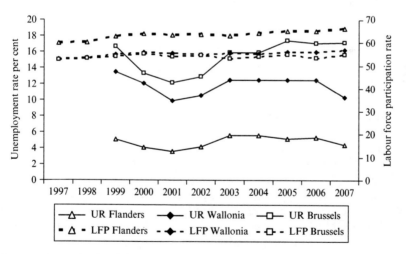

Figure 7.4   The development of unemployment and labour force participation in Belgium, by region

number of unemployed declined by 12 per cent during the period 1992–98, but this increased in Wallonia and the Brussels region by, respectively, 3.5 and 17 per cent.[10] As of 2007 the change toward a more active labour market policy in Wallonia is starting to have some effect.

Compared to other countries, Belgium still devotes more resources to direct job creation. The total costs of these programmes amount to 0.35 per cent of gross domestic product (GDP), whereas the OECD average is 0.06 per cent (2006). For Belgium, this is substantially lower than expenditure for such programmes in 1999, which were 0.49 per cent of GDP. When expenditure on direct job creation is compared with those on job placement and training and income maintenance for those out of work, a relative decline is observed, from 24 to 16 per cent. A comparison with the OECD as a whole shows that more resources continue to be allocated for such programmes. The distribution of 2006 expenditure on: (1) direct job creation; (2) placement services and training; and (3) income support for Belgium is 16:19:65, for the OECD on average 5:30:85, for the Netherlands 6:28:67 and for Germany 3:22:75.[11]

INTERACTION BETWEEN UNEMPLOYMENT PROTECTION, EMPLOYMENT PROTECTION AND ACTIVE LABOUR MARKET POLICIES

The Belgian system of unemployment support is often considered to be an example of the 'Ghent system'. However, the role of trade unions in the Belgian unemployment insurance system is quite different from what one would expect in a true 'Ghent system': the unions do not choose the type of insurance policy they administer, nor do they have a say in the entitlement conditions or the benefit levels; eligibility to benefits is not limited to union members, and it is not only union members who foot the bill of the insurance scheme. Rather, it is the state, together with both social partners (employers' associations and trade unions), who determine how to organize the insurance and how to administer it. All these three parties (the state, the employers and the wage earners) jointly finance the scheme. Who bears more of this financial burden is difficult to say, but formally the share paid directly by employees, in the form of contributions for the unemployment insurance system, is comparatively low. In the advent of high unemployment, nominal contributions rates were not increased, but recourse was first made to state subsidies, and later (when the EMU made it imperative to reduce the state debt) to special employers' contributions and to so-called wage moderation. The latter resulted in payments formally made by the employers, but these resources, in the end, came from a state-imposed wage moderation, at the expense of the purchasing power of employees. This wage moderation was the outcome of tripartite negotiations in which trade unions formed an essential negotiating party. But the conclusion seems warranted that employees and their unions have at best an indirect leverage on the streams that finance unemployment insurance and active labour market policies.

Within the system of so-called global financial management, adopted in 1996, employee contributions formally only play a minor role in the financing of unemployment benefits. Direct state subsidies and the revenues generated by so-called wage moderation carry the main burden, even if official accounting sees this as being part of the employer's contributions. There seem to be no reasons to expect a direct link between how much employees as a group pay into the system and successes in terms of labour market policy (lowering unemployment and/or increasing labour force participation), or the possible costs of employment protection (high unemployment and low labour force participation; and insider–outsider problems). But indirectly the neo-corporatist system may well feed such considerations into the governance system and into the process of rule making.

What, then, apart from being a partner in the corporatist system of intermediation, is the role of trade unions in the Belgian triangle of employment protection legislation, unemployment protection and labour market policies? Except for their formal role as a cash desk in the public unemployment insurance scheme, one could probably best describe the position of the unions as enacting the role of insurance brokers: they advise their members and help them with the paperwork to complete their application for unemployment benefits. They also provide legal assistance in cases of disputes with the unemployment insurance administration. More recently, they have started to assist their members to cope with the new system of the active monitoring of the job searching process.

In terms of entitlement, we have demonstrated that in the Belgian variant of the 'Ghent system' all wage earners are entitled to an unemployment insurance benefit. They have access to benefits either via their trade union, or via the public payment body. But the role of the union can be more important in the perception of employees. After all, insurance-like institutions thrive on trust, and union officials may reinforce this trust by standing closer to the insured than the officials of the state, who tend to have more of an arm's-length relationship with their 'clients'. The trade unions also form an important bridge between the insured and the public insurance system in that they help to complete dossiers, and they support their members if their entitlement claims are contested by the unemployment insurance administration. This may be one, but certainly not the only, reason for the comparatively high trade union density that one can continue to observe in Belgium.

When we look at what some consider to be an emerging 'market' for employment services, the Belgian reality confuses the models of an approach inspired by neoclassical economics: the neocorporatist actors who are involved in the 'supply' of unemployment insurance, are in part the very same as those who are active in the 'market' for employment services. On the other hand, they also 'contract' private companies for employment services; without, though, letting the market mechanism take over the coordination of the whole system. What is more important than to try to fit these complicated facts in a stylized model of a market is the reality of an institutional separation between, on the one hand, the compensation and control of the unemployed (which remains the responsibility of the federal RVA and the trade unions), and on the other hand, active labour market programmes, training and assistance to the unemployed in their job search (which since devolution has become the responsibility of the regional and language community authorities).

This does not mean that the regional governments have not been introducing market elements in their employment services, or that they allow for some competition within public labour exchanges, or that they might be working with private employers to further skill formation. Those governments might even have outsourced part of their job creation programmes to private sector providers (as, for instance, the service voucher scheme in effect did). In the end, though, all this is done with public money, and under the guidance of a public tripartite neo-corporatist administration, with administratively determined prices and subsidies. The principal actors in this game are not linked to each other by an amorphous market structure, in which the laws of supply and demand determine prices and equilibrium. The market mechanism only to a very limited extent guides the behaviour of the actors involved. Rather, they learn to respond to a series of administrative instructions which in essence are not very different from the former hierarchical bureaucratic structure. These instructions were often developed in a process of neocorporatist intermediation, which means that the actors that have to implement these instructions were in part also responsible for their very formulation.

In terms of employment protection the system has hardly changed since the late 1970s. There have been endless debates about harmonizing the system of individual dismissals. This debate seems to be in gridlock: employers want to lower the employment protection of salaried employees to the standard that now prevails for manual workers, and the unions want the opposite. No compelling evidence is found of a systematic link between reforms of the employment protection system and changes in unemployment protection. In the case of collective dismissals, there have been a number of changes that aim to keep people at work rather than parking them in the unemployment support system. An individual right to outplacement for older workers is legislated (sometimes extended to younger workers by industry-level collective agreements), and new tripartite institutions are created, such as the regional re-employment units, that can form public–private partnerships with outplacement offices. However, attempts to reduce individual employment protection, which in Belgium has never been that strong, has remained gridlocked because of a fundamental disagreement between the social partners, with the employer side seeking to harmonize the status of manual workers and salaried employees on the basis of the lowest common denominator, and the unions for obvious reasons objecting to such a change.

Active labour market policies in Belgium have traditionally consisted of various job creation programmes in the so-called 'social economy'. Recently, one can observe a trend towards establishing more partnerships with the commercial for-profit enterprises. The system of PWAs and the service voucher scheme in effect tries to offset the 'costs disease problem', by establishing public service companies and by subsidizing private service providers. More recently, Belgium has embarked on more supply-side activation programmes. On the one hand, there is a series of career guidance schemes, some of which are based on intensifying the cooperation with the private sector, but again with the public bodies still orchestrating the initiatives and providing the necessary funding. On the other hand, a more repressive system of monitoring the unemployed was established (with the possibility to suspend entitlement to a benefit – something which can be considered quite a novelty in a system in which there was no limit in time on the eligibility to benefits, except for those cohabiting with an earning partner).

Here one can observe an interesting – possibly unintended – outcome of how the distribution of responsibilities evolved into a complex web of institutions. In effect, there is a sort of division of labour in the Belgian chain of work and income, that is represented in Figure 7.5. The regional authorities are primarily responsible for assisting the unemployed to find a job or to retrain them in order to increase their labour market chances: the regional authorities offer the 'carrot'. Reintegration is being outsourced to private enterprises, and job creation is partly delegated to the municipally based PWAs and the service voucher scheme that again involves private firms organizing personal services. The federal agencies (and their local branch offices) are more holding the 'stick', in that they monitor and sanction the 'unwilling' unemployed. The unions, apart from being involved in the parity-based administration at both the federal and the regional

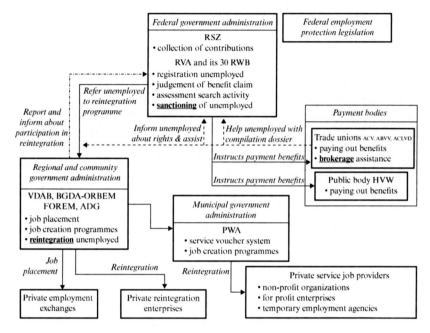

Figure 7.5   The division of labour in the Belgian chain of work and income

level, operate as a kind of 'broker', helping their members to find their way in this myriad of institutions, and making sure that their rights are not infringed upon by eager officials who want to score in terms of performance and report their 'successes' to the European Union's benchmarkers.

Because these functionally differentiated institutions are controlled by a tripartite governance structure composed of representatives of the very same collective actors, there seems to be a kind of network structure operating, which in addition to the formal coordination structures that have been set up, allows for an additional exchange of information.

The Belgian case also sheds an interesting light on employment successes by qualifying the importance of national labour market institutions and nationally embedded policy reforms. In spite of the fact that the three regions operate on the same unemployment benefit system, are subject to identical employment protection legislation and wage bargaining systems, and that the regional differences in activation policies are marginal (at best a matter of when they were introduced), persistent dramatic differences in terms of outcomes are observed. The Flanders region's unemployment rate is similar to a labour market 'success case' like Denmark, even if labour force participation, especially amongst elderly workers, is significantly lower. Wallonia, and even more so the Brussels region, have persistent unemployment well above the European average. One could argue, though, that it does not make that much sense to assess the Brussels region in isolation. Many inhabitants of the Flanders region only work, but do not live in Brussels. In addition, Brussels is not that different compared to other large metropolitan areas in Europe in that it has a large, low-skilled migrant population who, because they are mostly of North African origin, tend to become clients of the French-speaking Bruxelles Formation, not of the Flemish subsidiary of the VDAB in Brussels. In other words, while the Flanders region to some extent benefits from the employment opportunities that the capital city provides, it does not have to carry the burdens that such a position brings with it.

NOTES

1. Belgium is a federal state with three regions (Flanders, Wallonia and Brussels) and three language communities (Dutch, French and German) resulting in six governments: (1) the federal government; (2) the Flemish government (for the Flanders region and the Flemish (Dutch-speaking) community); (3) the government of the French-speaking community; (4) the government of the Walloon region; (5) the government of the Brussels capital region; (6) the government of the German-speaking community. The communities have competence over affairs relating to individuals and the regions for territorial matters. The Flemish and French communities have competence in Brussels for Dutch-speaking and French-speaking residents respectively. Another particular feature of Belgium's federalism is that this model works asymmetrically in the sense that in the Flemish area the community and regional areas of competence have been placed under one and the same authority, both regarding the legislative and the executive powers (in fact they have been merged), whilst on the French-speaking side, region and community remain clearly separate with two councils (parliaments) and two governments (executives).
2. This includes the costs of the early retirement system, interim pensions and career break schemes (such as parental leave and care leave), which in Belgium form a part of the unemployment insurance system.
3. The time credit scheme is a Flemish variation on the federal career break scheme. In contrast to the older federal scheme, the Flemish scheme no longer has a replacement condition, that is it no longer requires that beneficiaries of the sabbatical scheme are replaced by an unemployed person.
4. The Walloon *region* is responsible for the reintegration of the unemployed who live in the districts that are governed by the German *community*, but there is a separate Employment office for the German Speaking Community (ADG). In 2000 this institution replaced the Sankt Vith regional branch office of the FOREM. Unemployment in the German districts is comparatively low. In 2003, of a total of 70000 inhabitants less than 2000 were unemployed.
5. The following calculations of the replacement rate are based on the APW for Belgium for 2005 using the OECD's broad definition, amounting to €35578 per year. Even though unemployment benefits in principle are liable to an income tax of 10 per cent, most unemployed are exempt from this, such as singles, one-earner couples, and two-earner couples with the unemployed partner receiving the second-period benefits. As a matter of fact, the only category of the unemployed that does have to pay the 10 per

cent tax is the one that consists of those who are cohabiting with a working partner, and who receive the first-period benefit. For households with children, these net replacement rates can be higher because of the tax benefits they enjoy. Unemployed older than 50 also receive additional supplements which can increase the replacement rate up to 82 per cent.
6. It varied between 15 per cent in the UK and 26 per cent in the US, to over 52 per cent in Sweden and 66 per cent in Germany, to 74 per cent in Denmark and 76 per cent in the Netherlands. Only Switzerland, with 96 per cent came close to the Belgian ratio (calculations based on the SOCX OECD social expenditure data set and the LIS Comparative Welfare State Data Set), accessed at 18 July 2008 at www.lisproject. org/publications/welfaredata/welfareaccess.htm and http://stats.oecd.org/Index.aspx? datasetcode=SOCXAGG.
7. Which is why it is impossible to continue the time series of Figure 7.2 beyond the year 1995, because since that year there is no longer an earmarked revenue for the unemployment insurance system.
8. RSZ Data, www.rsz.fgov.be/Onssrsz/NL/Statistics/Brochures/Yellow/2003/xls/tabellen_20034_nl_wdn.xls.
9. These redeployment funds are financed by state subsidies and industry funds.
10. Calculations are based on RVA statistics www.rva.be/D_stat/Studies/2004/Serie_1992-2000/Publicatie_NL.pdf, accessed 10 August 2008.
11. Note that the OECD's ratio of active versus passive measures for some countries (Belgium) includes the cost of early retirement benefits, whereas for other countries (the Netherlands) these costs are excluded. Moreover, the OECD measure considers direct job creation as an active measure, similar to the typical EES activation programmes. All calculations are based on data from the OECD online database, accessed 10 September 2008.

REFERENCES

De Deken, J. (2007), 'Distribution of responsibility for social security and labour market policy. Country report Belgium', Amsterdam Institute of Advanced Labour Studies working paper 07/53, Amsterdam.
De Lathouwer, L. (1997), 'Het Belgische werkloosheidsstelsel in internationaal Perspectief', *Economisch en Sociaal Tijdschrift*, **2**: 295–238.
De Lathouwer, L., B. Cockx, K. Bogaerts, J. Ries (2003), *De impact van schorsing Artikel 80 in de werkloosheidverzekering op herintrede en armoede*, Studievoormiddag van 3 december, Ghent: Academia Press.
ESSPROS (European System of Integrated Social Protection Statistics) (2007), *European social statistics. Social protection expenditures and receipts. Data 1994–2004*, Luxembourg: Eurostat.
Gevers, A., A. van Pelt and A. Peeters (2006), *Evaluatie van het stelsel van de dienstencheques voor buurtdiensten en banen 2005*, Brussels: IDEA, in opdracht van FOD Arbeid en Sociaal Overleg.
GOM West Vlaanderen (2005), *Tewerkstelling van kansengroepen in West Vlaanderen. Een inventaris met cijfermateriaal*, Brugges: Gewestelijke Ontwikkelingsmaatschappij West Vlaanderen.
Mahy, B., Y.-B. Minette, L. Ockerman, V. Vandeville and D. Wala (1996), *Evaluation des politiques de résorption du chômage de longue durée: offre et demande de travail*, Brussels: DWTC.
NAR (Nationale Arbeidsraad) (2005), 'Rapport no. 66 van de Nationale

Arbeidsraad met betrekking tot de financiering van de sociale zekerheid', 12 June.

OECD (Organisation for Economic Co-operation and Development) (2004), *Benefits and Wages*, Paris: OECD.

Palsterman, P. (2003), 'La notion de chômage involontaire (1945–2003)', Centre de Recherche et d'Information Socio-Politiques (CRISP) Courrier Hebdomadaire, no. 1806, Bruxelles.

RVA (Rijksdienst voor Arbeidsvoorziening) (1997), 'De Functie verruiming vande Werkloosheidsverzekering en de financiering van het Stelsel', *Belgiach Tijdschrift voor Social Zekerheid*, **39**(2): 375–97.

RVA (2005), *Jaarverslag 2005*, Brussels, Centre de Recherche et d'Information Socio-Politiques (CRISP): RVA.

8. France

Jean-Claude Barbier

INTRODUCTION

As this chapter is written along the guidelines of a common analytical framework, a few methodological remarks are in place better to insert the presentation of the French case into this cross-national comparison. Cross-national comparison in general is a tricky business even among a relatively homogeneous European group of countries (Barbier 2005, 2008b). This justifies the presentation of cautionary methodological remarks especially valid in the empirical case of France.

The first concerns the notion of 'social security'. Especially in the French case, unemployment insurance is but one of the ways in which 'non-employment' is compensated for. Indeed, the comparatively rather late introduction of a mainstream minimum income benefit (MIB) in 1988 in France (*Revenu minimum d'insertion* – RMI) has rapidly functioned as a substitute for the shortcomings of the insurance scheme managed by social partners (established as a branch independent of Sécurité sociale in 1958). Moreover, France is certainly characterized, as we shall see, by a multiple system of minimum income benefits. Hence, looking in-depth at 'social security' for the present study entails dealing not only with unemployment insurance but also with MIBs across the board.

Second, the notion of active labour market policy, used in a decontextualized way, originates from the notion popularized in the Paris Organisation for Economic Co-operation and Development (OECD) headquarters by Gösta Rehn when he was head of its Directorate of Manpower and Social Affairs (1962–74). When researched in any national context, the programmes which can be put under the heading of active labour market policy are bound to vary because of different institutional settings; the very opposition between 'active' and 'passive' policies should be put in perspective. To take only one example, programmes exist which mingle 'active' and 'passive' elements. As will be seen in the French case, one important aspect of labour market policy has been the creation of subsidized jobs in the public and non-profit sectors since the early 1980s: seen in a cross-national comparative light, these programmes combine the attribution to beneficiaries of a wage-based contract, training and other supporting activities. Their substance is in a way hybrid, between 'passive' and 'active'. Moreover, the ability of any national system to produce some form of 'flexicurity' is also linked to its strategy for the activation of social protection in general (Barbier 2004) – which involves many more aspects of the system than the limited activation policies. In the present text, such aspects of the system which are also relevant for understanding our subject are mentioned only briefly.

Third, the notion of 'employment protection legislation' has mainly come to be seen today as the internationally decontextualized concept used by economists – who score it to benchmark countries against one another, according to the OECD selection of certain aspects of labour law or 'labour standards'. Consequently, I prefer here using 'labour law'. Finally, the notion of 'flexicurity' should also be taken with a pinch of salt. There are many meanings to it, which have been discussed in a comparative perspective by many scholars (Wilthagen 1998; Schmid 2008; Jørgensen and Madsen 2007; Bredgaard et al. 2007). Here again differences arise because of alternative disciplinary approaches, especially due to the distinctive positions in this respect of economics, political science and sociology. In strict sociological terms, because of its normative origin and its pervasive international political usage, 'flexicurity' cannot be seen as a rigorous sociological concept (Barbier 2007). I shall come back to this point in the last section of the chapter.

Numerous reforms have been implemented in France since the 1980s across all fields of social protection. Their sequencing should be seen in a macroeconomic context. The reforms were punctuated by the reappearance and recurrence of a business cycle alternating recovery and recession, as well as a succession of different economic policies associated with it: the 'stagflation' of the 1974–83 period, the 'competitive disinflation' of the 1984–93 period, economic policy governed by the Maastricht criteria from 1994 to the absorption of the shock created by the euro in 2002 and, at present, the prevailing dissociation of the territorial levels of monetary policy and fiscal policy. Each cycle can in fact be associated with one main type of reform: the pursuit of policy along Keynesian lines during 'stagflation management', parametrical reforms centred on a reduction of social expenditure with unchanged institutions during the period of 'competitive disinflation', or more structural reforms once the EU single market fully came into being. These adjustments in economic policy in the 1980s and the distinct reactions they have entailed among social actors have given rise to forward-looking reforms followed by setbacks or abrupt halts, transformations which were conceivable at a given time but which, held back by resistance, seemed less appropriate in the following period; to political learning processes involving trial and error; to innovations combining the new and the old. The discussion in this chapter concentrates on the last period, where again business cycles are important to take into consideration, after the booming years of the late 1990s and early 2000s, and into the second half of the 2000s. Notion is taken of the impressive list of reforms which have been put on the agenda and have started to be implemented since the election of a new president in 2007: the great majority of the latter are in their initial period and their legacy and effects are still to be observed in the future.

The French system has been in constant reform, from the late 1980s; its hybrid nature was in certain areas a positive factor facilitating this adaptation; and it has been in a way consistent with original republican choices as well as with choices made after the Second World War, for instance with regard to women's participation to the labour market, or to 'insertion' programmes (see later). The classic 'Beveridgean–Bismarckian' opposition has indeed remained adequate, especially when it comes to studying employment policies (Clegg 2007). Essentially, this does not add up to make all the reforms described here consistent. The most recent turning point in the reform debate in France was perhaps 2005, and this debate has been raging ever since, not only because of the long run-up to the presidential and parliamentary elections in 2007. Finally, there are many dimensions to the question of 'administration and responsibilities'; one is the question of funding mechanisms. It is important to stress from the beginning that one of the most crucial reforms in the French system has been its gradual shift from funding through social contributions to a mix of tax and contributions. In the early 1980s, social contributions amounted to 95 per cent of total social expenditure for the mainstream social insurance schemes (*régime general*), whereas their share in 2006 was down to less than 59 per cent. In the restricted field of 'unemployment' or 'employment policies', the influence of funding mechanisms has not been directly crucial, but this general transformation has had great influence upon the system as a whole.

UNEMPLOYMENT INSURANCE AND ASSISTANCE BENEFITS

Throughout the 1990s, a close interaction has existed between unemployment insurance[1] and minimum income benefits (MIBs), and, additionally, a strong relationship between the latter and employment programmes (*contrats aidés*) was constant, both in the public and non-profit sector and in the private sector (dealt with later in this chapter).

The Main Reforms since the 1990s

Three main reforms were implemented in the 1990s in the insurance system. In social assistance, it is also convenient to present the recent developments in stages.

In unemployment insurance, in 1992, AUD (Allocation Unique Dégressive) was introduced as the standard benefit: this meant tightening minimum entitlement conditions and introducing a new principle according to which the benefit was reduced by a fixed amount every four months (later, six months) until the end of entitlement.[2] The underlying rationale for the decreasing benefit was that it would foster job search. This justification had also a strong cost-containment motive. While the unemployment fund budget was balanced and money was spared, contrary to expectations this new design of benefits did not encourage leaving unemployment insurance. The rates of leavers to employment decreased over the period 1992 to 1996 and this was only marginally due to business cycle reasons (Dormont et al. 2001). In a way, this can be seen as an activation reform that failed. The 1992 reform caused the proportion of the unemployed eligible to insurance benefit to decrease from 62 per cent in 1991 to 52 per cent in 1998 and drove an increasing proportion of the unemployed to the MIBs (ASS, Allocation de Solidarité Spécifique,[3] and RMI) (see later). Nevertheless, this trend was later reversed during the employment boom. The share of the unemployed eligible to benefits rose from 54.9 per cent in July 2000 to a mean rate of 58.7 per cent for the year 2001 and, after a peak in 2003 (64 per cent), it has been rather stable at about 60 per cent since 2005.[4]

Since the mid-1980s, the idea that unemployment compensation should prompt job search and help enhance skills determined the orientation of both the National Union for Employment in Industry and Commerce (Union Nationale pour l'Emploi dans l'Industrie et le Commerce, UNEDIC)[5] and of employment policies (Daniel and Tuchszirer 1999; Barbier and Théret 2001). Measures fostering individualized training services delivered to jobseekers (for instance the retraining allowance scheme, AFR, Allocation Formation Reclassement) were implemented by UNEDIC from 1988. The principle of encouraging the return to the labour market was also illustrated from 1986 by the introduction of a disregard for part of the income gained from short-term, low-paid or part-time jobs. All these measures became obsolete with the introduction of a new programme in 2001. This reform, which triggered intense conflict, was not however a bolt from the blue in terms of 'activating' the unemployed. In October 2000, UNEDIC's reform was agreed by employers' organizations and three of the five French representative trade unions. In May

2001, corresponding legal provisions were approved by the government, especially the controversial 'back-to-work support plan' (PARE, Plan d'Aide au Retour à l'Emploi). Eventually, these were only implemented from July 2001, after more than one year of conflict among unions and between unions and employers' associations and the government. The AUD was abandoned and the total duration of entitlement remained unchanged. Insured people were offered a PARE, combining the benefit and a personalized action plan (PAP, Plan d'Action Personnalisé). The PARE mainly obliged the unemployed to have their skills assessed, to undertake training or to take an 'acceptable' job. The administration was committed to deliver a variety of active measures, including training and counselling. The implementation of individual projects was to be assessed in-depth at least every six months,[6] and was supposed to lead to various 'levels of services', according to the difficulties experienced by the beneficiaries. Because no comprehensive evaluation of the new benefit was published, it is still difficult to assess its overall effects, especially for the 'hard to place' or the potentially 'excluded' from the labour market.

With a new presidency in 2002, fresh reforms were mooted, which appeared difficult to legitimize. In 2004, the government suffered a first setback when the highest administrative court (Conseil d'État) censured it for having approved the new agreement by social partners, which decreased entitlement to benefits for PARE beneficiaries. When, in the 2004 elections, all regional councils but one were won by the opposition, the president decided to abandon the 2003 reform of the ASS, the entitlement to which was supposed to be shortened, leading to more people being transferred to the mainstream RMI benefit. In both cases, reforms were ditched. At the same time, the government was increasingly willing to find a breakthrough for the reform of the Public Employment Service (PES, *l'Agence National pour l'Emploi*) which in a way had been implicitly on the agenda since the early 1990s without materializing.

After the failed 2002–4 reform, a new agreement was passed between the social partners in January 2006 and approved by the government: the agreement was renegotiated in 2008 and brought fresh changes in 2009 (see below). The main changes agreed upon in 2008 by the majority of trade unions and employers' organizations were related to traditional adjustments of employers and employees' contributions to the fund in order to balance its budget. The duration of entitlement was also adjusted (see below). However, apart from balancing expenditure by adequate resources, probably the main stake of this new round of negotiations was a wider reform of the PES and its link to the social insurance system (dealt with in the section on active labour market policy).

In the area of social assistance, it is important to note that until 1988, the French 'Bismarckian' system had no mainstream safety net benefit. RMI was introduced that year and the benefit was endowed from its inception with a specific legacy of republican solidarity. The innovative motto of the 1980s was 'insertion', meaning that RMI beneficiaries were owed special attention by the state and local authorities (*départements*) to support their integration in society through a special contract associated with the benefit. Originating in civil society initiatives, the French doctrine of insertion was only at a second stage appropriated by the administration, which designed fully fledged 'insertion policies'. In the initial solidaristic insertion philosophy, 'social integration' was never meant primarily in terms of constraining people to take jobs on the market. In fact, due to the particularly low rate of job creation in France at that time, many programmes entailed the opposite function of keeping people in 'welfare' rather than transferring them over to work which did not exist (Barbier and Théret 2001). Although somehow watered down over recent years, this rationale can be interpreted in terms of 'republican' values, linked to the state's obligation to act as an employer of last resort. RMI was introduced in a time of '*nouvelle pauvreté*' when in many countries poverty was 'rediscovered'. In the previous years, three MIBs had been put in place, for special categories: one for mothers of young children (less than three years old) who were left with no resources because of widowhood or divorce (Allocation de Parent Isolé – API, in 1976) and one for disabled persons (Allocation d'Adulte Handicapé, AAH, in 1975). Moreover, as just mentioned above, ASS was introduced from 1984, in the unemployment insurance fund, but funded by the state budget. Hence, in the early 1990s, four MIBs were in place for working-age persons. With hindsight, well before the activation reforms were introduced in many countries, all four MIBs were framed within a 'solidaristic' perspective of activation. In particular, AAH and API benefits, because of their design, allowed a significant part of their recipients to be at least partly active or to return rather quickly to the labour market (this has always been the case for API recipients). On the other hand, for ASS, although in theory rules similar to the unemployment insurance have always applied, the majority of its older recipients have tended to be exempted from active job search, thus resembling early retirees.

However, despite its rhetoric and symbolic dimensions, RMI partly failed to live up to its initial ambitions. It nevertheless exemplifies the hybrid nature of the French system, enhancing particular features related to its history. Until 2009, no obligation was ever imposed on RMI recipients to register with the PES and to look for jobs.[7] In June 2009, as the new RSA benefit (*revenu de solidarité active*) (see below) is implemented, legal obligations are still ambiguous. It is an empirical question for future research to learn whether this special characteristic of the French system will remain in a comparative perspective. Local implementation obviously introduces differences as to the interpretation of the rules (Bouchoux et al. 2004).

However, nationally, a punitive orientation has never prevailed so far. Plans discussed with beneficiaries are on the basis of an individualized contract, where choices are taken into consideration. It is overwhelmingly assumed, however, that all recipients should engage in a series of activities, which, in the medium or long run, should result in integration into the labour market (*insertion professionnelle*).

In 2003, the government tried to introduce a new scheme for RMI recipients who had been eligible for two years, imposing contracts with lesser protection than ordinary employment (Revenu minimum d'activité – RMA).[8] However, because of intense political controversy over a programme that was intended to placate the right-wing section of the political majority, many of the French local authorities (*départements*) never really adopted the measure in 2004. It accounts for a tiny proportion of recipients engaged in this measure.[9] RMA was a fully fledged failure. Later, a new reform was announced during the 2007 presidential election, aiming at changing the system of MIBs more profoundly. In its initial design, all MIBs for working-age people were deemed to be included in a really ambitious reform. The rationale for the reform was twofold: to prevent working poverty, and to make incentives more credible (calculated as a differential, and allowing for the combination of the benefit and wages from employment). The reform essentially ensures that beneficiaries who take a job will always earn more than their previous benefit (at €454 for one person); however, the eventual scope of the RSA reform was less extensive than originally discussed: neither AAH nor ASS will be included in it. Hence a widely shared but still speculative assumption concludes that the final design of the reform will not alter the complexity and fragmentation of French social assistance.

The Current System: Main Characteristics

With regard to unemployment insurance, the general rule has been that social partners are competent and strike regular agreements (*conventions*) that have a limited duration (two or three years) and define levels of social contributions and of benefits. The last such agreement, in force since the beginning of 2006 was valid until early 2009. Generally, only a majority of unions accepted the agreement, with the Confédération Générale du Travail (CGT), one of the main French unions, declining to sign. Once the agreement is struck with employers' organizations, the French government is supposed to approve the agreement which subsequently acquires legal status. The general legal framework of the unemployment insurance is nevertheless the domain of legislation passed in parliament. Hence, three 'normative sources' coexist: the competence of social partners; government competence to approve agreements and the general competence of parliament for defining the unemployed's legal obligations; as well as the rules applying to the PES. Both employers and employees contribute to the fund: the current rates are at 6.4 per cent of wages (4 per cent for employers and 2.4 per cent for employees) and are calculated on the same basis as other social insurance contributions. In cases of financial problems, the state irregularly participates in the funding. In 2008, there were three variants of the benefit according to the duration of contribution: entitlement lasted for seven months for those who had contributed six out of the previous 22 months, 12 months for those having contributed 12 out the previous 20 months and 23 for those having contributed for 16 out of the previous 26 months. Additionally for the unemployed aged 50–60 having contributed 27 months out of the previous 36, the duration of entitlement was 36 months. However, the rule which allows insurance recipients aged 57+ not to seek work is supposed to be gradually phased out by 2011, after an August 2008 Act was adopted in parliament.[10] The 2009 agreement has essentially changed the situation of the younger unemployed who, from April, only have to contribute four months to be eligible for four months' income replacement.

The benefit is proportional to the previous wage, with a ceiling: 75 per cent of the previous gross wage up to a monthly €1040. The maximum benefit is at 57 per cent between €1928 and €11092. Workers covered are those in the private sector and some employees with short-term contracts in the public sector. Entitlement to the benefit is conditional upon abiding by the rules of job seeking and the acceptation of the Plan Personnalisé d'Accès à l'Emploi (PPAE), now the mainstream name for the implementation of PARE. When their rights are exhausted, unemployed people are presently eligible either to ASS or to RMI. This situation will be partly changed by the new reform passed into law in 2008, the RSA (Revenu de Solidarité Active), that prevents a decline of income when unemployed people get a job. At the same time sanctions were legally strengthened both in 2005 and in 2008. However, after the new definition of the unemployed's obligations as to the refusal of job and training offers, no evaluation was ever published by the government; hence proper comparable sanction figures are not available.

After the MIB reform introducing RSA, RMI and API recipients were requalified as RSA recipients while ASS and AAH remained separate benefits, the exact scope of the RSA benefit is still to be defined. Until the completed reform, mainstream MIBs remain RMI (administered by the local authorities) and ASS (administered by UNEDIC and ASSEDICs). Categorical MIBs remain in force for lone mothers (API) and for disabled persons (AAH). All these benefits are tax-funded. The question of funding RMI benefits has not yet been clearly fixed after the benefit was entirely decentralized to the local authorities in 2003. MIBs' rates are fixed nationally. In July 2008, the RMI benefit for a single person was €447 (€969 for a couple with two children). These rates are differential, meaning that other income is deductible, including a flat rate for housing benefits. Before the reform AAH and API rates were higher. The ASS benefit for a single person was €442 in 2008. AAH, API and RMI recipients are not obliged to register with the PES, nor to seek jobs, unless their contracts prescribe them to do so. What remains to be seen with the new RSA legal obligations is the extent to which RSA recipients will register in the PES, mainly because they can alternatively be taken in charge by other intermediaries linked to the local authorities' administration. Finally, it should be stressed that the system of evaluation of unemployment insurance and MIBs is very fragmented and irregular. For instance, the 2001 PARE reform, which was supposed to be evaluated by 2003, was never eventually assessed.

Administration and Responsibilities

As unemployment in the beginning of the 1990s was at record levels, all levels of government (local authorities, regions, municipalities) have increasingly been involved in some form of intervention: responsibilities fall mainly on the local authorities for MIBs, which they share with the family funds. However, the main reform currently being implemented is the merging of the UNEDIC/ASSEDICs and the PES (legalized in February 2008 Act). When the merger is completed (which in any case will take a long time), it means that placement and income replacement activities will be combined under the future single institution's responsibility. The new institution is called Pôle Emploi. Social partners are supposed to retain their competence in the management of unemployment insurance while, in theory, both the PES and ASSEDIC networks will be merged. In any case, this merger will be a gradual process, the bases of which are only generally laid out in the February 2008 Act. The reform of the PES and its predicted merging with the unemployment insurance fund, on the agenda for many years, has been presented by the new government as a key factor for enhancing the effectiveness of labour market policies and institutions.

LABOUR LAW ('EMPLOYMENT PROTECTION LEGISLATION')

With respect to 'flexibility' of work and employment, two aspects appear salient in the French context. One is the very fragmented nature of employment contracts; the second is the legislation about dismissals. In both areas, reforms occurred from the 1990s on, which remained unfinished and partly contradictory.

The Main Reforms since the 1990s

With regard to employment relations and contracts, a substantial difference exists between the public and the private sectors in France. However, in both, labour flexibilization has mainly happened by stealth (Barbier and Fargion 2004) from the late 1980s to the present day, through the introduction of a variety of contracts while standard ones were kept. Indeed, the most precarious contracts are found in the public sector and it is also in the public sector that the polarization of working conditions is the greatest, between highly paid officials with their job for life and employees whose contracts do not entail access to decent social protection (*vacataires*).

Two main kinds of contracts exist in the private sector: the open-ended contract is the first (Contrat à Durée Indéterminée, CDI). It has remained the legal norm, as was repeatedly accepted over recent years by MEDEF (Mouvement des Entreprises Françaises, the main employers' organization), and again clearly reaffirmed in the January 2008 agreement between the social partners, which was passed into law.[11] The second one is the fixed-term contract (Contrat à Durée Déterminée, CDD[12]) which was, along with agency work, regulated from the 1970s and 1980s.[13] Resorting to fixed-term contracts has always been limited to specific cases, although their legal use was reformed many times. For example, in 1986 the principle of a prohibition of usage in 'normal circumstances' was introduced and in 1990, after the return of a left-wing government, a new Act restricted the use of atypical contracts to only four cases: temporary absence of a permanent employee, temporary increase of the firm's activity, seasonal work and sectors where it is unusual to have regular open-ended contracts. At the same time, the use of these atypical contracts was explicitly forbidden in the following cases: a permanent job, replacing a worker on strike, dangerous tasks, and using temporary work or fixed-term contracts within six months after a redundancy plan. In January 2002, the French parliament finally passed a government bill on 'social modernization' (Loi de Modernisation Sociale), in order to promote more stable employment by limiting precarious jobs and redundancies as well as fostering the continuous adaptation of workers' skills. It was a key piece of labour legislation.

An already existing 'precarious employment bonus', paid to fixed-term employees at the end of their contract, was increased from 6 to 10 per cent of gross wages, in line with the bonus paid to temporary agency workers. The period between two successive fixed-term contracts was also extended, in order to limit their use, and to end what was seen as abuse of the system. Essentially, these provisions are still in force today, although an additional cause was added for the usage of fixed-term contracts (see next section).

In the public sector, the main difference in terms of social protection and protection against dismissal exists between civil servants (*fonctionnaires*) and those on non-standard contracts. Under active public sector unions' pressure, successive policies have been implemented since the 1980s on, which explicitly aimed at curbing the development of non-standard public contracts. Various Acts were passed between 1983 and 1986, in the three *fonctions publiques* (central state, local and regional authorities, hospitals). The principle that fixed-term contracts were the exception was reaffirmed in a June 1983 Act. Yet, these measures did not prevent atypical employment in the public sector from increasing and two further Acts were passed (Loi Perben, in 1996 and Loi Sapin, in 2001) to integrate non-standard employees into the regular civil service. All in all, the proportion of non-standard contracts has remained rather stable in the years since 2000, at around 20 per cent for central state administration, 33 per cent for local and regional authorities and 5 per cent for public hospitals.

The public sector has certainly been the place where flexibilization has happened through the introduction of a spate of 'special contracts', mostly subsidized contracts (*contrats aidés*), of which the Contrat Emploi Solidarité (CES), renamed many times, was typical. As a result, while measures taken to integrate atypical public sector employees into the civil service have prevented their share of the workforce from increasing, a supplementary source of flexible manpower was added via the implementation of special contracts from the 1990s onwards. Fixed-term contracts in the public sector enjoy higher duration limits than in the private sector. On top of that, distinctions among non-standard contracts make some of them highly flexible and with significantly lower legal protection and lower social protection rights. This is particularly the case of the so-called *vacataires*, a category of workers who can be dismissed at the drop of a hat and who are specially numerous in education, culture and the post office.

Finally, another failed reform was attempted by the government in 2005–6 in two stages in order to promote 'flexibility'. First, a special contract (Contrat Nouvelle Embauche – CNE) with a trial period of two years was implemented for small firms and it encountered temporary success.

However, when in 2006 the government decided to extend it to the young, with the Contrat Première Embauche (CPE), this measure sparked off a large social movement (with the unanimous support of trade unions) and the prime minister was obliged to abandon the project. The CNE was later censured by the International Labour Organization (ILO), to be finally scrapped from the labour code definitely in 2008.

With regard to dismissals and redundancies, after the Second World War, legal restrictions were strong, and submitted to mandatory prior administrative 'authorization' for hiring and firing. In 1970, these provisions were restricted to collective dismissals for economic reasons. The authorization was dispensed with in 1986, under the pressure of employers' organizations arguing that the main obstacle to hiring was the restriction on firing, in the case of an economic downturn. Meanwhile, labour courts (Conseils des Prud'hommes, with representatives of workers and employers) were given a larger role in dealing with redundancies. In August 1989, initiated by the Socialist government, a new Act introduced a requirement, a social plan. This social plan was deemed to contain dismissals by exploring other alternatives, especially internal flexibility and retraining. When redundancies were unavoidable, the employer had the legal duty to participate in the retraining and the redeployment of displaced workers. The requirements implied by the social plan were supposed to be based upon the promotion of employability and not only on income compensation. These requirements were strengthened in 1992 and in 1993, with detailed provisions. Later, the 2002 LMS Act, already mentioned, tried to strengthen redundancy legislation: a more restrictive definition of collective dismissals for economic reasons excluded all other justifications than: (1) serious economic difficulties which the firm had been unable to solve by any other means; (2) technological developments threatening the company's survival; and (3) reorganization requirements which were vital to keep the company in business. This last provision was censured by the Constitutional Court. The Act also enhanced the rights of the works councils (Comités d'Entreprise). With the return of right-wing governments, legislation was again changed, as is described in the next paragraph.

The Current System: Main Characteristics

With regard to contracts, variety has remained a special characteristic of the French system. This situation of fragmentation has only been changed slightly by the important social partners' agreement in January 2008, now turned partly into law in June. In the private sector, basic contracts still comprise both regular and fixed-term contracts, as well as special temporary agency contracts, and apprenticeship contracts for the young.

Subsidized contracts for the unemployed are also still in force. In the public sector, non-standard contracts comprise very flexible and unprotected contracts, as well as implicitly open-ended contracts (*contractuels*) and *vacataires*. A reform of subsidized contracts in the public sector was announced but it is not yet clearly designed.

Dismissals in France fall in three types: (1) individual dismissal for serious causes; (2) individual dismissal for economic reasons; and (3) collective dismissals for economic reasons. In the first case, the serious cause may be for disciplinary motives, refusal of a substantive modification of the contract or incompetence; the employee can go to the labour court. In the second case, additional conditions apply and the employee may benefit from priority rehiring. In the third case, two scenarios arise: less than ten or more than ten employees are fired. In both cases, the labour administration has to be notified, and the works council to be informed, but the procedure is stricter when more than ten people are fired. Economists advocating more flexibility in France have chiefly criticized two aspects of the French legislation: the power given to judges and courts to appreciate the substance of economic motivation of the redundancies for economic reasons, and especially in the case when more than ten employees are fired, on the one hand; and, on the other, the alleged strictness of dismissals in the case of fixed-term contracts. It is impossible to go into the legal details here and, for the sake of comparing the French case to others, we can draw on the mainstream economists' critics. They state that, comparatively, the French system, before the June 2008 Act, was stricter and burdensome in five respects: burdensome and too long procedures; excessive intervention by the local labour department inspectors; an absence of incentive for conciliation in case of litigation; the low level of compensation payments; and, as already mentioned, an excessive protection for fixed-term contracts (Cahuc and Kramarz 2004). Their advice was to create a single contract and to introduce a '*bonus-malus*' system for employers which fire employees.

In their agreement of January 2008, the social partners stated that the 'serious cause' was a mainstream provision, which was inserted in the June 2008 Act. Four main points drawn from their agreement were translated into legal provisions: (1) a mainstream trial period[14] was decided at between four months (workers) and eight months maximum (managers); (2) an individual possibility was introduced to negotiate an exceptional 'agreed break-up' (*rupture conventionnelle*); (3) a new fixed-term contract was added (*contrat à objet défini* – defined purpose contract) for engineers and managers, which can last up to three years. All these provisions have increased the legal flexibility of employment relations, yet it remains to be seen how they will be used in the future. Interestingly, provisions that the social partners included in their January agreement, as for instance increased rights to benefits for the young unemployed, or new rights portable from firm to firm for employees, have not been dealt with in the June Act. Hence, the translation from the social partners' agreement into law should be seen as unbalanced, at least for the moment.

Legislation on redundancies has not been changed significantly. Labour market authorities have to be notified, and the social plans are still in force (labelled plan de sauvegarde de l'emploi since 2002).

Administration and Responsibilities

As for administration and responsibilities, it should briefly be said that the main responsibility stays with the Ministry of Employment, as the June Act illustrated. Social partners are invited to negotiate beforehand and legislation now recognizes their systematic involvement as of principle but, de facto, government retains (and uses) the arbitrary possibility of going against the rule, as has been constantly manifest in the years since 2000. Even in 2008, the government passed an Act in August, which dealt with provisions concerning unemployment insurance, without consulting social partners. Two other important actors are directly concerned with the administration of labour law, namely the works councils and the labour courts. Their role would be too complex to detail here and the recent reforms have not changed it significantly, with the exception of course of a general tendency to decentralize bargaining towards the firm level.

'ACTIVE' LABOUR MARKET POLICIES AND ACTIVATION STRATEGIES

As was already mentioned before, active labour market policies (ALMPs) are to be considered in a wider 'activation' perspective (Barbier 2004). PES activities as such are not always directly included under the ALMP heading; yet we will see in this section that PES reform is now essential.

The Main Reforms in the 1990s

The fact that France since the 1990s has failed to achieve full employment and has seen its unemployed population grow and remain stable is very well documented. Except for two periods (1988–90 and 1997–2001), unemployment rates were always high in European comparative terms. The unemployment rate was still over 7 per cent (mid-2008) before the crisis. Hence, for most of the period, French governments were confronted with the 'employer

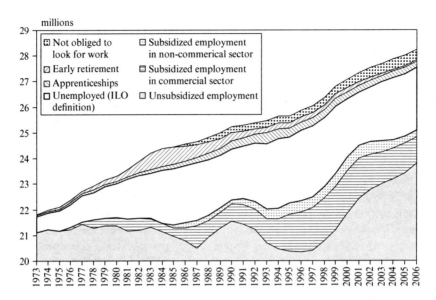

Source: DARES (2008), Statistics, Research Institute of French Ministry of Labour, France Metropolitaine (2008), Paris

Figure 8.1   Employment, inactivity and active labour market programmes in France, 1973–2006 (yearly mean stocks, millions)

of last resort' question (a question that has run through French history more or less since the French Revolution), the state being expected to provide temporary jobs when the market failed to deliver them. As a result – although never reaching levels observable in Sweden and Denmark – a significant proportion of gross domestic product (GDP) has been constantly devoted to employment expenditure (Barbier and Gautié 1998). From the 1980s on, as Keynesian full employment policies became obsolete, *politiques de l'emploi*[15] gradually emerged as a new and consistent policy area for social protection. Throughout the 1980s and into the early 2000s, programmes mixing both minimum income benefits and 'job creation' schemes were seen as one the main elements of *politiques de l'emploi*. In a nutshell, a mean yearly stock of 400 000 to 500 000 places was funded between 1993 and 2003 (see Figure 8.1).[16] Even in 2006, after a gradual decline, their stock figure was still close to 300 000. This provision was, however, never able to accommodate all target groups, thus ruining the programmes' claim to 'universal solidarity'. With the economic crisis, the government announced in the autumn of 2008 that the figure will rise again to more than 300 000.

Moreover, these programmes are but one of the elements to consider in painting a broader picture of French reform strategies. In a nutshell, up to 2007, the French 'activation strategy' was a combination of four more or less interlinked and more or less consistent actions. First, as already mentioned, was sustaining or enhancing the activation logic in the domain of income compensation, along with the management of insertion MIBs. Second, the central leg of active labour market policies has been the emergence and stabilization of a sector of employment programmes, well entrenched, mostly wage-based, with training programmes for the unemployed (this sector bears some resemblance with Scandinavian programmes and corresponds to the function of 'employer of last resort'). The implementation of this important provision of subsidized contracts was not inconsistent with the aforementioned PARE–PPAE reform in the unemployment insurance system. Third, a most consistent strategy has been pursued to foster the gradual decreasing of employers' social contributions, in the double goal of overhauling the funding principles of social protection as a whole (substituting taxes for social contributions), and of fostering employment creation. Fourth, a protracted, and mostly ineffective, strategy was initiated in the 1990s to reform labour market institutions: in 2008, this strategy eventually resulted in a major reform of these institutions, with the apparent support of social partners.

In a first period, from the late 1980s, programmes were gradually extended. They encompassed: (1) training schemes for the unemployed; (2) temporary subsidized employment in the public and non-profit sectors; and (3) subsidized contracts in the market sector for certain hard-to-place groups. Training programmes aside, almost all participants enjoyed a employee status (*statut de salarié*) and, consequently, were entitled to standard social protection rights (nevertheless, there has been a clear relationship between these schemes and the emergence of a 'working poor' stratum in France). The number of participants in the various employment programmes increased to about 11 per cent of the active population in the late 1990s (a stock of 3 million in 2000, if 330 000 older unemployed allowed not to seek work were included). Table 8.1 displays the main components of these programmes, including those for an early exit from the labour market, while Figure 8.1 puts them into a broader perspective.

Table 8.1 includes a stock of about 300 000 to 500 000 places for the temporary subsidized jobs in the public and non-profit sector, of which the CES (Contrats Emploi Solidarité) was emblematic.[17] As a result, during the period, all governments – despite obvious reluctance from the more liberal ones – have stuck to the logic of the state as an employer of last resort to a certain degree, for fear of being confronted with even higher unemployment figures and with recurring social demonstrations, such as those that occurred in 1995 and 1997. Overall, over the period,

Table 8.1   Employment programmes in France, 1995–2005 (end-of-year stocks of participants, 000s)

	1995	1998	1999	2000	2005
Subsidized contracts (private)[1]	1415	1689	1694	1573	1015
Subsidized contracts in the public and non profit sectors	458	438	493	521	275
Training schemes	344	316	315	287	262
Early retirement	195	185	173	164	67
Older unemployed allowed not to be active	279	276	300	335	405
Total	2692	2905	2975	2975	2147

Note: [1] Includes targeted subsidies and not general social contributions breaks.

Source: Ministry of Labour.

these programmes nevertheless failed to actually provide hard-to-place people (and the unemployed more generally) with effective transitions to conventional market jobs. Only a minority of CES participants succeeded in gaining such access. Other forms of temporary subsidized jobs, like the *emplois jeunes*,[18] have nevertheless yielded positive outcomes for participants (although net effects were controversial). Additionally, subsidies targeted to contracts for the long-term unemployed or RMI beneficiaries in the private sector have proved effective. Yet, while more similar to the Scandinavian 'employer of last resort' rationale than to a liberal one in this domain, the overall French policy appears to be only half-implemented, because of limited funding and quality. Hence, a significant proportion of employment programmes could certainly not be viewed as effective but, as in many other countries, they have certainly acted as ways of decreasing 'open unemployment'. These discouraging outcomes are a constant difficulty for politicians to legitimize programmes which they nevertheless continue to promote; such programmes also function as a tool for making the labour market more flexible, at its margins. They also concur to the increasing prevalence of inequality and segmentation and certainly foster the special relationship French society has built since the 1990s with the concept of *précarité* (Barbier 2008a).[19] Subsidized contracts in the private sector (Table 8.1) include all sorts of contracts with various types of social contributions breaks for targeted groups, for instance the long-term unemployed or apprentices, but these figures do not include general social contributions breaks,[20] which have represented the main element of the activation strategy in France for nearly ten years.

Indeed, although it has now become history, one should not forget that the socialist government implemented a new form of employment policy from 1998, namely the reduction of working time (RWT). Its rationale was job creation (RWT combined with social contributions reduction). With the return of a conservative government from May 2002, as the RWT was abandoned, it retained and even extended the logic of social contributions' reduction. In 2006, the overall expenditure devoted to 'active programmes' was estimated by the Ministry of Labour at about €13 billion, a sum which is about half the total cost to the budget of the general reduction of employers' social contributions (nearly €30 billion in the future for 2008).[21]

In the 1990s, both sums were comparable: this considerable change stresses how important it is to situate active labour market policies in a restricted sense, within the broader strategy of activating the system of social protection (Barbier 2004). Indeed, a short-sighted view of the 'activation' dynamics currently developing across EU countries would miss the connection between elements often referred to as 'workfare', and much wider-ranging reforms of 'tax and benefit' systems. In France, the activation dynamics has been implemented through an extensive reduction of labour costs and, only recently, emerging tax credits. On the reduction of social contributions side, there has been a gradual move from initially targeted measures to their 'quasi-generalization', accompanying the RWT for the lower-paid segments of the labour force. Debates and controversies exist over the estimated outcome of the protracted reduction of indirect labour costs. Finally, in 2001, the Jospin government added a tax credit, the Prime pour l'emploi (PPE), which is currently included in the RSA reform presented above. The PPE was supposed to function as an instrument against poverty and to represent an incentive for work. It was reformed in 2009 and merged with the new RSA. Contrary to analogous credits in other countries, the French programme was inserted as a new element into an already complex system. In 2007, 9 million persons were eligible on the basis of their 2006 income, about 33 per cent of employed people; the mean amount of the credit was €480 (about 4 per cent of their annual income derived from employment). It was estimated at that time that the impact of the PPE on the reduction of poverty was marginal and that its theoretical 'incentivizing' dimension was also marginal.

The Current System: Main Characteristics

In a nutshell, and in anticipation of the future adoption and subsequent implementation of the 2008 reforms, the French system can be seen as combining far-reaching and costly measures intended to foster job creation through decreasing labour costs, with traditional active labour market policies combining subsidies in the private and public sector with training schemes for the unemployed.

The insured unemployed persons are supposed to look actively for jobs, and, since the 2005 reform, sanctions have been strengthened, introducing new possibilities for the local state authority (the Préfet) of suspending and reducing benefits for non-compliance and for refusing offers from the PES. Before the 2005 reform, the Labour code essentially stated that the unemployed person had to accept offers in relation with their previous wage and occupation and according to their ability to be mobile. New opportunities were also included for the long-term unemployed and other targeted categories, subsidized contracts or training activities. Arguing that the labour code was not clear enough, and with comparison with other provisions in other countries, like Germany, a 2005 Act detailed the cases where refusals to comply were not acceptable and led to suspension (or reduction) of the insurance (or, for that matter, the ASS) benefits. However, no data about the effects of this reform were ever published. The sanction system remained in any case complex, because it involved many actors: the PES (Agence nationale pour l'emploi, now renamed Pôle Emploi after the merger described above), the ASSEDIC regional branch, and the employment department under the responsibility of the Préfet. Hence, deregistrations by the PES do not lead to homogeneous sanctions; this is even truer than, as was mentioned before, almost 40 per cent of the unemployed are not eligible to insurance or ASS benefits. Without waiting for evaluation data, in August 2008 the government passed a new Act, this time defining an 'acceptable offer' (*offre raisonnable*). Implementation of the new rules is still pending. After six months of unemployment, insured unemployed people will have to accept offers at 85 per cent of their previous wage and up to 30 km from their domicile (or one hour's travel, to and from). After one year, the offer will be deemed 'acceptable' at a wage equivalent to the benefit. Rights to appeal against the Préfet's decision will be curtailed.

This reform will be only one among others to be implemented in the context of the merging of ANPE and ASSEDIC networks. Given the difficulties encountered by any merger of two large organizations, the process will be painstaking. Adding that employment opportunities are insufficient, trade unions fear that the new reform will oblige the harder-to-place people to take precarious jobs and increase their work-poor situation. Against this, the government argues that the new RSA benefit will help them out of poverty. The answer lies in the future functioning, not of the sanctions, but of the new systemic consistency of reforms taken together: RSA reform, the merging of the PES and ASSEDIC networks, the subsidized contracts reform, and so on. Not to mention their interaction with the permanent reduction of employers' social contributions. The situation is further complicated by the fact that, most probably, only some of the RSA beneficiaries will be obliged to register at the newly merged PES, and to seek jobs. One should also remember that the current reforms[22] leave out AAH and ASS from their scope. ASS is the only MIB where claimants are, in theory, obliged to look for work, but only a minority (the younger) do so, older claimants being exempted when they are 57 until they become eligible for their pension. True, the August Act also provides, as was mentioned, for the gradual phasing out of the exemption by 2011.

In a way, although not presented together by the government, the 2007–8 reforms have certainly tended, in theory, to render unemployment policies much more systemically consistent. Before such consistency is actually translated into realities, the system will in any case take a long time to adjust. Moreover, old MIBs will remain in force, and the sustain-ability of the funding of the RSA reform – a significant extension of tax credits in a way, including the previous tax credit (PPE) – cannot be taken for granted.

Administration and Responsibilities

Finally, a supplementary condition for the success of these far-reaching reforms, currently under design and implementation, lies in the smooth cooperation between levels of government, most especially the local authorities (*départements*), but also the regions. The former have now acquired full responsibility for social assistance. The latter were given full competence in the area of occupational training. Many uncertainties still exist as to how compromises will eventually be struck, especially about the question of funding. Another great uncertainty lies in the final agreement and cooperation between the social partners (still competent for adminis-tering unemployment insurance) and the new agency which results from the merging of ASSEDIC and ANPE networks. To sum up: on paper, consistency has increased, but on paper only, and important elements of fragmentation remain.

CONCLUSION: A FRENCH PATH TO 'FLEXICURITY'?

What can be concluded from the analysis of the three policy areas in France? Our survey has amply documented the fact that all three are closely interlinked. Does this amount to 'French flexicurity'? Answering this question presupposes a definition of what 'flexicurity' is. 'Flexicurity' is not acceptable as a sociological concept for two fundamental reasons: contrary to economics, a discipline with highly stylized models, in sociology and political science the empirical documentation of an existing 'trade-off' between flexibility and security requires identifying the relevant social actors who, via their assessments and their individual and collective actions, accept that a balance exists in such and such a society; moreover the situation is more complicated than identifying 'trade-offs' as Schmid (2008) has rightly noted. If ample empirical evidence shows that in some countries policies referred to as 'flexicurity' policies are considered legitimate, and linked to active participation of the social actors (social partners, essentially), this has never been the case in France (Barbier 2007), and the main elements now stressed in this conclusive section show that a French version of 'flexicurity' is something yet to happen in the future.

France's labour market performance has tended to be among the laggards in the EU-15 in the 1990s–2000s. There prevails a structural difficulty in terms of labour market participation of the young and the older, and a clear inability so far to reforming early exit from the labour market. Moreover, whatever the reforms, they have occurred on the background of low employment creation and of an increased segmentation of the labour market, with certain categories in the workforce particularly affected by insecurity and instability, and low quality of jobs, while the majority have retained significantly better security and social protection rights. This situation is an additional facet of the French inability to achieve universalism. It bears many aspects: the fragmentation of the benefits system, the large variety of formal institutions involved in the treatment of 'non-employment' and the great variation of status among the unemployed and the assisted, as well as their labour market participation. As is typically illustrated in the case of the minimum income benefits, and especially RMI, whereas entitlements and rights are theoretically designed as universal, de facto eligibility is selective. This situation can be explained by many reasons: overload of services, scarcity of resources, actual targeting mechanisms.

A similar situation applies to the unequal access to places in employment or vocational training programmes. It leads to fragmentation rather than clear polarization (the opposition between better-quality mainstream insurance-linked provision and the lower quality of many assistance-linked provisions, but also to the increasing emergence of a 'working poor' stratum in French society) and labour market segmentation, along with the very high share of the French civil service in the labour force.

Finally, sweeping reforms are ongoing in the PES and the unemployment insurance fund. In the domain of assistance benefits and temporary subsidized jobs in the public and non-profit sector, results have really been disappointing. However, always in a significant number of cases, such subsidized jobs help transitions to the conventional labour market and are a source of income (albeit limited and increasing the number of the working poor); they also help beneficiaries keep contact with some forms of employment, and who express satisfaction at that. Insertion *sociale et professionnelle* has retained a positive function of political integration, but groups are excluded from access to it. One part of the French employment and assistance policy emerges as trying to implement a function of second-rate 'employer of last resort' which, only for some, opens the way to mainstream participation in the labour market, while a significant part of the population (with turnover) suffers from inequality and the increased complexity of subsidized contracts.

Altogether, in sociological terms, this cannot be termed '*flexicurité à la française*', because two ingredients are still lacking for this: the first is the documentation of the legitimacy of the system as it is, and as it is being reformed: legitimacy among social partners' elites and organizations, but also among employees, and especially the most exposed to the negative sides of employment and labour flexibility. The second aspect is the eventual sharing and implementation of the 'security' aspects of the current reforms: in this respect, inequality is overtly prevailing in the French arrangement.

NOTES

1. Strictly speaking, unemployment insurance is outside the scope of the social security system (*sécurité sociale*) which was established in 1945.
2. The minimum requirement for contribution to the fund was four months within the past eight months, thus excluding people in short-term employment from compensation. As for the duration of benefits, it was linked to the duration of contribution, with a maximum of 15 to 30 months: 15 months for those contributing for eight out of 12 months; 30 months for those having contributed for 14 out of 24 months.
3. Since its introduction in 1984, the insured unemployed who had exhausted their right to the mainstream insurance benefit and who had a sufficient employment record in the previous ten years became eligible to the ASS benefit, one of the MIBs.
4. Forty-eight per cent were eligible for the mainstream insurance benefit and 12 per cent for ASS in 2007.
5. UNEDIC is the national fund managed by the board of social partners who make all strategic decisions; the Associations pour l'Emploi dans l'Industrie et le Commerce (ASSEDICs) are the regional agencies which are present over the whole territory.
6. The 2007 target decided for the PES was contact with the unemployed on a monthly basis.
7. Indeed, successive 1988 and 1992 RMI Acts established RMI as an unconditional citizenship right. At the end of 2006, there were about 2.8 million MIB working-age recipients.
8. The Raffarin government introduced new legislation for RMI recipients after a certain period of eligibility. These individuals were supposed to be transferred to the RMA.

However, out of 1 million recipients at the end of 2005, about 15 per cent of RMI recipients had access to special employment programmes.

9.   The 2008 number of participants is still marginal at less than 15 000.
10. In 2007, there were still 360 000 people in this situation.
11. 'Accord sur la modernisation du marché du travail', 11 January 2008: although CGT participated in its negotiation, it did not eventually sign the agreement. The June 2008 Act turned only some of the provisions of the agreement into law.
12. The proportion of fixed-term contracts (in stocks) has been rather stable at around 9–10 per cent of the workforce in the years since 2000.
13. An 1979 Act limited the duration of fixed-term contracts to one year. A 1982 ordinance extended this duration to 18 months.
14. Exceptions are admitted for existing collective agreements. For fixed-term contracts the period is between two and four months. Mainstream notice periods after the trial period (which may be longer in collective agreements) are two weeks after one month, and one month after three months of employment. Severance payments are defined in collective agreements; they vary according to the type of dismissals and cannot be inferior to one-fifth of a month per year of employment, after one year of seniority.
15. The term used in French for an equivalent of active labour market policies.
16. The active population in France has been in the range of 24 million to 25.5 million in the 1990s. See Figure 8.1, which shows the evolution of the main elements of employment and labour market programmes in the last 30 years (Ministry of Labour figures).
17. From 2004–2005, this contract was reformed and renamed, but its basic rationale was not changed.
18. The *emplois-jeunes* (or nouveaux services-emplois jeunes, NSEJ) programme was one of two flagship programmes introduced by the Jospin government in 1997, along with the reduction of the working time. NSEJs were five-year 'temporary' contracts, signed by young people under 25 in associations and in the public sector. Whatever its final net outcome, and efficiency balance, the NSEJ programme showed that the French government could create and manage an important programme of public and non-profit jobs in times of a labour market boom, a programme not targeted at the low-skilled or the excluded and certainly not 'workfare'-like. The programme was cancelled by the Raffarin government in 2003. In summer 2005, the de Villepin government eventually reintroduced a similar programme in the public sector, although on a much smaller scale.
19. The English word is 'precariousness', it applies not only to employment but also to living conditions.
20. Employers' social contributions breaks apply under 1.3 minimum wage (SMIC) in 2009. Levels of reductions differ, but are at the highest at SMIC level (around 30 per cent of gross labour costs).
21. When the first social contributions reductions were implemented, a part was not compensated by the state budget. From 1995, it was decided that all reductions were to be compensated by transfers from the state budget to the *sécurité sociale* funds.
22. At the time of writing (October 2008).

REFERENCES

Barbier, J.-C. (2004), 'Systems of social protection in Europe: two contrasted paths to activation, and maybe a third', in J. Lind, H. Knudsen, and H. Jørgensen (eds), *Labour and Employment Regulation in Europe*, Brussels: PIE-Peter Lang, pp. 233–54.

Barbier, J.-C. (2005), 'Dealing anew with cross-national comparison: when words matter', in J.-C. Barbier and M.-T. Letablier (eds), *Politiques sociales/Social*

Policies: Enjeux méthodologiques et épistémologiques des comparaisons internationales/Epistemological and methodological issues in cross national comparison, Brussels: PIE Pieter Lang, pp. 45–68.

Barbier, J.-C. (2007), 'From political strategy to analytical research and back to politics, a sociological approach of "flexicurity"', in H. Jørgensen and P.K. Madsen (eds.), *Flexicurity and Beyond: Finding a New Agenda for the European Social Model*, Copenhagen: DJØF Publishing, pp. 155–88.

Barbier, J.-C. (2008a), 'There is more to job quality than "precariousness": a comparative epistemological analysis of the "flexibility and security" debate in Europe', in R. Muffels (ed.) *Flexibility and Employment Security in Europe*, Cheltenham, UK and Northampton, MA USA: Edward Elgar, pp. 31–50.

Barbier, J.-C. (2008b), *La longue marche de l'Europe sociale*, Paris : PUF, Le lien social.

Barbier, J.-C. and V. Fargion (2004), 'Continental inconsistencies on the path to activation: consequences for social citizenship in Italy and France', *European Societies*, **6**(4): 437–60.

Barbier, J.-C. and J. Gautié (eds) (1998), *Les politiques de l'emploi en Europe et aux Etats Unis*, Paris: PUF, Cahiers du CEE.

Barbier J.-C. and B. Théret (2001), 'Welfare to work or work to welfare, the French case', in N. Gilbert and R. Van Voorhis, *Activating the Unemployed: A Comparative Appraisal of Work-Oriented Policies*, Rutgers, NJ: Transaction Publishers, pp. 135–83.

Bouchoux, J., Y. Houzel, and J.-L. Outin (2004), 'Revenu minimum d'insertion et transitions: une analyse des inégalités territoriales', *Revue française des affaires sociales*, **4**: 107–32.

Bredgaard, T., F. Larsen and P.K. Madsen (2007), 'The challenges of identifying flexicurity in action – case study on Denmark', in H. Jørgensen and P.K. Madsen (eds), *Flexicurity and Beyond: Finding a New Agenda for the European Social Model*, Copenhagen: DJØF Publishing, pp. 365–90.

Cahuc, P. and F. Kramarz (2004), 'De la précarité à la mobilité, pour une sécurité sociale professionnelle', rapport commandé par F. Fillon, Paris: Documentation française.

Clegg, D. (2007), 'Continental drift: on unemployment policy change in Bismarckian welfare states', *Social Policy and Administration*, **41**(6): 597–617.

Daniel, C. and C. Tuchszirer (1999), *L'Etat face aux chômeurs, l'indemnisation du chômage de 1884 à nos jours*, Paris: Flammarion.

Dormont B., D. Faugère and A. Prieto (2001), 'L'effet de l'allocation unique dégressive sur la reprise d'emploi', *Economie et Statistique*, **343**: 3–28.

Jørgensen, H. and P.K. Madsen (2007), *Flexicurity and Beyond: Finding a New Agenda for the European Social Model*, Copenhagen: DJØF Publishing.

Schmid, G. (2008), *Full Employment in Europe: Managing Labour Market Transitions and Risks*, Cheltenham, UK and Northampton, MA, USA: Edward Elgar.

Wilthagen, T. (1998), 'Flexicurity: a new paradigm for labour market policy reform?' WZB papers FS I 98-202, Berlin.

9. Conclusion: is there a golden triangle?

Paul de Beer and Trudie Schils

In the preceding chapters the particular combination of unemployment insurance, employment protection and active labour market policies in seven European countries was examined. In this final chapter we summarize the main results and draw some overall conclusions from this overview. In the introductory chapter we noted that the empirical literature on the effectiveness of these policy instruments is at best mixed, but in general not very positive. In addition, we showed that a statistical analysis of the labour market performance of Organisation for Economic Co-operation and Development (OECD) countries based on global indicators of these three policy fields only gives limited insight into the effectiveness of the policy instruments. As we explained, this is probably due to the fact that it is much more the actual implementation and administration of these policies that matters, than some formal characteristics or the budget spent on these policies. Consequently, the main part of this volume comprises an extensive discussion of unemployment insurance, employment protection and active labour market policies in seven European countries, namely Belgium, Denmark, France, Germany, the Netherlands, Sweden and the United Kingdom. In each of the chapters the actual policies in the three areas are described, along with the main reforms since the 1990s and the coherence between the three policy areas. From these chapters it has become clear that, despite some similarities, the policies of these countries differ widely. However, since the number of characteristics in which the countries differ exceeds the number of the countries covered in this volume by far, it is not easy to pin down which factors are responsible for the differences in policy outcomes. In this final chapter we nevertheless attempt to trace some patterns and regularities which may give a clue as to which elements of the social policy triangle matter most. Thus, we hope to contribute to both the academic and the political debate on the optimal social policy mix.

We first discuss the similarities and differences between the seven countries for each of the policy areas separately. Next, we compare the countries with respect to the administration and coordination of social policy. Then we examine whether the policy reforms sinces the 1990s point towards convergence or divergence of social policy in these seven countries. In the next two sections we compare the output and outcomes of social policy and its impact on flexicurity. Finally, we try to answer the question of whether there is a golden triangle of social policy, after all.

UNEMPLOYMENT BENEFITS

The unemployment insurance schemes of the seven countries differ in many respects, which are only very partially reflected by the replacement rates (average benefit levels), as calculated by the OECD, which are often used to compare the generosity of unemployment benefits. Unemployment benefit schemes can differ in many more dimensions, namely:

- eligibility conditions, such as the required work record to qualify for a benefit, minimum working hours, or membership of an unemployment insurance fund;
- benefit level: flat rate or earnings-related (percentage of previous earnings), taking into account any income ceiling;
- benefit duration, depending on work record and/or age, and sometimes on the family situation;
- job search requirements, including the frequency of job applications required, the obligation to participate in activation programmes and the kind of job offer the unemployed person has to accept;
- existence of a means test;
- application of sanctions in case of non-compliance with the eligibility conditions;
- supplementary benefits and subsidies on top of the legal unemployment benefit, including semi-public and private employee benefits;
- benefit available after expiration of the earnings-related benefit and for those who are not entitled to an earnings-related benefit;
- funding: through payroll contributions, state subsidies or general taxes.

Even if two countries score equally on the replacement rate indicator of the OECD, the unemployment benefit schemes of these countries may differ considerably. Table 9.1 gives an overview of the main characteristics of the unemployment benefit schemes in the seven countries.

Exact information on some of the characteristics of the unemployment insurance schemes, such as work requirements, application of sanctions

Table 9.1 Main characteristics of unemployment benefits legislation in seven European countries

	Belgium	Denmark	France	Germany	Netherlands	Sweden	United Kingdom
Work record (% of previous period)	56.8	33.3	a. 27.3 b. 60.0 c. 61.5	50.0	a. 72.2 b. 80.0	50.0	96.2
Benefit level (if possible expressed for single person)	40–60% to flat-rate	a. 90% b. €18 725 p/y	75%	a. 60/67% (net) b. €351 p/m	a. 75% b. 70%	a. 80/70% b. €33 p/d	a. €76 p/w b. €76-194 p/w
Maximum yearly benefit	€13 728	€23 278	€11 092	€19 248 (W) €16 116 (E)	€33 928	€18 744	€10 103
OECD gross summary RR (%)	40.9	48.9	39.0	24.2	35.3	23.8	12.4
Benefit duration	phased, but infinite	a. 4 y b. infinite	a. 7 m b. 12 m c. 23 m	a. 6–18 m b. infinite	a. 3 m b. 38 m	300 d	a. 6 m b. infinite
Funding	contrib. + state subsidy	contrib. + state subsidy	contrib.	a. contrib. b. taxes	contrib.	contrib. + state subsidy	a. contrib. b. taxes

Note: Denmark: a. uninsured workers, b. insured workers. France: a. when contributed 6 out of 22 months, b. when contributed 12 out of 20 months, c. when contributed 16 out of 26 months. Germany: a. Arbeitslosengeld-I, b. Arbeitslosengeld-II. Netherlands: a. short-term benefit, b. extended benefit if both work conditions are fulfilled. Sweden: a. universal basic unemployment insurance, b. voluntary income-related unemployment insurance. United Kingdom: a. contribution-based Job Seekers Allowance, b. Income-based Job Seekers Allowance.

Source: Chapters 2–8.

and existence of supplementary benefits, is not available, so the differences between the schemes are even larger than can be read from Table 9.1. The conditions one has to fulfil to be eligible for an unemployment benefit vary strongly. In Denmark it is rather easy to claim a benefit, even with a brief or interrupted work career, while the English scheme requires an almost continuous work history. Most countries have a combination of flat-rate and earnings-related benefits, depending on one's work history and/or membership of an insurance fund. Even though the formal replacement rates of the unemployment benefit lie within a rather narrow range (from 60 per cent to 90 per cent), the actual benefit level may vary more widely, due to the applicable income ceiling and/or supplemental benefits. This is illustrated by the wide dispersal of the maximum benefit level, which ranges from a little over €10000 a year in France and the UK to more than €30000 in the Netherlands. There are also large differences in maximum duration of the unemployment benefit, which ranges from three months to 'infinity'. Although most unemployment insurance schemes are contribution-based, in most countries there is also some kind of state support, either directly from taxes or as a subsidy to the insurance funds.

If one tries to arrange the unemployment insurance schemes in order of generosity, the Danish unemployment benefit appears to be the most generous (weak eligibility criteria, high replacement rate, long duration) and the British the least generous (strict eligibility criteria, flat-rate benefit and short duration for the contribution-based benefit). However, one should take into account that there are some supplementary benefits in the UK, such as housing benefits, which raise the effective replacement rate in cases of unemployment. The other countries are more difficult to rank, since most of them are relatively generous in one respect (for example, replacement rate) and rather harsh in another (for example, maximum duration).

EMPLOYMENT PROTECTION LEGISLATION

The well-known OECD employment protection indicator is a summary measure for a large number of characteristics of the employment protection legislation of different countries. However, it does not include all elements of employment protection legislation and the weighing of the elements is rather arbitrary. Moreover, it is based purely on legal characteristics at the national level. This means, for example, that the weight attached to the maximum duration of temporary contracts is independent of the number of temporary workers in a country. Neither does the indicator take into account that, in most countries, the social partners are allowed to deviate from the legal rules by collective agreement, in some cases even to the detriment of the employees.

It can, thus, be rightfully questioned whether the OECD indicator really measures the strictness of employment legislation in various countries. Although some initiatives are being taken to improve the OECD indicator, these will probably not neutralize all its drawbacks. It is even doubtful whether it makes sense at all to try to summarize the information on employment protection in one figure. Therefore, Table 9.2 gives an overview of the main characteristics of employment protection legislation – and the possibility of social partners to deviate from it – in the seven countries.

In all countries, notice periods depend on the seniority of the worker, but while the difference between workers with long tenure and with short tenure is very large in Belgium, Germany, Sweden and the UK, it is much smaller in Denmark, France and the Netherlands. Remarkably, in Belgium and Denmark the notice period also differs considerably between blue-collar workers and white-collar workers. The maximum notice period varies from three months in the Netherlands and the UK to 15 months in Belgium. Only in France and in the UK are employers legally obliged to pay severance pay. In the Netherlands this is only the case if employers dismiss employees via the court route, while in Denmark severance pay is regulated by collective agreement. In four countries there is a legal trial period, while in the other three countries this is agreed upon in individual contracts or collective agreements. An important distinction between the countries concerns the existence of legal restrictions on the use of fixed-term contracts. In Belgium, France and Sweden, employers are allowed to hire temporary workers only in specific circumstances. The other four countries only have legal restrictions on the maximum duration or the maximum number of consecutive temporary contracts. Finally, an important but often overlooked point is whether social partners are allowed to deviate by collective agreement from the legal regulations regarding dismissals and fixed-term contracts. In Belgium, Denmark, France, Germany, the Netherlands and Sweden this is indeed the case, which means that national law only partially defines the practice of dismissal regulation in these countries.

On the basis of Table 9.2 it is not easy to rank the seven countries with respect to the strictness of employment protection. Although the UK and Denmark are, according to the OECD employment protection indicator, considered to have relative weak employment protection, this is not immediately apparent from the other information in this table. And although Belgium, France, Germany and the Netherlands score relatively high on the OECD indicator, they do not differ that much from Denmark with

Table 9.2 *Main characteristics of employment protection legislation in seven European countries*

	Belgium	Denmark	France	Germany	Netherlands	Sweden	United Kingdom
Average notice period after:							
– 9 m tenure	bc: 35 d wc: 3 m	bc: 3 w wc: 3 m	1 m	4 w	1 m	1 m	0.2 m
– 5 y tenure	bc: 35 d wc: 3 m	bc: 8 w wc: 4 m	2 m	1 m	1 m	3 m	0.9 m
– 20 y tenure	bc: 112 d wc: 15 m	bc: 10 w wc: 6 m	2 m	7 m	3 m	6 m	2.8 m
Average severance pay after:							
– 9m tenure	0	0	0	0	0	0	0
– 5y tenure	0	0	0.6 m	0	6 m[a]	0	1.1 m
– 20y tenure	0	bc: 0 wc: 3 m	4 m	0	18 m[a]	0	4.6 m
Average trial period	no law, practice: bc: 7-14 d wc: 1–6 m	bc: 9 m wc: 12 m	no law, practice bc: 1-2 w wc: 1–3 m	6 m	1–2 m	max 6 m	agreed in individual contract

Table 9.2 (continued)

	Belgium	Denmark	France	Germany	Netherlands	Sweden	United Kingdom
Legislation on fixed-term contracts	Restricted use, max 4 successive contracts	Allowed for specific periods of time or tasks, max 2–3 years	Restricted use, max 2 successive contracts	Allowed for max of 2 years and 4 renewals	Allowed for max of 3 years or 3 renewals	Restricted use, objective situations	Allowed for max of 4 years
Deviation by collective agreements?	yes, but limited	yes	yes	yes	yes	yes	no
OECD EPL indicator (2003):							
– regular workers	1.7	1.5	2.5	2.7	3.1	2.9	1.1
– temp. workers	2.6	1.4	3.6	1.8	1.2	1.6	0.4
– overall	2.2	1.4	3.0	2.2	2.1	2.2	0.7

Notes:
bc: blue-collar workers; wc: white-collar workers.
[a] Netherlands: only in case of dismissal through Court.

Sources: Chapters 2–8 this volume; and OECD (2004), *Economic Outlook*, Paris: OECD.

respect to notice period, severance pay and trial period. It thus strongly depends on which elements of employment protection legislation one focuses on, as to whether the employment protection in a particular country is to be considered stricter or looser than in another country.

ACTIVE LABOUR MARKET POLICIES

Active labour market policies include a broad range of activation measures, from registration and counselling to workfare and subsidized employment. Most countries employ a number of instruments. Usually, it is left to the professionals of the Public Employment Service (PES) or the administrative body of the unemployment benefit to decide in which kind of programme an unemployed person – or someone else who seeks work – participates. The official labour market policy of the national government is, thus, often not very relevant in comparing the active labour market policies of different countries. That is why total expenditure on active labour market policy is most often used as a measure to compare the effort of different countries (see Table 9.3). However, this figure hardly informs us about the real effort, since the costs of activation programmes may differ enormously. A country that focuses on costly measures, such as subsidized jobs, may spend more on active labour market policies and at the same time reach much fewer unemployed than another country that spends less on such policies but concentrates on cheaper measures, such as job counselling. Apart from the kind of activation programmes, it is also of interest which body administers and implements the programmes and whether benefit recipients are obliged to take part in these programmes.

It is not possible to summarize this qualitative information in the form of a table. However, from the description of active labour market policy in the country chapters it is warranted to conclude that Denmark and Sweden have the most extensive activation programmes, including counselling, training and employment subsidies. The United Kingdom is generally thought to rely more on an unfettered market mechanism than on state intervention. Nevertheless, since the late 1990s the British government has implemented a rather ambitious activation programme. So it is questionable whether the UK should still be considered a laggard with respect to active labour market policy. For a long time, the conservative welfare states of Belgium, France, Germany and the Netherlands focused much more on passive, income-protection measures than on active labour market policies. However, this has changed largely since the 1990s. So, arguably, there is no longer a large gap between the activation efforts of the Scandinavian countries and of the Continental welfare states.

Table 9.3 Output of social policy in seven European countries (averages for 1991–95 and 2001–2005)

	BE		DE		DK		FR		NL		SE		UK	
	91–95	01–05	91–95	01–05	91–95	01–05	91–95	01–05	91–95	01–05	91–95	01–05	91–95	01–05
Unemployment benefits														
Expenditures (% GDP)	3.1	3.2	1.6	1.7	4.8	3.1	1.7	1.7	2.7	1.4	2.3	1.2	0.7	0.3
Benefit claimants (% of labour force)	n.a.	10.1	n.a.	4.6	n.a.	5.5	n.a.	7.6	n.a.	4.3	n.a.	3.9	n.a.	3.1
Employment protection legislation														
Average job tenure	10.7	11.6	10.0	10.6	7.9	8.3	10.2	11.4	8.4	10.1	10.3	10.9	7.8	8.1
Active labour market policy														
Expenditures (% GDP)	1.1	1.1	1.3	1.1	1.3	1.9	1.1	1.1	1.4	1.5	2.6	1.4	0.5	0.5
Number of participants (% of labour force)	n.a.	8.3	n.a.	4.8	n.a.	5.3	n.a.	2.9	n.a.	4.2	n.a.	5.6	n.a.	0.6
Ratio of participants ALMP to benefit claimants	n.a.	0.82	n.a.	1.04	n.a.	0.96	n.a.	0.38	n.a.	0.98	n.a.	1.44	n.a.	0.19

Source: OECD (2004), *Employment Outlook*, Paris: OECD; data taken from chapter in this volume.

ADMINISTRATION AND COORDINATION OF THE POLICY INSTRUMENTS

Although, in theory, unemployment insurance, employment protection legislation and active labour market policies can be considered as the angles of a social policy triangle, in practice they usually do not form a well-designed and logically consistent policy mix. With respect to the implementation and administration of unemployment insurance and active labour market policies there is some coordination in most countries. Indeed, in five of our seven countries one public body at the local (mostly municipal) level is responsible for the administration of both instruments. Still, the funding of the benefits and of the activation measures is often separate. The administration of employment protection legislation is usually assigned to separate bodies (such as labour courts). Political debates about reforms of the social security system and active labour market programmes are seldom connected to reforms of employment protection legislation. Even in Denmark, whose particular combination of policy instruments is lauded as a golden triangle, the three policy areas have a very different history and cannot be considered to be a consciously designed policy mix.

In most countries there is also a rather sharp dividing line between the administration of unemployment insurance and the administration of the means-tested benefit (social assistance or otherwise) for the unemployed who do not comply with the eligibility criteria for the unemployment insurance or whose earnings-related benefit has expired. As a consequence, there is often a lack of coordination between the administration of policy instruments for the short-term unemployed on the one hand and for the long-term unemployed and the unemployed with limited work history on the other hand.

In three of the seven countries considered, namely Belgium, Denmark and Sweden, the trade unions play a role in the administration of unemployment insurance. This involvement of trade unions is often referred to as the Ghent system. However, as the description of the unemployment insurance in the country chapters shows, the role of the trade unions in the administration of unemployment benefits is actually very limited. They act primarily as a kind of broker between the insured employees and unemployed and the insurance system, but they do not have the authority to decide on either the insurance policies or the actual granting of benefits.

Perhaps more important, but often overlooked in the literature, is the competence of the social partners in six of our countries (Belgium, Denmark, France, Germany, the Netherlands and Sweden) to overrule the national legislation with respect to employment protection by collective labour agreement. This means that the legal characteristics of employment protection legislation, as measured in the OECD employment protection indicator, may be of limited relevance in practice.

POLICY REFORMS SINCE THE 1990S

All seven countries covered in this book have revised their social policies considerably in the past 10–20 years. Although it was impossible to give a complete overview of the policy reforms since the 1990s, each country chapter enumerates the main policy changes. From these overviews we can conclude that there are some common elements in the policy reforms since the 1980s.

The most general statement one can make about these reforms is that they embody a general shift from passive to active measures. By this we do not so much refer to the ratio of expenditure on active versus passive measures, which has risen in only four of the seven countries (Table 9.3). We mainly point to the stronger emphasis on the obligations of benefit claimants. Many countries have tightened eligibility conditions, either by making it harder to claim a benefit or by strengthening the requirements on benefit recipients with respect to search effort, participation in training and/or accepting job offers. In some cases recipients are even required to perform unpaid work (workfare) in exchange for their benefit.

Although only four of the seven countries have actually increased their spending on active labour market policy, relative to unemployment benefits, the linkage between participation in such policies and benefit eligibility has become stronger in most countries. Thus, the motivation effect of active labour market policy has become more important in comparison to the qualification effect.

Although eligibility conditions for unemployment benefits may have become stricter, the income protection offered to those unemployed who are eligible does not seem to have changed much in most countries. This is shown by the replacement rates as calculated by the OECD, which have only changed a little since the early 1990s. Two notable exceptions are the Netherlands and Germany. In the Netherlands, the main change was a considerable reduction of the maximum duration of the earnings-related unemployment benefit. This reform primarily affects older workers. In the early 1990s an employee aged 57.5 years or older could apply for an earnings-related benefit until the official retirement age of 65; nowadays the maximum duration of the earnings-related benefit is 38 months, after which he or she has to apply for social assistance. In Germany, the so-called Hartz reforms included a radical change of the unemployment benefit system (Hartz IV). Overall, this change meant a reduction of the generosity of the benefits for the long-term unemployed. In the other countries, there were only minor changes in benefit generosity. In Sweden, for example, compensation rates were reduced during the 1990s, but this is hardly visible in the OECD replacement rates.

Perhaps the most controversial element of the policy triangle is employment protection legislation. Most economists and employers consider employment protection legislation (EPL) to be a formidable obstacle to a flexible labour market and are thus in favour of loosening employment protection as much as possible. Most trade unionists and even a majority of the population usually consider employment protection to offer essential protection against the vicissitudes of the free market, and therefore strongly resist any attempt to reduce employment protection, at least for regular workers. It is thus not surprising that governments that wanted to relax employment protection have focused on the regulation of temporary employment. Employment protection legislation for temporary work has thus been deregulated in all the countries considered, with the exception of France and of the UK, in which temporary work was hardly regulated at all in the early 1990s. Insofar as governments tried to reform employment protection legislation for permanent workers since the 1990s, they were not very successful in doing so. Best-known are the riots in the *banlieus* of Paris after the announcement by the government of the introduction of a new flexible contract for youngsters. But also the Dutch government met with fierce resistance from the trade unions and the left-wing parties in parliament when it announced a reform of EPL in 2007. In 2008, it finally reconciled itself with a marginal change of the legal system.

A final common trend in social policy is the attempt of various countries to increase the coordination between the administration of unemployment benefits and active labour market policy. In Germany, the Federal Employment Office (BA) has for a long time been responsible for both the payment of unemployment benefits (ALG I) and the implementation of labour market programmes for the short-term unemployed. In Belgium, the local employment offices perform the administration of unemployment benefits and part of the activation instruments. In 2006, the administration of unemployment benefits (by Benefit Agencies) and labour market policies (by Employment Services) at the local level in the United Kingdom was merged into so-called Jobcentres Plus. Very recently, in January 2009, the public bodies responsible for administration of the unemployment benefits and for activation measures in France and the Netherlands have been merged. Although the other countries still have separate bodies for these two parts of social policy, cooperation between these bodies has been strengthened.

At the same time the responsibility of the social partners for the admin-istration and supervision of social insurance and labour market policies was restricted in a number of countries. In the Netherlands, the social partners were completely banned from the administration; in Germany and Sweden their role was considerably limited.

THE OUTPUT OF SOCIAL POLICY

In this section we give an overview of what might be called the direct output of social policy. By this we refer to some variables which are directly related to the policy, although we readily concede that they are also affected by other factors.

The output of unemployment benefit systems can best be measured by total expenditure on unemployment benefits and by the number of benefit claimants. The first two rows of Table 9.3 give figures for these two indica-tors for our seven countries, for both the early 1990s and the early 2000s. The expenditure and the number of beneficiaries vary widely between these countries. Belgium and Denmark lead the pack both with respect to expenditure and benefit claimants, while the UK lags behind. This is not unexpected in view of the characteristics of the benefit systems as described in the country chapters. Denmark and Belgium have quite generous unem-ployment benefits systems, although in Belgium this refers primarily to the unlimited duration of the benefit and in Denmark to the replacement rate. The very large number of benefit claimants in Denmark is probably due to the loose employment protection and flexible labour market, which causes a large inflow into (but also a large outflow from) unemployment (see next section). Germany, France, the Netherlands and Sweden take an intermediate position. The rather low expenditure on unemployment benefits in Sweden is remarkable, since Sweden used to be one of the most generous welfare states in the world. Since the relative number of benefit claimants in Sweden is larger than in Germany, while expenditure is lower, this suggests that the Swedish unemployment insurance is rather austere. However, one should take into account that in Sweden many of the unemployed receive supplementary benefits, often agreed upon in col-lective labour agreements or paid out by voluntary trade union insurance schemes, which are not included in the OECD figures for unemployment compensation in Table 9.3. Hence, expenditure on unemployment benefits in Sweden might be substantially higher if these supplementary benefits are included.

The only indicator for the output of employment protection for which we have international comparable data is average job tenure. (Unfortunately, no figures on the numbers of dismissals are available.) Average job tenure of the seven countries lies within a rather narrow band from about eight to 11 years. Nevertheless, there is a clear dividing line between Denmark and the United Kingdom, with average tenure around eight years, and the other five countries with tenure around 11 years. Since Denmark and the UK have the least strict employment protection legislation of the seven countries, this is exactly what could be expected.

Similarly as with unemployment benefits, the output of active labour market policies (ALMPs) can be measured by expenditures (in percentage of gross domestic product, GDP) and by the number of participants (expressed as a percentage of the labour force). Denmark spends by far the most on ALMPs, namely 1.9 per cent of GDP, while the UK spends the least, namely 0.5 per cent. Again, this is what could be expected from the description of ALMPs in the country chapters. Although Belgium, Germany, the Netherlands and Sweden spend considerably less on ALMPs than Denmark, the numbers of participants do not differ much from the Danish number. This suggests that Denmark exerts more effort (in terms of expenditure) per ALMP participant than the other four countries. The same appears to apply to French ALMP. In all countries, with the exception of France and the UK, the number of unemployment benefit claimants and the number of participants in activation programmes are similar. In Sweden, even more people participate in ALMP than claim unemployment benefits. In France and the UK the relative number of participants in activation measures is much smaller, which suggests that many unemployed are not reached by ALMP. Overall, the output of the three policy areas is consistent with what one would expect on the basis of the qualitative description of these policies in the country chapters. Generous unemployment benefit systems result in high expenditure and a large number of benefit claimants; strict employment protection legislation translates into long job tenure; and intensive ALMPs result in high expenditure and many participants.

THE IMPACT OF SOCIAL POLICY ON LABOUR MARKET PERFORMANCE AND INCOME SECURITY

The output indicators discussed in the preceding section do not really inform us about the effectiveness of social policy with respect to its ultimate goals: a well-functioning, flexible labour market and sufficient protection of workers against the income and employment risks of a market economy. In Chapter 1 we introduced a number of indicators for flexibility and security. In this section we show the outcomes of these indicators for the seven countries that this study focuses on in more detail.

As we noted above, the large number of characteristics in which the policy triangles of the seven countries differ make it almost impossible to determine which elements are crucial in explaining the differences in outcomes of social policy in these countries. Indeed, it is very possible that other policies outside the social policy triangle, such as general economic policy, tax policies, education policies, wage formation and industrial relations, and exogenous factors such as demographic developments and economic structure, also influence the outcomes. Thus, our attempt to connect characteristics of the social policy triangle to some socio-economic indicators serves only an illustrative purpose. We certainly do not claim to explain the differences in outcomes from particular elements of the social policy triangle. Nevertheless, it is certainly informative to examine to what extent the socio-economic performance of the seven countries differ. In this way we want to illustrate to what extent the variation and similarities in the policy mix of the seven countries are reflected in their labour market performance. This gives us at least an indication of the extent to which social policy matters, but also to what extent other factors have to be brought into the picture to understand the differences in performance between the countries.

Table 9.4 gives an overview of some indicators for employment security, labour market flexibility and income security, respectively, for the seven countries. We calculated average figures for the early 1990s (1991–5) and for the most recent five-year period (2003–7) in order to minimize the effect of the business cycle on the outcomes. We first focus on the outcomes for the most recent years and then discuss the changes that have taken place since the 1990s.

If we take the employment rate (measured as the number of employed as a share of the population aged 15–64) and the unemployment rate (the number of unemployed as percentage of the labour force) to be the best available indicators for employment security, then Table 9.4 shows that there are considerable differences between the seven countries. Overall, Denmark, the Netherlands, Sweden and the UK score best on these indicators and Belgium, Germany and France the worst. In the first three countries the employment rate is on average about ten percentage points higher than in the other four countries, while the unemployment rates in the latter group are about one and a half time the figures for the first group.

With respect to labour market flexibility again two groups can be distinguished, but this time the Netherlands falls into the group of Belgium, Germany and France, with rather small inflows into both employment and unemployment and, consequently, a rather large share of long-term unemployed and long average unemployment duration. The inflow

Table 9.4 Indicators for employment protection, labour market flexibility and income security for seven European countries (averages for 1991–5 and 2003–7ᵃ)

	BE		DE		DK		FR		NL		SE		UK	
	91–95	03–07	91–95	03–07	91–95	03–07	91–95	03–07	91–95	03–07	91–95	03–07	91–95	03–07
Employment security														
Employment rate (% of population 15–64)	56	61	66	66	74	76	59	63	64	72	75	74	69	73
Unemployment (% of labour force)	8	8	7	10	9	5	11	9	6	5	8	7	9	5
Labour market flexibility														
Inflow into employment[b]	11	13	14	14	22	23	14	15	13	9	14	18	17	19
Inflow into unemployment[c]	8	6	9	6	19	12	5	4	5	2	16	17	12	10
Share of temporary work (% of dependent employment)	5	9	10	13	12	10	11	13	10	16	.	16	6	6
Share of long-term unemployment (% of total unemployment)	59	51	40	54	29	21	38	41	48	38	19	17	39	23

213

Table 9.4 (continued)

	BE		DE		DK		FR		NL		SE		UK	
	91–95	03–07	91–95	03–07	91–95	03–07	91–95	03–07	91–95	03–07	91–95	03–07	91–95	03–07
Average unemployment duration (months)	12.7	11.5	10.0	12.0	8.3	6.8	9.3	10.0	10.8	9.7	6.5	5.7	9.8	7.0
Income security														
Average income loss due to unemployment[d]	62	33	66	72	15	4	73	68	37	26	50	70	83	90
Expected income loss due to unemployment[e]	7.2	2.4	4.9	6.8	1.4	0.2	7.2	5.8	2.5	1.1	4.1	4.3	7.7	4.3

Notes:
[a] Average for 2001–5 for income security
[b] The number of employed who have their present job for less than one year as a percentage of the labour force. These figures are an estimate of the average annual inflow into employment from 1992 to 1996 and from 2003 to 2007, respectively
[c] The number of unemployed who are unemployed less than one month, multiplied with 12 as a percentage of the labour force. These figures are an estimate of the annual inflow into unemployment
[d] Calculated as the average replacement rate for all unemployed as a percentage of the average wage. This percentage is subtracted from 100 to get the average income loss as a percentage of the average wage. The average replacement rate is calculated as the average expenditure on unemployment benefits per unemployed person (including those without a benefit) divided by the total compensation for employees per full-time employee.
[e] Calculated as the unemployment rate multiplied by the average replacement rate for all unemployed (see note c) as a percentage of the average wage. This percentage is subtracted from 100 to get the expected income loss as a percentage of the average wage.

Source: OECD (2008) Labour Force Statistics and author's calculations taken from chapters in this volume.

into employment and into unemployment in the other three countries, Denmark, Sweden and the UK, is much larger. There is however no systematic difference in the share of temporary employment between the two groups. The relatively small labour market flows in Belgium, France, Germany and the Netherlands are consistent with the rather strict employment protection legislation in these countries. Likewise, the large flows in Denmark and the UK can be explained by the very loose employment protection. However, the high labour market flexibility of Sweden is surprising in view of the fact that the level of employment protection legislation in Sweden is, according to the OECD employment protection indicator, the second highest of the seven countries.

When it comes to income security, the dividing line runs between Belgium, Denmark and the Netherlands on the one hand, and the other countries on the other hand. In Denmark and the Netherlands both the average income loss in case of unemployment and the expected income loss due to unemployment (which takes the probability of unemployment into account) are by far the lowest of the seven countries considered. This is explained by the combination of a high replacement rate and a high coverage rate of unemployment insurance and a relatively low unemployment rate. To be sure, the unemployment risk in Belgium is much higher, but thanks to the generous unemployment benefit system, and the high coverage rate in particular, the expected income loss due to unemployment is quite small.

In the other four countries, the average income loss in cases of unemployment is much larger, either due to low replacement rates or low coverage rates of the unemployment benefit schemes. Since Germany and France also have a relatively high unemployment rate, the expected income loss due to unemployment is even higher than in the UK, where the unemployment risk is considerably smaller. It should be noted, however, that the figures in Table 9.4 exclude supplementary benefits, such as housing benefits, which can make up a substantial part of total compensation of the unemployed, especially in Germany and the UK.

If we take all flexicurity indicators in Table 9.4 into consideration, we can conclude that Belgium, Germany and France show the worst overall performance of the seven countries considered. Denmark scores best, overall. Sweden and the UK follow closely behind, but do not perform very well with respect to income security. The Netherlands, too, lags only a little behind Denmark with respect to the security indicators, but it stays far behind with respect to the flexibility indicators.

The distinction between Belgium, Germany and France on the one hand and Denmark, Sweden and the UK on the other is not surprising, in view of our analysis of the social policy mix. The former countries are typical examples of the conservative Continental welfare regime (according to Esping-Andersen 1990, 1999) which focus primarily on securing the position of the insiders on the labour market (male breadwinners in particular) and not on promoting labour participation of 'marginal' groups (women, youth, older persons) or stimulating flows between employment and unemployment. Thus, strict employment protection results in long job tenure and small inflows into unemployment, but also into unemployment. However, for workers who lose their job all the same, and for those who are not able to find a job, income protection is rather austere. Belgium is an exception in this respect, since the unlimited duration of unemployment benefits provides more income protection than the unemployment benefits of the two other conservative welfare states.

Denmark and Sweden are the exemplary social-democratic welfare states, which stress the importance of labour participation for all. This is expressed in the high employment rate and relatively low unemployment rate in these two countries. More remarkable is the high labour market flexibility of both countries, as shown by large inflows into employment and unemployment. In the case of Denmark this is understandable on account of the rather loose employment protection legislation. The large flows between employment and unemployment in Sweden are harder to explain, since employment protection is rather strict in this country. Perhaps the large share of temporary work might be the explanation, but then it is surprising that the Netherlands, which has the same share of temporary work, has the smallest inflows into employment and unemployment of all seven countries. A remarkable finding is that income security in Sweden is rather low. In the past Sweden used to be the most generous welfare state which provided extensive income protection to all who lost their job. However, in the 1990s, after Sweden went through a deep recession, benefit eligibility and benefit levels were considerably curtailed, resulting in much less income protection than before. Thus, average income loss in cases of unemployment increased from 50 per cent in the early 1990s to 70 per cent in 2007. However, one should take into account that in Sweden many unemployed receive supplementary benefits, often agreed upon in collective labour agreements or paid out by voluntary trade union insurance schemes, which are not included in the OECD figures for unemployment compensation in Table 9.4. Hence, income security in Sweden might be substantially higher if these supplementary benefits were included.

The Netherlands is unique among the seven countries in combining high levels of both employment security and income security with a very low labour market flexibility, at least with respect to regular work. Apparently, the rather large number of temporary workers absorbs most of the flexibility of the Dutch labour market. Probably, this also explains why the inflow into employment fluctuates strongly over the business cycle. In the years 2000 and 2001 the inflow into employment in the Netherlands was comparable to that in Denmark and the UK. So, the fluctuation of employment over the business cycle seems to be largely cushioned by temporary work in the Netherlands. This might be caused by the fact that, while employment protection for regular contracts in the Netherlands is the second strictest of the seven countries considered, the protection of temporary workers is the most lenient after the UK. Although this large gap in employment protection between permanent and temporary workers has met with a lot of criticism in the Netherlands lately, it does not seem to be a real barrier to a good performance with respect to overall employment and income security. Apart from temporary work, the large and increasing share of part-time work in the Netherlands might also contribute to a smooth adjustment of employment to the needs of companies.

If we now focus on the outcomes for the early 1990s the overall picture does not change much. Denmark was already the best-performing country with respect to employment security, labour market flexibility and income security in the beginning of the 1990s, while Belgium, Germany and France were already lagging behind in most respects. The only exception regards the unemployment rate, which was the second highest in Denmark in the first half of the 1990s. Since the unemployment rate is often taken as the most obvious indicator for the functioning of the labour market, it is understandable why in the 1990s Denmark was not yet recognized as an example for other countries. The Netherlands was the most successful in raising the employment rate since the early 1990s, followed by Belgium and the UK. It is not easy to connect this improvement to the policy reforms in these countries, since they were quite dissimilar. The rise of the employment rate in the Netherlands is explained primarily by the strong growth of female labour participation, which was not directly related to the social policy triangle. It is remarkable that the flows between employment and unemployment in the Netherlands dwindled at the same time, although the share of temporary work increased quite strongly. In the other countries, labour market flows and temporary work did not change significantly often the early 1990s. With respect to income security, the changes diverge. In Belgium, Denmark, France and the Netherlands both the average income loss and the expected income loss due to unemployment diminished, while they rose in Germany and Sweden. In the latter countries this was caused by both a reduction of the generosity of unemployment insurance and an increase of the unemployment risk.

Overall, it is quite difficult to explain the changes of the flexicurity indicators in our seven countries from the policy reforms that were implemented since the 1990s. This suggests that the evolution of labour market performance is also strongly influenced by factors that lie outside the social policy triangle.

A GOLDEN TRIANGLE AFTER ALL?

Since the 1980s a number of countries have been bestowed the (dubious) honour of being named the paragon country of effective labour market policies. In the 1980s Sweden represented the most successful labour market policy, then attention shifted to Japan; in the 1990s New Zealand and Finland were in the focus of attention; and most recently, Denmark is hailed as the exemplary welfare state that best succeeds in combining security and a flexible labour market in a harmonious way. However, depending on one's political inclination, either the loose employment protection legislation or the generous unemployment benefits and intensive active labour market policies are lauded by the admirers of the Danish model.

The figures in the preceding section showed that of our seven countries Denmark indeed scores best on the indicators for flexibility and security. There are large flows between employment and unemployment, there is a high labour participation and workers enjoy large income security, while unemployment is limited and the share of long-term unemployment is small. It is, thus, not surprising that the combination of loose employment protection, generous benefits and intensive labour market programmes that constitute the Danish policy triangle has been labelled a 'golden triangle'.

However, it remains rather difficult to establish the importance of the various elements of the policy triangle and their combination for the performance of our countries. This becomes particularly clear if we compare Sweden and the United Kingdom. These two countries are generally considered to be prototypical examples of the social-democratic welfare state and of the liberal welfare state, respectively (at least in Europe; the USA may be even more 'prototypical' liberal). Nevertheless, if we look at the outcomes of their social policies in Table 9.4, they are remarkably similar. Both countries have a high employment rate, moderate unemployment rate, flexible labour market and offer at most moderate income security. These comparable results are, however, the outcome of a completely different policy mix. Sweden is well known for the active involvement of the state in promoting labour participation and reducing (long-term) unemployment, in combination with an earnings-related unemployment benefit system. The United Kingdom, in contrast, focuses strongly on stimulating a flexible labour market. The high employment rate, moderate unemployment rate and large flows between employment and unemployment are, thus, primarily the result of the absence of state interference with the labour market. It thus appears that two completely different social policy models can result in remarkably similar results.

A different image arises if we compare the Netherlands with Germany. The social policy triangles of these two countries have a lot in common (see Table 9.3). They spend a similar share of GDP on unemployment benefits and active labour market programmes, and both have rather strict employment protection legislation. Nevertheless, the outcomes are much more favourable for the Netherlands than for Germany. The Dutch employment rate is much higher and the unemployment rate much lower than in Germany, while the Dutch benefit system offers considerably more income security. Only with respect to the lack of labour market flexibility are both countries similar. Thus, apparently, this lack of labour market flexibility does not explain the weak performance of Germany with respect to employment and income security. It is not completely clear what, then, explains the difference in outcomes between Germany and the Netherlands. Probably some other factors, outside the realm of the policy triangle, play a role. For example, quite typical for the Netherlands has been the very strong increase of female labour participation in tandem with the strong growth of part-time employment since the 1980s, which cannot be explained by the reforms of unemployment insurance, employment protection legislation or active labour market policies.

If, however, we compare Germany with Belgium and France, then both the policy mix and the outcomes in terms of security and flexibility are comparable. Thus, the combination of rather generous and lax unemployment insurance, strict unemployment protection legislation and moderate active labour market policies appears not to be very successful in achieving employment and income security and a flexible labour market.

Our study has also shown that it is not possible to characterize the social policy mix of a country with a few quantitative indicators such as, for example, the OECD indicators for the replacement rate, the employment protection legislation and spending on active labour market policies. These indicators neglect the numerous qualitative differences between policy instruments which cannot be simply summarized in one figure. Indeed, we found it quite hard to understand the changes in the scores on the OECD indicators from the description of policy reforms in our country chapters. Moreover, the implementation and administration of the social policy instruments might be just as important as the formal characteristics. For instance, it can make a lot of difference whether the qualifying conditions for unemployment benefits are applied very strictly or rather loosely. What is more, in many countries the legal conditions for unemployment benefits and employment protection are supplemented or even surpassed by collective agreements between the social partners. As a consequence, the actual income and employment protection for many workers may differ considerably from the legal regulations at the national level. This might also result in substantial differences between sectors, so that it does not make sense to assume that the same conditions apply to all employees in a country. Finally, all these qualitative features and sub-national variations might interact and might determine the final outcome in terms of employment and income security and labour market flexibility. Thus, it makes little sense to ask which element of the social policy mix is crucial in explaining the differences in performance between countries. Eventually, it is the complete policy triangle, including the administration, the distribution of responsibilities and additional clauses in collective agreements, that explains the successes and failures of social policy in the various countries.

To conclude, on the basis of our comparison of seven European countries we assess that the combination of unemployment benefits, employment protection legislation and active labour market policies does indeed matter when it comes to labour market performance. However, we are somewhat sceptical about the claim that there is an optimal combination of policy instruments which will yield the best results under all circumstances. The good performance of Denmark with respect to both employment and income security and labour market flexibility might justify the epithet 'golden triangle'. But the comparison of Sweden and the UK shows that widely different policies can result in similar outcomes, while the comparison of the Netherlands and Germany shows that similar policies can result in strongly diverging outcomes. So, apparently, there is no direct link between the policy mix and the labour market outcomes. This raises the question whether copying the Danish policy mix by another country would produce just as favourable outcomes as in Denmark. Probably, it is not only the particular policy mix, but also the specific conditions that apply in Denmark (for example the large share of small companies which makes external labour mobility more important than in other countries), that explains the Danish success. Although the governments and social partners of other countries can surely learn from the Danish experience – but also from less successful countries, for that matter – they will also have to take the particular circumstances in their own country into account in designing the optimal policy mix, not only in terms of instruments, but also with respect to coordination and administration. There are no simple recipes to improve socio-economic performance. And one day the successful Danish model, too, will probably have to give way to another, even more successful paragon.

Index